Resettled Iraqi Refugees in the United States

FORCED MIGRATION

General Editors: Tom Scott-Smith and Kirsten McConnachie

This series, published in association with the Refugee Studies Centre, University of Oxford, reflects the multidisciplinary nature of the field and includes within its scope international law, anthropology, sociology, politics, international relations, geopolitics, social psychology, and economics.

Recent volumes:

Volume 47
Resettled Iraqi Refugees in the United States: War, Refuge, Belonging, Participation, and Protest
Jared Keyel

Volume 46
Cosmopolitan Refugees: Somali Migrant Women in Nairobi and Johannesburg
Nereida Ripero-Muñiz

Volume 45
Refugees on the Move: Crisis and Response in Turkey and Europe
Edited by Erol Balkan and Zümray Kutlu-Tonak

Volume 44
Durable Solutions: Challenges with Implementing Global Norms for Internally Displaced Persons in Georgia
Carolin Funke

Volume 43
Mediated Lives: Waiting and Hope among Iraqi Refugees in Jordan
Mirjam Twigt

Volume 42
Outsiders: Memories of Migration to and from North Korea
Markus Bell

Volume 41
Latin America and Refugee Protection: Regimes, Logics, and Challenges
Edited by Liliana Lyra Jubilut, Marcia Vera Espinoza, and Gabriela Mezzanotti

Volume 40
Un-Settling Middle Eastern Refugees: Regimes of Exclusion and Inclusion in the Middle East, Europe, and North America
Edited by Marcia C. Inhorn and Lucia Volk

Volume 39
Structures of Protection? Rethinking Refugee Shelter
Edited by Tom Scott-Smith and Mark E. Breeze

Volume 38
Refugee Resettlement: Power, Politics, and Humanitarian Governance
Edited by Adèle Garnier, Liliana Lyra Jubilut, and Kristin Bergtora Sandvik

For a full volume listing, please see the series page on our website:
https//www.berghahnbooks.com/series/forced-migration

Resettled Iraqi Refugees in the United States

WAR, REFUGE, BELONGING, PARTICIPATION, AND PROTEST

Jared Keyel

berghahn
NEW YORK • OXFORD
www.berghahnbooks.com

First published in 2023 by
Berghahn Books
www.berghahnbooks.com

© 2023, 2025 Jared Keyel
First paperback edition published in 2025

All rights reserved. Except for the quotation of short passages
for the purposes of criticism and review, no part of this book
may be reproduced in any form or by any means, electronic or
mechanical, including photocopying, recording, or any information
storage and retrieval system now known or to be invented,
without written permission of the publisher.

Library of Congress Cataloging-in-Publication Data

A C.I.P. cataloging record is available from the Library of Congress
Library of Congress Cataloging in Publication Control Number: 2022045364

British Library Cataloguing in Publication Data

A catalogue record for this book is available from the British Library

ISBN 978-1-80073-842-3 hardback
ISBN 978-1-80539-753-3 paperback
ISBN 978-1-80073-843-0 epub
ISBN 978-1-80539-054-1 web pdf

https://doi.org/10.3167/9781800738423

An electronic version of this book is freely available thanks to the support of libraries working with Knowledge Unlatched. KU is a collaborative initiative designed to make high-quality books Open Access for the public good. More information about the inititative and links to the Open Access version can be found at knowledgeunlatched.org.

This work is published subject to a Creative Commons Attribution Noncommercial No Derivatives 4.0 License. The terms of the license can be found at http://creativecommons.org/licenses/by-nc-nd/4.0/. For uses beyond those covered in the license contact Berghahn Books.

For Ilana and Olivia

So they might live in a more peaceful world

Contents

Acknowledgments   viii

Introduction   1

1. Seeking Refuge amid Decades of American War against Iraq   23

2. How Does it Feel to Be a Refugee? Belonging, Precarity, and Cultural Exchange   49

3. Enacting Democratic Membership: Finding Time, (Re)Distributing Resources, Building Knowledge, and Protecting Rights   95

4. Forms of Participation: Dialogue, Civil Society, and Resistance   124

Conclusion. The Local, National, and Cosmopolitan Work to Be Done   151

References   161

Index   183

Acknowledgments

I would like to thank the many people who have made this work possible. First and foremost, I want to express my sincere gratitude to the individuals who generously agreed to be interviewed for this project. Each one shared their time and their often difficult and painful experiences with me. Many also went above and beyond to reach out to their colleagues, friends, and family to assist me in connecting with others. This project could not have been realized without them. I hope that I have honored and accurately represented the complexities of their experiences.

I want to express my deepest thanks to Max O. Stephenson Jr. for his unfailing support and guidance throughout this project. He has continuously pushed me to become a better writer and clearer thinker. A sincere thank you, too, to Christian Matheis, who has consistently encouraged me to think seriously about liberation and how we reach it. Thank you as well to Deborah Milly and Katrina Powell for their helpful feedback as this project took shape from a rough sketch in 2016 to the present book. To the anonymous reviewers of this work, thank you for your insightful suggestions on clarifying and improving the manuscript.

Thank you to my family for being constant sources of joy and support: my partner, Zibby, my daughters, Ilana and Olivia, my parents, Ellen and Wayne, and my sisters, Becca and Aryn. I want to thank the wonderful and diverse community of friends and colleagues I made while at Virginia Tech. Thank you for the hikes, the conversations, the TOTS nights, the late-night waffles, the cat sitting, and most especially for the delicious potlucks and Friendsgivings. I cannot list everyone here, for fear of leaving someone out, but I hope you all know who you are. I am grateful to the members of the Blacksburg Refugee Partnership as well, particularly Scott Bailey, for the continuous reminder that we can choose to act with care and compassion toward newcomers in American society, rather than exclusion and violence.

Last, but certainly not least, a huge thank you to the friends who offered me lodging and meals and acted as—possibly reluctant, but always gracious—sounding boards as I conducted this research: Jen Cohn, Rama Issa-Ibrahim,

Stephanie Sacco, Sony Rane (and everyone at the Bowers House Cooperative), and Tamar Frolichstein-Appel.

Introduction

The United States has been waging war against Iraq since 1991. The intensive six-week bombing campaign of the Gulf War was the first phase of a conflict that has continued for three decades. Throughout the 1990s, American and allied warplanes patrolled the skies of Iraq, regularly bombing the country (Ali 2000). The 2003 American-led invasion was an escalation of an ongoing conflict. The "shock and awe" bombing and subsequent large-scale military occupation of Iraq between 2003 and 2011 as well as the cross-border campaign from 2014 to the present targeting the so-called Islamic State in Iraq and Syria (ISIS) have caused hundreds of thousands of deaths and precipitated, directly or indirectly, the displacement of millions of individuals in that country. Between 20 March 2003 and 30 September 2017,[1] more than 172,000 Iraqis left their country and resettled in the United States. This book examines the displacement and resettlement experiences of a cohort of fifteen such individuals, placing their personal narratives within the larger context of the war in their country and daily life as resettled refugees in the United States.

The Iraqis seeking refuge who came to the United States during that nearly fifteen-year period included not only those who arrived through the United States Refugee Admissions Program (USRAP) (143,165), but also those who qualified for a Special Immigrant Visa (SIV) as a result of their work with the US military or government during the war (21,961), and individuals who were granted asylum (7,189) (Bruno 2019; US Department of State 2019; US Department of Homeland Security 2004, 2014, 2017). Iraqis who entered the United States via the USRAP, SIV, or asylum were eligible for work authorization, permanent residence, and, eventually, citizenship. In short, these populations were granted a status that may lead to full legal membership in the country.

Individuals who arrive in the United States seeking refuge must navigate social and political contexts rife with tensions and contradictions. Iraqis who came to the United States entered a society that had been at war with their country for decades. Moreover, many Iraqis are Arab and Muslim, groups against whom significant numbers of Americans hold negative and prejudiced views. As a result, legal residence or citizenship does not necessarily guarantee substantive possibilities to engage in American society or politics (Brubaker 2010). Substantive membership and belonging in a society involve significantly more than formal legal rights and are enacted and enhanced through both formal and informal processes (Carens 2013; Crane 2021). Social and political exclusions, whether socially imposed or legally rendered, can be challenged by newcomers as well as native citizens. Belonging is not only granted to newcomers but is claimed and enacted by them (Crane 2021). Contestations to expand the right to belong to those formerly excluded can happen at varied and overlapping sites within society, for example: workplaces, neighborhoods, community organizations, protests, schools, and within and between families (Brubaker 2010).

This book explores these issues through the narratives and experiences of fifteen resettled Iraqis. Scholars have identified a tendency among analysts and policymakers to talk *about* refugees, rather than listen to those individuals' experiences, needs, and desires (Fiddian-Qasmiyeh et al. 2014; Szczepanik 2016). Similarly, Horst (2006) has emphasized the importance of recognizing, (re)valuing, and including the knowledge of refugees in developing strategies and solutions to the challenges created by forced migration. This book addresses a group of Iraqis' interpretations of what it was like to leave their homes in Iraq and to relocate and live in the United States. The core of this text examines those individuals' thoughts and narratives about belonging and participation in American society and politics. As a diverse group of individuals, they did not offer unanimity in their perceptions, interpretations, or recommendations. Nor do the stories of these fifteen people represent an exhaustive picture of "the Iraqi refugee experience" (Crane 2021, 8). However, by drawing their narratives together, this book offers a set of themes and threads about the experience of seeking refuge in the United States. Across interviews, those with whom I spoke elaborated both opportunities and challenges to belonging that they encountered as well as possibilities for democratic participation in formal institutions and informal settings. Their experiences demonstrate that those who resettle as refugees can exercise agency "within the limitations that have been constructed around them" (Inhorn and Volk 2021, 115).

I situate this book in the refugee and forced displacement literature, which is highly inter- and trans-disciplinary. Understanding refugees' experiences requires engaging with questions of war and conflict, global ethics, and democratic belonging and citizenship. As such, I draw methods, concepts, and theories from political science, sociology, and anthropology. This book contributes an empirical exploration of the lived experiences of resettled Iraqis as well as theoretical insights into the complexities of agency and democratic engagement for newcomers in American society.

What follows is also a critical and normative work of interdisciplinary social science. Critical social theorizing presumes that historically situated knowledge can be mobilized for emancipatory aims (Agger 1998). Existing conditions, social systems, and political institutions are neither necessary nor predetermined. Societies can be otherwise, and the task of critical social science is to locate where opportunities for change exist (Nickel 2012). Building understanding about the conditions of life for newcomers is important. However, it is also important that that knowledge furthers understanding to improve those conditions.

I root this book in a normative commitment to democracy and a political commitment to working to radically democratize American society. This effort entails vastly expanding the substantive opportunities for all members of society to participate in the decisions that affect their lives in their households, workplaces, and political organizations and institutions. It also incorporates a commitment to challenging xenophobia and exclusions as incompatible with a democratic society. A central aim for those concerned with democratizing the United States should be to create a more open society that also welcomes newcomers. Empirically, the book seeks to represent the range of views and experiences shared by interviewees. As other recent studies of resettled Iraqi refugees have found (Campbell 2016; Crane 2021; Inhorn 2018), the individuals I spoke with expressed mixed views of the war in their country and nuanced interpretations of the experience of seeking refuge in the United States. As a result, it is important to note at the outset that not everything interviewees said points in emancipatory directions. In fact, some of the thoughts that my interlocutors shared challenged the political aims of this project. Individual agency can resist power but also reinforce it (Campbell 2016). Nonetheless, I have sought to represent the full range and subtlety of views of those I interviewed.

Finally, this book is also an antiwar work, grounded in a pacifist ethic that maintains that war can never be justified. Such an ethical orientation incorporates both "a negative refusal to participate in organised [sic] political violence or offer it legitimacy, and a positive determination to actively build more peaceful and cooperative forms of political life and find ways of resolving contemporary threats and challenges employing alternative, realistic non-violent means" (Jackson 2019, 216).

The American war waged against Iraq since 1991 has always been an imperial war, launched to project and maintain American dominance in the Middle East (Kinzer 2007; Kumar 2012). The war has caused immense and ongoing harm to millions of people. No study of those displaced by that conflict can be complete without directly engaging with American military violence and imperial ambitions to dismantle Iraqi society and rebuild it according to its own aims. There is an urgent need for social scientists to engage more directly with the effects of political and military violence (Blain and Kearns-Blain 2018; Inhorn 2018) and to offer critical interventions that challenge the assumptions of global American military dominance (Espiritu 2014; Nguyen 2012).

Despite a growing interdisciplinary literature exploring displacement and refugees (Cameron 2014), relatively few studies have focused on the experiences of individuals from the Middle East who have been displaced by American wars and resettled in the United States (Shoeb, Weinstein, and Halpern 2007), particularly Iraqis (Black et al. 2013). Dewachi (2017) argues that Iraq is the most understudied country in the Middle East. Several recent monographs have begun to fill this lacuna, using ethnographic methods to explore the experiences of Iraqis who have resettled in the United States, and to examine the moral obligations Americans have to redress the harm they have caused to millions of Iraqis (Campbell 2016; Crane 2021; Inhorn 2018). Much like this book, these works delve into the challenges and difficulties facing Iraqis who now live in a society that is often actively hostile to them as well as the opportunities for resettled individuals to contest negative assumptions and exclusions. Overall, the findings in this book strongly accord with the experiences of resettled Iraqis considered in those earlier works.

Within the literature on resettled Iraqis in the United States, there is a strong focus on individuals' emotional, mental, and physical health and experiences of trauma (Arnetz et al. 2014; Elsouhag et al. 2015; Jen et al. 2015; Kira et al. 2012; Black et al. 2013; Gangamma 2018; Harding and Libal 2012; Hauck et al. 2014; Jamil et al. 2012; LeMaster et al. 2017; Haldane and Nickerson 2010; Nelson et al. 2016; Saadi, Bond, and Percac-Lima 2015; Taylor et al. 2014; Willard, Rabin, and Lawless 2014; Wright, Aldhalimi, et al. 2016; Wright, Dhalimi, et al. 2016; Yako and Biswas 2014; Inhorn 2018). Such inquiries are important and provide much-needed insights. However, a narrow focus on the needs and achievements of refugees locates the problem of displacement within those individuals, rather than in the political and historical conditions that produced their situation (Espiritu 2014).

With several notable exceptions of works that directly confront the violence of American war (Inhorn 2018; Crane 2021; Campbell 2016), much of the extant literature concerning resettled Iraqis cited here either omits or only obliquely describes the American-led war that caused their displacement. By focusing strongly on trauma and simultaneously failing to acknowledge the role the US military and government have had in causing it, such research on Iraqi refugees can reproduce status quo understandings of the United States as a neutral or benevolent country accepting refugees, rather than as a state whose military violence caused that displacement. As Crane argues, the "brute fact" of resettled Iraqis in the United States is a "testimony to the enduring [effects] of *our* war, rather than to the generosity of *our* humanitarian ideals" (2021, xv). This book, particularly its first chapter, similarly directly faces the brutality of the American war waged against Iraq and challenges the assumption and assertion of American humanitarian commitments.

Overall, I make three primary arguments in this book. First, the American war against Iraq is a crime against humanity. The architects of this conflict must be held to account, and Americans must make urgent reparation to the people of Iraq. Second, within the constraints constructed around them (Inhorn and Volk 2021), those who seek refuge can create and enlarge spaces to belong in, and alter, their new host societies through intentional and reciprocal social exchanges with members of the native-born population and other newcomers with diverse backgrounds. Many of those interviewed for this book were engaged in such exchanges. Creating opportunities for this kind of interaction is one potential approach those committed to creating a more open and diverse society can pursue to further those goals. Such work requires intentionality (Benhabib 2006) and, at minimum, a democratic commitment by all parties involved to mutual adjustment (Carens 2013). Third, in addition to interpersonal interaction, collective action undertaken together by newcomers and native-born citizens (leveraging their relatively more secure social and legal positions) is critical to defending and expanding the rights of refugees and other marginalized groups. Collective political engagement is also important if resettled refugees are to build power and contest exclusions.

Contextualizing the Book: Competing Conceptions of American Society

The United States is a settler-colonial society with a transnational genealogy (Dewachi 2017). The interconnected processes of violent dispossession of its territory's Indigenous inhabitants, forced relocation and labor of enslaved Africans, and expansionist European settlement of the continent are foundational to its development as a political, economic, cultural, and social project. The historical and ongoing voluntary and involuntary movements of people within and across the country's borders are a central phenomenon to understanding American society.

Despite its history of dispossession, expulsions, and genocide against the Indigenous inhabitants of what became its territories (Madley 2016), a "grand narrative" persists that frames the United States as an "immigrant country" that has been exceptional–and in some versions unique–in its incorporation of diverse newcomers throughout its history (Alba and Foner 2015). Although there has long been significant scholarship that challenges such claims, offering much more nuanced analyses, many public figures have continued to perpetuate a mythology of American exceptionalism concerning immigrant incorporation (Obama 2010; Kennedy 2006). This narrative persists in popular discourses as well.[2]

Moreover, as Cristina Beltrán argues "much of US immigration law is a history of racialized assaults on particular segments of the American immigrant population" (2020, 25). Nativism, fear, and exclusion of assumed others have long existed alongside the prevailing "America is an immigrant country" narrative. I undertook the research for this book during a period of acute anti-immigrant sentiment and policies emanating from the Republican presidential administration of Donald Trump (2017–2021) and expressed by his supporters. On 26 September 2017, I drove to Upstate New York, ready to conduct my first interview for this research the following day. As I drove north on Interstate-81, I passed another vehicle with a decal that read: "Fuck off, We're Full," spelled out in the shape of the continental United States. This incident is illustrative of the sentiments expressed by some segments of American society and members of government during the Trump administration. Echoing the bumper sticker's sentiment, in April 2019, Trump declared, "our country is full," to justify reductions in immigrant admissions and increased militarized border enforcement (Irwin and Badger 2019).

Trump campaigned on a nativist, anti-immigrant, and anti-refugee platform (Beinart 2018; Huber 2016) that directed ire at Muslims in particular. In late 2015, for example, as a presidential candidate, Trump called for a "total and complete shutdown of Muslims entering the United States" (Johnson 2015). Trump's campaign and government drew on deeply rooted Orientalist myths about Islam, and those who practice it, as inherently different, dangerous, and irrational (Said 2003), and stoked the fears, prejudices, and nativist sentiments of his supporters.

The Trump administration pursued an anti-refugee agenda both domestically and internationally during its tenure. In addition to drastically reducing refugee resettlement in the United States through the USRAP (Davis 2021), it also cut US funding for the United Nations Relief and Works Agency for Palestine Refugees in the Near East (UNRWA) (Inhorn and Volk 2021), the international agency that supports Palestinians forced to flee their homes by Zionist militias in 1947–48 (Pappe 2006) and later the Israeli military in 1967. Trump's administration also intentionally created dangerous and traumatizing conditions for children seeking asylum in the United States, separating them from their parents and jailing them in unsafe facilities in efforts to deter asylum-seekers from entering the country (Ainsley 2017; Long and Alonso-Zaldivar 2019; Seville and Rappleye 2018). Moreover, in one of his first acts as president, Trump signed an Executive Order that attempted to ban refugees from seven predominately Muslim countries from entering the United States, including Iraq (K. Liptak 2017). This "travel ban" was initially blocked by legal challenges and later superseded by additional Executive Orders. At the time of this study's interviews, the travel ban's final status was uncertain. However, in late 2017 the United States Supreme Court of the United States allowed a revised version to go into effect while legal actions continued (A. Liptak 2017). The Court ultimately upheld the ban's legality (Totenberg and Montanaro 2018). Although Iraq was removed from the final list of banned countries, the uncertain climate Trump's actions created cruelly affected many of this study's participants' lives and became an important topic of this research.

This book explores such discriminatory and exclusionary rhetoric and policies, but also the (re)actions of many who opposed them. Significant numbers of Americans challenged the "we're full" ethos, articulating as an alternative what might be called a "refugees welcome" orientation. The work done on behalf of and with newcomers to resist exclusion and xenophobia to create a more open and diverse society is central to the analysis offered in this book as are the ways that participants found to navigate and ameliorate the tensions of living in a society alongside a significant portion of the population that was working to exclude them.

2021 and Beyond: Biden Administration Reversals and Continuities

Trump lost his re-election bid in 2020 and a new presidential administration led by Joe Biden, a Democrat, assumed office in January 2021. Biden had previously served for eight years as vice president under Trump's predecessor, Barack Obama. The Obama administration (2009–2017) took a decidedly different rhetorical approach to immigration than Trump, leaning heavily into the immigrant country narrative and meritocratic discourses of the contributions newcomers make to American society and economy (Obama 2010). Despite its rhetoric, the record of its policies is mixed. That administration pursued stable refugee resettlement policies throughout its tenure. It also took executive actions, such as the Deferred Action for Childhood Arrivals (DACA) program, to provide limited protections for immigrants who had arrived as children without legal status. However, that administration simultaneously forcibly deported significantly more people than the previous two presidential administrations had expelled.

It is too soon to definitively assess the Biden administration's approach to migration and resettlement. To date, there have been shifts from the previous administration's approach, but also continuations of its exclusionary policies. Upon Biden's assumption of the presidency, he signed an Executive Order reversing the 2017 travel ban (Meng 2021). His administration has also pledged to return refugee resettlement numbers to pre-Trump levels. However, at the time of writing in spring 2022, full implementation of that reversal is still pending (IRAP 2022). Despite these changes, there are significant continuities between Biden's policies and Trump's. Throughout its first year in office, the Biden administration continued the Trump era use of Title 42, a legal provision used to expel asylum-seekers ostensibly on public health grounds due to the COVID-19 pandemic that began in 2020 (BBC 2021). Moreover, although the total number of migrants and asylum-seekers held in US Immigration and Customs Enforcement (ICE) jails has decreased from a peak of 55,000 in August 2019, that number increased again from 15,000 when Biden took office in January 2021 to more than 27,000 in August 2021.

Persistent Exclusionary Policies and Sentiments in American Society and Government

The Trump administration's overtly anti-refugee and anti-Muslim rhetoric and policies are only the most recent manifestation of a long-standing bipartisan policy consensus among the Republican and Democratic parties that has made "life more violent and precarious for immigrants" (Beltrán 2020, 9). The presidential administrations of "Ronald Reagan, George H. W. Bush, Bill Clinton, George W. Bush, and Barack Obama all supported legislation and policies making migration a more punitive and perilous process" (Beltrán 2020, 9). Moreover, significant percentages of Americans have long expressed exclusionary attitudes. For example, Gallup surveys dating back to 1939 suggest that Americans have largely disapproved of allowing refugees seeking safety from violence to resettle in the United States.[3]

Negative perceptions of Arabs and Muslims are widespread among members of American society as well. For example, when polled in 2010, only 43 percent of respondents had a favorable view of Arabs and only 35 percent of Americans polled viewed Muslims positively (Zogby International 2010). When polled again in 2017, even fewer respondents had a favorable view of Arabs (35 percent) and Muslims (34 percent) (Zogby Analytics 2017). Muslims and Islam are also perceived the least positively of any religious group or tradition in the United States (Pew 2017a; Sides and Mogahed 2018; Telhami 2015). Moreover, since the beginning of the American war against Iraq in 1991, majorities of Americans—an average of 80 percent across thirty years of surveys—have held unfavorable views of that country (Gallup 2021).

In addition to negative perceptions of Arabs, Muslims, and Iraqis, pluralities of Americans report support for discriminatory policies targeting those individuals. For example, after Trump declared in 2015 that he would require Muslims living in the United States to register with the government (Hillyard 2015), 27 percent of respondents told YouGov that they "strongly" supported and 13 percent "somewhat" supported a national registry of Muslims (YouGov, 20–23 November 2015). In 2017, 37 percent of Americans polled supported law enforcement profiling of Arab and Muslim Americans. Thirty-five percent agreed that the United States should ban immigrants from Middle Eastern countries and 31 percent said Muslim immigrants should be prohibited from entering the country (Zogby Analytics 2017). While such views are held by a minority, one in three Americans supporting discriminatory policies is still a significant segment of the population.

Moreover, Trump's proposed "Muslim registry" and the 2017 travel ban are only the most recent discriminatory policies targeting Arabs and Muslims living in the United States.[4] In 2002, for example, the George W. Bush administration created the National Security Entry-Exit Registration System (NSEERS), which required male immigrants sixteen years old and older from twenty-five countries, all of which, except North Korea and Eritrea, were Muslim majority, to submit to "special registration" and government tracking. By the end of 2003, 83,000 individuals had voluntarily done so, nearly 13,800 of whom were then placed in deportation proceedings (Kumar 2012). Similarly, the Federal Bureau of Investigation (FBI) and the New York City Police Department (NYPD) devoted significant resources to surveil individuals and infiltrate Arab and Muslim organizations in the years after the 11 September 2001 attacks. Working with the Central Intelligence Agency (CIA), the NYPD spent at least a decade illegally spying on Arabs and Muslims in dozens of mosques, community organizations, restaurants, stores, and schools in New York City, New Jersey, and Connecticut. The program failed to uncover any evidence of criminal activities by any of the people or organizations illegally surveilled (Pilkington 2018; Goldman and Apuzzo 2012). Thus, while Trump certainly imposed discriminatory and violent policies, he did so by building upon similarly cruel precedents set, and platforms constructed, by previous presidential administrations and other agencies of the American government.[5]

The United States has also pursued discriminatory and violent policies directed against Arabs, Muslims, and Iraqis within and beyond its borders. For example, the CIA carried out a global kidnapping program euphemistically called "extraordinary rendition" through which its agents abducted individuals and flew them to secret prisons in fifty-four different countries to be tortured. At least fourteen people were kidnapped and transferred to Egypt during Bill Clinton's presidency (1993–2001) and at minimum 136 individuals were abducted under his successor, George W. Bush (2001–09). The vast majority of the known victims resided or originated in majority Arab and/or Muslim countries, including Iraq (Singh 2013). While Bush's successor, Barack Obama, took limited steps to curtail torture, he refused to hold anyone who participated in these cruel–and illegal–programs accountable.

And although there are differences in the strategies and tactics used by Bush, Obama, Trump, and now Biden, each administration has continued to project American hegemony violently throughout the Middle East and parts of Africa. In addition to its thirty-year war against Iraq, in the years since 2001 the United States has also launched and participated in wars against six other majority Arab and/or Muslim countries including Afghanistan, Libya, Pakistan, Somalia, Syria, and Yemen (Crawford 2018a; Scahill 2015; Guilliard et al. 2015).

As of this writing in spring 2022, except for formally ending the US war in Afghanistan in August 2021, the Biden administration has thus far continued the rest of those military campaigns launched by previous administrations and has proposed further increasing the already colossal US military budget (Greve 2022).[6] After the February 2022 Russian invasion of Ukraine, the Biden administration ramped up US support for Ukrainian forces, sending funds and weapons, and providing intelligence to strike Russian targets. In May 2022, US Congressman Seth Moulton, a Democrat from Massachusetts, acknowledged that these actions are in service of an American proxy war against Russia (Brands 2022; Democracy Now 2022). American wars have led directly and indirectly to the displacement of millions of people in those countries and beyond. The individuals interviewed for this book were forced to seek safety in the United States as a direct result of continued American militarism and imperial wars.

Speaking with Iraqis

A recounting of the narratives and experiences of fifteen individuals from Iraq whom I interviewed between 27 September 2017 and 27 February 2018 constitute the core of this book. When I began this research, I had been working in the nonprofit sector for ten years, primarily with organizations that serve immigrants and refugees to the United States. In many ways, this research project and my interest in understanding the complex experiences of newcomers to the United States grew out of that work. This book is also informed by a lifelong opposition to war. Marching against the 2003 invasion of Iraq was one of my first political acts. This commitment informs my desire to understand the ways in which American war has harmed so many people in Iraq and beyond.

I began seeking study participants by contacting my professional and personal networks in immigrant and refugee serving nonprofit organizations in the Chicago, Illinois, metropolitan area (colloquially known as Chicagoland), Upstate New York State, and New York City. I used those connections as a foundation on which to locate the first group of individuals who agreed to be interviewed for this research. I then connected with additional interviewees using a snowball method. This initial strategy helped me find four individuals, who in turn connected me with six more interviewees.

As interviews proceeded, I widened my geographical search for participants to other locations to which I could feasibly travel and that have significant resettled refugee populations. With those expanded recruitment parameters, I contacted additional organizations in Illinois, New York State, Virginia (where I lived at the time of this research), and the Washington, DC, metropolitan area. I was able to connect with individuals in the Shenandoah Valley Region of Virginia, and the Washington, DC, metropolitan area. To ensure the confidentiality of interviewees, I refer to broad geographic regions and large metropolitan areas rather than identify exactly where they live.

Contacting potential interviewees through my existing personal and professional contacts proved significantly more successful than cold-calling immigrant or refugee service organizations. As one interviewee told me, it is unlikely that he would have agreed to an interview if his friend, with whom I had already spoken, had not connected us. I identified only two interviewee possibilities through cold contacts, each of whom connected me with an additional individual. Finally, I secured one interview through a serendipitous personal connection. Over the course of five months, I traveled to and conducted interviews in Chicagoland, Upstate New York, New York City, the Shenandoah Valley Region of Virginia, and the Washington, DC, metropolitan area. I refer to interviewees by pseudonyms throughout this book. I also assigned pseudonyms to all friends, family members, and in some cases obscured other details about topics we discussed to protect the confidentiality of research participants.

I spoke with seven individuals who arrived in the United States via the United States Refugee Assistance Program, five SIV recipients, two people who claimed asylum, and one young man who had refugee status in Syria, but journeyed to the United States on a student visa. Each one of these people, and in many cases their families, left their country after the 2003 US-led invasion and came to the United States seeking safety. Although this book frames the American violence against Iraq as one long conflict with multiple phases that began in 1991, when I began planning for this research project, I conceived of the 1991 Gulf War and the 2003 American-led invasion as two separate conflicts. It is for that reason that I recruited participants who left Iraq after the 2003 invasion, understanding this population as distinct from Iraqis who left the country between 1991 and 2003.

Iraq is a multicultural and diverse society. The modern Iraqi state was created by the British Empire after World War I by stitching together three former Ottoman provinces in which an Arabic-speaking majority (75–80 percent of the population) lives alongside a Kurdish-speaking minority (15–20 percent). In addition to the Arabic-Kurdish ethnolinguistic cleavage, Iraq's society can be broadly divided into adherents of one of the two major sects in Islam: Sunni or Shi'a. The majority of Muslims worldwide is Sunni, however, Sunni Muslims only make up approximately 15 to 20 percent of Iraq's Muslims, while Shi'a are the majority. As most Kurds are Sunni, Marr and al-Marashi (2017) argue that Iraq can broadly be understood as segmented into three major groups: Arab Shi'a, Arab Sunnis, and Kurds. There are also much smaller numbers of Iraqi Christians, Yazidi, and Jews.

Because of Iraq's long history and diverse population, the idea of an Iraqi nation and identity is contested (Marr and al-Marashi 2017). Moreover, terminology and concepts such as "the Middle East" are fraught with Orientalist and imperialist histories (Campbell 2016). While remaining aware of these difficulties, I make use of such concepts in this book in large part because they were understood by the individuals with whom I spoke and because interviewees themselves used such terms.

I spoke with four women and eleven men ranging in age from twenty-seven to fifty-seven at the time of their interview. Those I interviewed came from multiple cities in Iraq. All identified themselves as either Muslim or non-religious, but Muslim by background. Only a few of the individuals I spoke with identified themselves as either Shi'a or Sunni. Several characterized themselves as of mixed ethnolinguistic background (Arabic and Kurdish) or religious background (Sunni and Shi'a). I conducted interviews in English with individuals who felt comfortable expressing themselves in that language. The quotations drawn from those interviews that appear in this book have been edited lightly for clarity and readability. However, I sought to minimize edits to maintain and reflect everyone's words as closely as possible.

Who Is a Refugee?

Each of those with whom I spoke identified themselves as either a refugee or former refugee. Yet, there is significant disagreement among scholars, legal experts, and practitioners concerning how to define that term. A number of overlapping and contrasting definitions exist in scholarship, domestic and international law, and popular understanding (Lister 2013; Shacknove 1985; Haddad 2008; Bakewell 2008).[7] Volk and Inhorn argue that the central concepts scholars use to understand displacement: refuge, refugee, internally displaced persons, and asylum-seeker have "frayed edges" (2021, 10). Indeed, as Cameron (2014) has argued, the complexity of refuge situations and experiences makes building a grand or meta-theory of "refugeeness" difficult.

For this analysis, I distinguish between refugee—and related concepts such as refuge, asylum, asylum-seeker, and resettlement—as analytical categories and as policy or legal categories (Bakewell 2008). I primarily use these concepts as analytical categories throughout this book, particularly refugee. I employed an expansive definition of refugee as an individual who has left their home due to insecurity and sought safety elsewhere, irrespective of legal, visa, or immigration status.

Despite the multiple programs and paths through which participants arrived in the United States, each decided to leave their country and seek safety abroad. As explored in more detail in later chapters, the status each individual sought or achieved was a result of assessing their situation and seeking out whatever means might bring safety. The ongoing violence and instability of the American war against Iraq prompted each to leave their homes and seek security and better conditions elsewhere. Therefore, irrespective of their legal categorization—or lack of such status—by state agencies or international institutions, the individuals who participated in this study have experienced being refugees. Likewise, although the choice to remain permanently was not entirely in their control for some of the individuals with whom I spoke, they had all resettled in the United States, and almost all sought to stay in the country and pursue education, work, and (re)establish their lives.

Introducing Research Participants

Throughout this book, I organize participants' experiences around key themes. As a result, the narratives, interpretations, and opinions of all fifteen interviewees are interwoven throughout the chapters of this book. Here I provide short introductions to each of the individuals with whom I spoke and indicate who was connected to whom in each of the geographic locations where interviews took place. I also provide a summary table of demographic information at the end of this section.

Upstate New York

Walid, 39, was born in Karbala, a city two hours south of Iraq's capital, Baghdad. Before leaving Iraq, Walid worked as a middle school teacher and owned a business. Walid's father was killed by the Ba'ath regime, and his mother, brother, and a sister chose to remain in Iraq. Another sister sought refuge in Germany. He and his family left Iraq in 2006, first seeking refuge in neighboring Syria. They stayed in Syria until 2008, when they applied for resettlement in the United States. He and his family resettled in Upstate New York. Walid is active in his community, working with, founding, and leading various nonprofit initiatives supporting other refugees and immigrants in the area.

Marwa, 48, is from Baghdad. She is a friend and colleague of Walid. Marwa left Iraq in 2006 and lived in Egypt for three years. She arrived in the United States in 2009 through the USRAP with her three children. Her husband joined them the following year. Marwa settled in Upstate New York with the help of another Iraqi family her husband knew. She has a degree in physics and worked as a math and physics teacher for eleven years in Iraq. After resettling, she studied at a local college to train as an optician. When we spoke, she had left optometry and was working as a case manager at the same organization as Walid.

Mohammed, 38, volunteers with Walid and Marwa for a community organization assisting resettled refugees in Upstate New York. He is from Karbala originally, where his mother and siblings still live. Mohammed sought refuge in Syria for four years before coming to the United States. He arrived in the United States through the USRAP in 2011. He and his wife and fourteen-year-old daughter resettled in Upstate New York because his friend Walid was already there. Both Mohammed and his wife work as case managers for a social service organization in the area.

Tariq, 33, lives in Upstate New York with his wife and children. He is originally from the Babylon Province in central Iraq. He identified himself as a Shi'ite Muslim. After the 2003 invasion, Tariq joined with the US Marines as a translator. He later faced danger because of this work with the United States and decided to apply for the SIV program. He received his visa and resettled in the United States in 2012. Tariq has a degree in physics from Iraq and was working as a sales representative at an automobile dealership in Upstate New York at the time of our interview. He was also enrolled in an MBA program at a local university.

New York City

Nada, 57, resettled in the United States in 2013. She was the last member of her family to leave Iraq. First her daughter and her daughter's husband left Iraq for the United States, then her son. After that, her husband and other children came to the United States. Finally, her documents were ready, and she left Iraq for New York City. Nada was eligible for an SIV because her husband worked for an American company in Baghdad and faced threats as a result. Her brother-in-law, who had come to the United States twenty-five years earlier, sponsored Nada and her family to come. When we spoke, Nada was taking English as a second language (ESL) classes at a local college. Nada and her husband had worked as engineers in Iraq. When she resettled in New York, she began volunteering at a local nonprofit assisting other immigrants and refugees and, at the time of our interview, worked as a teacher at the organization. Nada introduced me to Sarah.

Sarah, 39, is from Baghdad. After leaving Iraq in 2005, she lived in Syria for eight years with her brother and sisters. From Syria, her brother went to Germany and she and her sisters resettled in the United States in 2013. They first arrived in Arizona, where they lived for three years. Sarah and one of her sisters moved to New York City while her other sister and her four children stayed in Arizona. At the time of our interview, Sarah had just started taking English classes at a local college to improve her communication.

Ali, 37, was born in Iraq but spent some of his childhood in the United States. His father worked for the Iraqi Ministry of Foreign Affairs under Saddam Hussein. He and his family lived for a time in Virginia in the 1980s.

Ali identified himself as a Sunni Muslim. He left Iraq in 2006 and spent time in Jordan, Syria, and Egypt before resettling in the United States through the SIV program in 2012. He worked as a dishwasher when he arrived before finding a job at an Arab American serving nonprofit. He lives with his wife, two children, and parents. His daughter was born in Damascus and his son in New York City. Ali's sister lives in the New York area as well, and at the time of our interview, he was working to complete his brother's immigration process to bring him to the United States. Ali introduced me to Abdullah.

Abdullah, 28, arrived in New York City in 2010. An outlier among those interviewed for this research, he came to the United States on a student visa. Abdullah had sought refuge in Syria after leaving Iraq. While there, he heard about an American nongovernmental organization that offered scholarships to study in the United States. He applied twice to this program and, after the second attempt, received funding to travel to New York City and study civil engineering at a local university. When we spoke, Abdullah was working for a company in the area on an Optional Practical Training immigration status and hoping to receive a Green Card, which would allow him to stay longer in the United States and work without sponsorship.

Chicagoland

Ahmed, 34, grew up in Baghdad. He first arrived in the United States in 2015 but went back to Iraq after three months. He then returned to the United States in 2016 with the intention of staying permanently. He and his daughter arrived in Chicago through the SIV program. At the time we spoke, he had lived in the United States for approximately one year and was working for a nonprofit organization that serves immigrants, refugees, and asylum-seekers in the Chicagoland area. Ahmed connected me with both Hashim and Wissam.

Hashim, 34, was born and raised in Baghdad. He and Ahmed attended high school together and remained friends. In 2006, he moved to Erbil, the capital of Iraqi Kurdistan, in the north of the country to escape the violence in Baghdad. While in Erbil, Hashim worked with the United States Agency for International Development (USAID). This work made him eligible for a Special Immigrant Visa. In 2014, he received an SIV, and he and his wife left Iraq for the United States. Hashim resettled in Chicago, Illinois, and some of his wife's family followed thereafter. His parents remained in Baghdad. Two of his brothers resettled in Texas. At the time of our interview, Hashim worked for a university hospital system, serving as a bilingual point of contact for international medical patients who traveled to the United States for care.

Wissam, 35, is originally from Sulaymaniyah, in the Kurdish region of Iraq. He described his background as mixed, with Kurdish and Turkman grandparents, and an Arab mother. He lived in Baghdad before leaving the country. Wissam worked with the US government after the 2003 invasion. In 2005, he went to Jordan to study at an American university program. In 2009, he traveled to the United States for his graduation ceremony. While he was in the country, he and his parents claimed asylum, fearing his work with the United States put his family at risk. After Wissam claimed asylum, his wife left Iraq for Jordan, where she applied for refugee resettlement in the United States. Wissam's asylum claim was approved in 2012. Wissam is an entrepreneur. When we spoke in 2017, he was working to launch a food service and restaurant business.

Shenandoah Valley Region of Virginia

Omar, 42, is from Basra. He described himself as Sunni. He left Iraq for Lebanon in 2006 and stayed there for two years. Deciding he could not return to Iraq or stay in Lebanon, he applied for resettlement through the USRAP, and he and his wife and first child arrived in the United States in 2008. He now lives in the Shenandoah Valley Region with his wife and four kids. Omar is involved with, and has founded, multiple initiatives to support refugees and immigrants in the area. Working with other members of the local immigrant and refugee communities he has created ESL classes, translated government documents, and held civic engagement activities. Omar connected me with Nora.

Nora, 27, was born in Yemen while her father was working there. She described her background as both Kurdish and Arab with family members who are both Sunni and Shi'a. Nora has four brothers and four sisters. Two of her brothers live in Baghdad, one lives in Jordan, one in Ohio. Three of her sisters live in Iraq, one lives in Fairfax, Virginia. Nora is a lawyer who practiced family law before leaving Iraq. In what became her last case, she represented the wife of a militia leader. The militia threatened Nora's life to scare her away from the case. In 2014, Nora and her parents received visas to visit her brother and his children who live in Ohio. While in the United States, Nora decided to seek asylum due to the ongoing threat posed by her client's husband. At the time of our interview, Nora was completing a graduate degree, working, and volunteering with Omar and in several other capacities in the area.

Washington, DC, Metropolitan Area

Kasim, 45, originally from Baghdad, left Iraq for Jordan in 2006. He stayed in Jordan for a year before coming to the United States as a refugee. Kasim briefly lived with a sponsor in Virginia before moving to the DC area. He has a background in architecture and worked in that field when he first arrived in the United States. When we spoke, Kasim was working for a DC-based NGO with a focus on peacebuilding and addressing post-traumatic stress disorder (PTSD) for those affected by war. He lives with his wife and three children. His first child was born in Jordan and his two younger children were born in the United States. Unique among those interviewed in this book, Kasim is a Trump supporter, a topic we spoke at length about. Kasim connected me with Zaid.

Zaid, 35, comes from a mixed Sunni/Shi'ite family. He completed his medical training in Baghdad and worked as a doctor in Iraq. In 2007, he left the country for Jordan. He first applied for visas to go to the United Kingdom, where his older brother lives. Zaid was unable to secure a visa to the UK, so he applied for refugee status and resettlement in the United States. He arrived in the DC area in 2010. He wanted to work as a doctor but did not have the time or resources to complete the lengthy and expensive process of having his medical credentials accredited in the United States. When we spoke, he was working at an embassy in the medical attaché office. His work involves supporting nationals of the embassy's country who come to the United States for medical treatment.

Organizing Displacement and Resettlement Narratives around Belonging, Democratic Membership, and Participation

This book examines the experiences of individuals who have left their homes as refugees and resettled in the United States. Such experiences are complex and entail navigating entrance into a new society and processes of engaging with that society as a newcomer. I have sought to conceptualize those processes along three key axes: belonging, democratic membership, and participation in democratic processes.

Each of these ideas is, in turn, embedded in the concept of democracy. Democracy is both an empirical practice and a normative set of commitments. For this book, I use democracy to denote the activities and institutions that give members of a society not only legal standing, but also substantive opportunities to engage in the processes of deciding the rules and laws that govern their lives (Benhabib 2006; Pateman 1970, 2012). Therefore, participation in such processes at every level (in the home, in the workplace, and in public institutions, for example voting in elections or joining a school board) is essential to the functioning of a democratic society. Moreover, in a democratic society, members have a right to public provision of the individual and collective material resources needed to live full and meaningful lives, and a parallel right to engage in decision-making concerning how those resources are produced and distributed (Pateman 2012; Wolff 2012).

Table 0.1. Summary interviewee demographics

Pseudonym	Sex	Age	Program	Arrival	Status	Location	Interview Date
Walid	M	39	USRAP	2008	Citizen	Upstate NY	9/27/2017
Hashim	M	34	SIV	2014	Resident	Chicagoland	10/1/2017
Ahmed	M	34	SIV	2016	Resident	Chicagoland	10/2/2017
Wissam	M	35	Asylum	2009	Resident	Chicagoland	10/22/2017
Nada	F	57	SIV	2013	Resident	NYC	11/1/2017
Tariq	M	33	SIV	2012	Resident	Upstate NY	11/2/2017
Mohammed	M	38	USRAP	2011	Citizen	Upstate NY	11/2/2017
Marwa	F	48	USRAP	2009	Citizen	Upstate NY	11/25/2017
Sarah	F	39	USRAP	2013	Resident	NYC	11/30/2017
Omar	M	42	USRAP	2008	Citizen	Shenandoah Valley Region	12/14/2017
Ali	M	37	SIV	2012	Resident	NYC	1/14/2018
Abdullah	M	28	OPT	2010	Resident	NYC	1/14/2018
Nora	F	27	Asylum (Pending)	2014	Resident	Shenandoah Valley Region	2/6/2018
Kasim	M	45	USRAP	2007	Citizen	Washington, DC, Metro	2/27/2018
Zaid	M	35	USRAP	2010	Citizen	Washington, DC, Metro	2/27/2018

Because everyone who lives in a given society is subjected to decisions and structures that affect their lives each of those individuals *ought* to have an equal right to participate in those decision-making processes and structures, regardless of their formal legal status.

This book is concerned with democratizing democracy (Pateman 2012), that is to say, identifying opportunities to increase participation in existing institutions and creating new modes and sites for members to participate in making the decisions that affect their lives. A robust democratic society incorporates such structures and opportunities at every level, and in the multiple sites in which people live, work, and spend their time. The forms of participation in a democratic society are manifold and include both formal and informal structures and processes as well as deliberative engagements and agonistic struggles among its members.

With this in mind, I have adopted a normative orientation that "democracies require porous borders" (Benhabib 2006, 68). That is, there must be a way for "outsiders" to cross the boundaries of a democratic society, figuratively and literally. This access requires ongoing contestations to determine who has a right and standing to participate, and how those formerly excluded can become full members of a social and political community should they so choose. The politics of membership can play out at various sites and scales within society, including the family, neighborhood, city, nation, and beyond (Brubaker 2010).

As noted above, belonging to a political community involves much more than legal status and formal rights (Carens 2013). Belonging requires not only a right to reside in a particular place but also a right to act (Crane 2021). There is a distinction between belonging *to* a nation-state (or other sociopolitical community) and belonging *in* a nation-state (Brubaker 2010). The former typically refers to citizenship, a legal status conferring formal rights to political membership. The latter can be understood as the informal possibilities for individuals to exercise their rights substantively and to obtain acceptance as full members of the society (Brubaker 2010), should they choose to seek it. As the majority of those interviewed for this book either had US citizenship at the time of interview or had a path to gaining it, this analysis focused on belonging *in* the United States. Belonging understood this way also incorporates the reciprocal feelings of acceptance, and the processes and possibilities for interviewees to identify and build relationships with members and institutions of American society at multiple levels. As a minimum normative standard, developing a robustly democratic society requires mutual adjustment among existing members and newcomers (Carens 2013), in which all parties are willing to accept some changes to their lives and practices as a result of living in that society together.

Just as there can be tensions between formal legal status granting belonging to a state and the informal substantive experience of belonging in a nation-state, there is also tension in the substantive exercise of democratic membership. A normative presupposition of democracy is that members of a democratic community have opportunities to engage in making the decisions that affect their lives. However, there has never been a perfect overlap between those governed by the rules and laws in societies and those recognized as legitimate members of those communities. Every political community, democratic or otherwise, has disenfranchised some of its members (Benhabib 2006). Therefore, I have sought to explore the barriers, again primarily informal, to the substantive exercise of democratic membership for resettled Iraqis.

Guiding Questions

The questions that guided this project included:

- In what ways do resettled Iraqis see themselves as current or future members of a social and political community in the United States?
- What challenges and barriers existed to their gaining and exercising membership?
- Did legal residence and/or a path to citizenship translate into substantive opportunities to engage with and influence the culture, policies, and laws that affected their lives?
- In what ways were resettled Iraqis engaged in processes of democratic (re)negotiations or (re)interpretations in the United States?

Chapter Organization

This book, organized into four chapters, explores these questions through participants' observations, narratives, and experiences. Chapter 1 focuses on the 2003 American invasion of Iraq, the social, economic, and political breakdown that it precipitated in that country, and the decisions study participants made to leave their homes and resettle in the United States as a result. It details the violence unleashed by the occupation—particularly that committed by the American military and its allies—and traces the connections between the erosion of interviewees' personal safety and their decisions to seek refuge abroad.

Chapter 2 delves into study participants' assessments of postresettlement opportunities for belonging in American society and analyzes their perceptions of how negative media and government discourses and policies concerning refugees, Arabs, and Muslims shaped and constrained their life experiences. This chapter explores how those interviewed articulated the importance of finding opportunities to engage in personal and cultural exchange with friends, neighbors, and colleagues to create a more open and diverse society. I argue that such sustained efforts, while potentially constrained, can be important factors in challenging discriminatory treatment and policies and mitigating persistent negative attitudes toward these groups held by a share of America's citizens.

Chapter 3 describes study participants' understandings of democratic membership, formal and informal, in the United States. It considers interviewees' critiques of American political institutions and problematizes the possibilities for democratic governance in the United States. It then investigates four key requirements to democratic participation that interviewees identified: sufficient time to engage in democratic processes and activities; public provision of resources; adequate information to make informed decisions and participate productively; and substantive protections of rights and safety to attenuate suspicion of government officials and institutions, in part resulting from living under authoritarian rule in Iraq.

Chapter 4 elaborates on multiple sites and modes of participation in which interviewees engaged and that they identified as desired future activities. The three primary sites and modes were engaging in dialogue, debate, and discussion concerning the decisions, policies, and laws that affect their lives; volunteering with–and, in some cases, founding–community and nonprofit organizations focused on various types of (typically) refugee and immigration-related activities; and activism and protest in response to the Trump 2017 travel ban. I argue that participants' experiences demonstrate that social and political mobilization and public demonstration of norms of welcoming and diversity, and against xenophobia, undertaken jointly by resettled refugees and native-born Americans can protect and enlarge spaces for belonging and democratic participation for refugees and other groups targeted by discriminatory politics and policies.

The concluding chapter underscores the importance of deliberate, daily interactions, exchange, and organizing among newcomers and native-born Americans to expand spaces for resettled refugees to engage in, and, potentially, reconstitute, American society. Through these multifaceted social and political processes, newcomers can contest exclusions and fictive insider/outsider boundaries. It also considers how such processes might catalyze emerging and new practices of cosmopolitan democracy. The book closes by reiterating the key implications for policy and activism that the resettled Iraqis' experiences explored here illuminate, including the need to generate alternatives to American military violence; create and enlarge spaces for diversity, difference, and exchange; understand the interconnected relationships between barriers and requirements for democratic participation; and engage in struggles for justice in and across multiple sites and modes of action with varied strategies and tactics.

Notes

1. This date coincides with the end of US Federal Government fiscal year 2017 and the beginning of interviews conducted for this research.
2. See long-time National Public Radio (NPR) host Tom Gjelten's *A Nation of Nations: A Great American Immigration Story* for a recent example of work that perpetuates the discourse that the United States has "demonstrate[d] the exceptionalism it has long claimed for itself" through "enlightened" immigration policies (2015, 344).

3. In only one of eight cases polled, the 1999 proposed resettlement of several hundred individuals from Kosovo, did a clear majority of Americans support resettlement (66 percent). In 2018, a slight majority (51 percent) indicated support for accepting several thousand Central American individuals fleeing their countries. Only minorities approved in all other cases polled: Syrians in 2015 (37 percent), Vietnamese in 1979 (32 percent), Hungarians in 1958 (33 percent), Europeans including Jews in 1946 (16 percent) and 1947 (24 percent), and German children in 1939 (26 percent) (J. McCarthy 2018).
4. Anti-Arab and anti-Muslim rhetoric propagated by American political leaders dates back as far as the late eighteenth century, when conflict broke out between the newly established United States government and the Barbary states encompassing present-day Morocco, Algeria, and Tunisia (Beydoun 2013).
5. Importantly as well, there is a long history of violent and exclusionary US government policies targeting (im)migrants. For example, the United States expelled more than one million Mexican immigrants in the 1930s, 60 percent of whom were American citizens (Valenciana and Ordoñez-Jasis 2012).
6. Negotiated under Trump and carried out under Biden, in August 2021, the United States officially ended its twenty-year war against Afghanistan and evacuated its remaining troops from the country. However, the repeated declarations of war's end in Iraq, and continuing bombing and US special forces campaigns around the world, provide significant reason to assume that this decades-long war will not end, but rather morph into a continued military engagement waged by clandestine forces, private mercenaries, and aerial bombardment by drones and warplanes.
7. For example, most Palestinian refugees—one of the world's largest displaced populations—are excluded from the (limited) protections afforded by the international legal regime established by the 1951 Convention Relating to the Status of Refugees and the programs run by the United Nations High Commissioner for Refugees (UNHCR) that assist displaced persons.

1

Seeking Refuge amid Decades of American War against Iraq

Everyone knows . . . there were no good reasons to destroy the country and to make the people immigrants and . . . kill so many . . . people in Iraq just because of Saddam Hussein and his administration at that time. The country is completely destroyed. . . . I mean, the Iraqi people didn't deserve that.

–Hashim, 1 October 2017

Introduction

The study of displacement and refugee resettlement is also the study of war.[1] Addressing how those who resettle as refugees view belonging and democratic membership in societies of refuge requires first considering the question of what compelled them to leave their homes in the first place. For this reason, it is crucial to examine the connections between the American war in Iraq and the effects that conflict has had on millions of people in that country, in the region, and around the world. The ongoing American war fought against their country forced the individuals who participated in this study to leave their homes and resettle in the United States. As Omar, 42, originally from Basra and now living in the Shenandoah Valley Region of Virginia, told me, for example, "I came here because of the war that I didn't create" (14 December 2017).

The United States has been fighting a war against Iraq for thirty years. Since 1991, its government and military have inflicted massive, widespread, and ongoing harm to the Iraqi people. Conservatively, the American war has caused hundreds of thousands of deaths, and many times that number of physical and psychological injuries. Millions have been displaced from their homes, some temporarily and many others permanently. American soldiers and their allies have committed numerous atrocities during the war as well, including rape, torture, murder, and massacres. Extensive bombing and battles have caused catastrophic destruction throughout the country. Although many other countries have fought against Iraq during this conflict, particularly the United Kingdom, the United States has led the war since its inception and overwhelmingly caused the most harm.[2]

The US government's justifications for continued violence have shifted over time–stopping Iraqi aggression against Kuwait in 1991, weakening the Saddam regime in the 1990s, liberating the people of Iraq in 2003, and defeating ISIS in 2014. However, beyond the public rhetoric and propaganda campaigns calibrated to gain support for conflict from the American population (Kellner 2004, 1992), the war in Iraq–like so many other conflicts before and since–has been fought to project and maintain American imperial hegemony in the region and beyond (Kumar 2012; Kinzer 2007). The American war against Iraq has been, since its inception, a crime against humanity. The architects and leaders of this war, who have thus far evaded any responsibility for their crimes, must be held to account. Americans broadly must grapple with and make reparations for the immense ongoing harm the US-led war has caused the Iraqi people since 1991 and the mass displacement that was among its predictable consequences.[3] This chapter sketches the violent realities of the US-led war, particularly the 2003 invasion and occupation, without which millions of individuals would still be living in their homes in Baghdad or Fallujah, rather than seeking refuge in Amman, Berlin, or New York.

This chapter begins by establishing the context that the United States, as well-articulated by one of this study's participants, is not a "normal" country; rather, it is an empire that has violently pursued its imperial designs throughout the world, including Iraq. The chapter then explores the thirty-year American war against Iraq, focusing particularly on the harms caused by the 2003 invasion and subsequent occupation. That discussion is followed by interviewees' observations concerning the corrosive effects the invasion inflicted on their lives and the lives of millions of other Iraqis. Finally, this chapter explores interviewees' decisions to leave their homes and seek refuge in the United States.

The United States: Not a Normal Country

On 14 January 2018, I spoke with a young man named Abdullah, 28, who lived in New York City at the time of our interview. During our conversation, he said of the United States: "It's not a normal country, it's a superpower country. . . . It's not like a country that is just, interfering inside its own borders. It's a major power" (Abdullah 14 January 2018). His characterization of the United States as a superpower is commonly accepted by those both supportive and critical of its role in the world (Ullman and Wade

1996; Ó Tuathail 2003; Kagen 2021; Boot 2019). Put more directly: the United States is an empire.

The United States as a political and social formation is a historically and contemporary expansionist and imperialist project, striving to conquer territory, maintain military dominance, and extend economic and cultural hegemony, first in what is now called North America and thereafter around the globe (Brown 1970; Kinzer 2007; Kumar 2012; Immerwahr 2019). According to the US Department of Defense, for example, the United States now operates 4,800 "Defense Sites" in 160 countries located on all seven continents (US Department of Defense n.d.). This includes maintaining eight hundred military bases in dozens of countries (Vine 2015). In comparison, all other countries in the world maintain a combined total of seventy military bases beyond their own borders (Slater 2018).

To maintain and expand its influence and control, the United States has a long and ongoing history of military invasions, covert and overt assassinations, training and funding of paramilitary forces, and coups against other governments. In the decades after World War II, the United States worked to overthrow the governments of Iran, Guatemala, Congo, Dominican Republic, South Vietnam, Brazil, and Chile (Stuster 2013). In the second half of the twentieth century, it bombed and/or invaded North and South Korea, North and South Vietnam, Laos, Cambodia, Panama, Grenada, and Iraq (Kinzer 2007). To enumerate only a partial list of the conflicts it has waged in the twenty-first century, in addition to the war in Iraq described in this chapter, the United States waged a war against Afghanistan from 2001 to 2021, participated in the 2011 North Atlantic Treaty Organization (NATO) naval blockade and aerial bombardment of Libya, and has fought an air war in Syria since 2014. The United States also supports, funds, and arms the Israeli military occupation of the West Bank and its blockade and regular bombardment of Gaza (Sharp 2022). The US military and Central Intelligence Agency (CIA) have also carried out large-scale drone assassination programs and air wars in Pakistan, Somalia, and Yemen, begun in 2002 under George W. Bush, intensified under Barack Obama, and continued under Donald Trump and Joe Biden (Guilliard et al. 2015; Scahill 2015). The United States has launched at least 947 drone, fighter jet, and cruise missile attacks since 2002, killing between 4,569 and 6,605 people in those countries.[4] In 2020, the United States deployed special forces to 154 countries, approximately 80 percent of the nations in the world (Turse 2021). Abdullah emphasized his point about the global reach of American power and violence by observing: "[Americans] might not feel it, but whatever decision politically you take, it could affect the lives of millions of other people. . . . It did affect my country and it's affecting other countries. I know it's hard to tell from living here and the media you have. . . . But that decision you make to elect someone, it has a direct influence on other people's lives" (14 January 2018). It is to the devastating effects of the American war on Abdullah's home country that I now turn. The next section is not a thorough history of the American war against Iraq; rather, it is a sketch meant to demonstrate the character, scale, and duration of the violence of American geopolitical maneuvering and military conflict and the tremendous harm the United States has caused to the people of Iraq.

Decades of American Geopolitical Machinations and War against Iraq

Like the United States, Iraq has a transnational genealogy (Dewachi 2017). Successive imperial powers have controlled and shaped the country as a social and political community–the Ottoman Empire, the British Empire, and most recently the American empire. The movements of people into and out of Iraq's territory have fundamentally shaped and reshaped it. In recent decades, Iraqis have experienced prolonged insecurity and violence under authoritarian and repressive governments as well as multiple, consecutive conflicts. Sarah, 39, an interviewee living in New York City, explained there was a "very bad situation there because before 2003, before the American war, [Iraq] had another war with Kuwait, with Iran, and all the wars affected the people. So, this suffering is not from just 2003. Before, it was very hard for these people to live this destroyed life" (30 November 2017).

The United States has supported multiple repressive Iraqi regimes. It is implicated in all the conflicts Sarah referenced and began interfering in Iraq's internal affairs more than half a century ago. In 1960, for example, the CIA attempted to assassinate Iraqi prime minister Abd al-Karim Qasim (Wise 2009). It then built links with the then-marginal Ba'ath Party, supporting its 1963 coup to remove Qasim. Seeking to purge leftist opposition in the country, the CIA provided lists of Iraqi Communist Party members and their allies to the Ba'athists, which that faction used to track and murder at least seven hundred people (Frontline 2014). The Ba'athists remained in power for the next forty years, with Saddam Hussein rising to the Iraqi presidency in 1979. The American government supported Saddam's brutal regime while it carried out many of its worst crimes. During the 1980–88 Iran-Iraq War, for example, the United States provided Saddam with economic aid, battlefield intelligence, and components to build chemical weapons (Tucker 2014). It simultaneously supplied Iran with weapons in violation of an international arms embargo and American law (Cleveland and Bunton 2009). US intelligence provided critical targeting information for Iraqi sarin gas attacks on Iranian forces (Harris and Aid 2013). Saddam remained a US ally throughout his government's genocidal campaign against Iraq's Kurds between 1986 and 1989 (Roth 2004).

When Saddam invaded Kuwait in 1990, however, the United States turned on its former ally and led a multicountry coalition in an air war against Iraqi forces in Kuwait and Iraq. The massive six-week bombing campaign that began in January 1991 killed as many as eighty-two thousand Iraqi soldiers and seven thousand civilians (Cleveland and Bunton 2009) and destroyed thousands of buildings (Ahtisaari 1991). The now-infamous "Highway of Death" events demonstrate the one-sided nature of the conflict. As Iraqi soldiers retreated from Kuwait, US warplanes destroyed vehicles at the front and rear of the column of forces before heavily bombing along the highway. Blocked by ruined vehicles, Iraqi soldiers were trapped under the assault. American pilots who participated described the attacks as "shooting ducks in a pond" and "shooting fish in a barrel" (Coll and Branigin 1991). Coalition forces also intentionally and extensively bombed civilian infrastructure in Iraq including roads, power plants, food warehouses, and water purification facilities (Sherry 1991). As Dewachi describes the assault:

> Coalition forces devoted their energies to the strategic destruction of Iraq's physical infrastructure. Aerial bombardment and cruise missiles hammered Iraqi cities for forty days, dropping more than 90,000 tons of bombs. In Baghdad, bridges linking the two banks of the Tigris River were demolished, power stations were destroyed, and water sanitation systems across the country were ruined. Decades of infrastructure work had been undone. For months, Iraqis living in the capital had no electricity, no clean water, and no telephone lines. (2017, 148)

In one instance, American warplanes dropped laser-guided "smart" bombs on a civil defense air-raid shelter in Baghdad, killing two to three hundred civilians. The United States knew the structure had been used as a civilian air-raid shelter during the Iran-Iraq War—and it was clearly marked as such in 1991—yet warplanes intentionally bombed the shelter without first issuing warnings to evacuate as mandated by international law. Human Rights Watch called the attack a "serious violation of the laws of war" (Sherry 1991). A United Nations humanitarian mission report filed in 1991 characterized the level of devastation inflicted by the American-led bombing in the following way: "The recent conflict has wrought *near-apocalyptic* [emphasis added] results upon the economic infrastructure of what had been, until January 1991, a rather highly urbanized and mechanized society. Now, most means of modern life support have been destroyed or rendered tenuous. Iraq has, for some time to come, been relegated to a pre-industrial age" (Ahtisaari 1991).

Wissam, 35 originally from Sulaymaniyah and now living in the Chicago area, argued that Saddam made a mistake when he invaded Kuwait in 1990: "If he didn't do that, maybe Iraq will be even better than Qatar or Kuwait or Saudi Arabia" (22 October 2017). Saddam had ruled a strong centralized state; Iraq had a large, highly educated population, a powerful military, and a relatively high healthcare standard (Sanford 2003; Dewachi 2017; Inhorn 2018). Wissam, no supporter of Saddam, said that although there were no political freedoms in Iraq under the Ba'athist regime, "It was the peak state in the area . . . but now, it has the opposite" of those strong social and economic structures (22 October 2017).

During the conflict, more than one million Iraqis sought refuge in neighboring countries, including Jordan and Iran (Public Information Section 2003). The majority eventually returned to their homes. However, in the decade following the conflict, approximately forty-nine thousand Iraqis resettled in the United States (Grieco 2003).

Soon after the Iraqi invasion of Kuwait, the United Nations imposed, and the United States supported and enforced, unprecedented, comprehensive sanctions on Iraq that remained in place until 2003. That sanctions regime, compounded by the destruction of essential infrastructure, shattered the Iraqi health system (Gordon 2010). Lack of food, clean water, and healthcare led to the deaths of hundreds of thousands of children under age five between 1990 and 2003 (Dyson 2006). Journalist Jeremy Scahill (2018) said of his time reporting from Iraq during this period that "hospitals were like death rows for infants. There were no medical supplies. Birth defects that weren't found in modern medical journals were appearing. Syringes were being reused and hospital floors were being cleaned with gasoline."

In 1996, when confronted with the prospect that sanctions had killed half a million Iraqi children, US ambassador to the United Nations and later secretary of state under President Bill Clinton, Madeleine Albright said, "We think the price is worth it" (Mahajan 2001). In 1999, former UN humanitarian coordinator in Iraq Denis Halliday, who resigned in protest of the enormous suffering caused by the sanctions, described these measures as "deliberately, knowingly killing thousands of Iraqis each month. And that definition fits genocide" (Siegal 1999). An "undeclared conventional war" continued between 1991 and 2003 (Anderson 2014, 111). American and British warplanes dominated Iraqi airspace, flying hundreds of thousands of sorties, dropping thousands of bombs and missiles, and killing and injuring hundreds of civilians (Ali 2000).

Shortly after George W. Bush's election to the US presidency in 2000, preparations began for a large-scale escalation of conflict against Iraq. One of Bush's first acts as president was to authorize joint US/UK bombing raids in February 2001 to disable Iraq's air defense network ("US and British Aircraft Attack Iraq" 2001). The administration spent the next two years waging a propaganda campaign to convince domestic US and international audiences that Saddam Hussein presented a global threat (R. C. Kramer and Michalowski 2005; Kellner 2004). Despite unprecedented worldwide antiwar protests (Chrisafis et al. 2006; CNN 2003b) and opposition by the United Nations, Arab League, and the European Union (CNN 2003c, 2003a; MacAskill and Borger 2004), the United States and its allies launched a large-scale assault on Iraq on 20 March 2003.

After more than a decade of low-level conflict, the 2003 invasion began a new destructive phase of the war. As Nora, 27 and living in the Shenandoah Valley Region of Virginia, succinctly put it, "The US said that they're liberating [Iraq], but they were invading actually" (6 February 2018). The initial aerial bombardment and ground attack killed more than seven thousand civilians and many more Iraqi combatants defending against the invasion. The US military targeted fifty Iraqi leaders, including Saddam Hussein, for "decapitation" airstrikes during the assault. The initial bombings killed none of those original targets, but did kill dozens of civilians. Although on a smaller scale than in 1991, American warplanes again targeted infrastructure such as the country's media outlets, telecommunications, and the electrical grid (Docherty and Garlasco 2003).

The invaders quickly defeated the Iraqi Army, overthrew the government, and dismantled the state. The Americans and their allies then restructured the Iraqi government and economy, privatizing public goods and resources for the profit of United States and other foreign companies (R. Kramer, Michalowski, and Rothe 2005). A US occupation regime directly ruled the country until June 2004, after which a provisional Iraqi government formed the basis for a newly established parliamentary system. Although Saddam Hussein escaped the initial invasion, American forces captured him in December 2003. Saddam was tried and convicted of crimes against humanity in an Iraqi court and executed in 2006.

Unlike in 1991, the 2003 escalation involved a large-scale military occupation by American soldiers and mercenaries–euphemistically referred to as "contractors"–as well as much smaller numbers of allied forces. Four individuals with whom I spoke–Ahmed, 34, a Special Immigrant Visa (SIV) recipient now living in Chicago; Ali, 37, now residing in New York City; Hashim, 34, and living in Chicagoland; and Tariq, 33, now living in Upstate New York–worked with the US government and military in different capacities, such as translators and interpreters, in the years after 2003. The husband of Nada, 57, an SIV recipient now living in New York City, did as well.

Sarah told me that after the invasion there was "No education. No electricity. No stable life. No jobs. The war destroyed the country" (30 November 2017). Nada said of life after 2003 in Iraq: "The situation in Iraq is so, so difficult. . . . During one year in my country, I couldn't sleep. I feel always I'm very scared of everything. Who's knocking on the door? When my kids or my son or my husband went to college or school or his work, really, sometimes when they went, I heard some bombs. I didn't know what I will do at that time" (1 November 2017). Violence in Iraq continues today. Conservatively, since March 2003, the American-led invasion and subsequent occupation have killed between 275,000 and 306,000 people, including approximately 186,000 to 209,000 civilians (Crawford and Lutz 2021). Hundreds of thousands more have been injured. These numbers include people killed directly by violence committed by the United States and its allies as well as by anti-occupation forces and groups such as al-Qa'ida and later ISIS.[5] The figures cited here are certainly incomplete; destroyed infrastructure, lack of healthcare, and inadequate food access caused by the invasion have killed as many or more people than these totals. Multiple studies conducted in the years since 2003 have estimated a significantly higher civilian death toll (Hagopian et al. 2013; Burnham et al. 2006; Guilliard et al. 2015).

Since 2003, American and allied bombardment and battles have destroyed tens of thousands of homes, hospitals, mosques, and other buildings throughout the country. In 2004, for example, US forces twice laid siege to Fallujah. On April 1, Marines surrounded the city and launched an assault that killed hundreds of civilians, destroyed thousands of homes, and forced the majority of the city's two hundred thousand residents to flee (R. McCarthy and Beaumont 2004; Rayburn et al. 2019). American and allied forces again attacked the city on 8 November 2004. A US Army Captain who led a thirteen-day tank assault on the city, told *The Boston Globe,* "I really hate that it had to be destroyed. But . . . [t]he only way to root them out is to *destroy everything in your path*" (Barnard 2004; emphasis added). The second assault killed more than one thousand civilians and damaged or destroyed 70 percent of the homes in Fallujah, thousands of businesses, one hundred mosques, and multiple government buildings (Jamail 2012). The siege killed so many civilians that the city's soccer stadium had to be converted into a graveyard (Glantz 2017).

Shelling and bombing from ground and air—first against Saddam's government, then anti-occupation fighters, and most recently ISIS—has repeatedly reduced large sections of major Iraqi cities, including Ramadi and Mosul, to rubble (Sim 2017; George 2016). According to Amnesty International (2017), the US-led aerial assault against ISIS in Mosul demonstrated an "Alarming pattern" of "destroy[ing] whole houses with entire families inside. The high civilian toll suggests that coalition forces . . . have failed to take adequate precautions to prevent civilian deaths, in flagrant violation of international humanitarian law." The massive debris created by heavy bombardment and the use of weapons such as cluster bombs and depleted uranium munitions have left many areas contaminated and polluted with toxic and radioactive materials (Inhorn 2018).[6] Epidemiological studies since have found a correlation between this pollution and significantly increased birth defects and cancer rates among Iraq's population (Busby, Hamdan, and Ariabi 2010; Chulov 2010; Zwijnenburg and Weir 2016).

Between 2003 and 2011, the United States maintained a large occupying army in Iraq. As Abdullah argued in his interview, "If the military, they go to a civilian place, any military, they wouldn't act nice. They would be rude. They would attack people. They would be aggressive" (14 January 2018). The occupying army battled individuals and groups resisting its presence and policed the country. American and allied occupiers belligerently patrolled Iraqi streets,[7] shooting, injuring, and killing thousands of civilians (Zielbauer 2007b). In the months after the 2003 invasion, American soldiers fired upon crowds of anti-occupation protesters on at least five separate occasions, killing dozens of people and injuring many more (Amnesty International 2004a; Howard and McCarthy 2003; Bouckaert and Abrahams 2003). For example, on 15 April 2003, soldiers fired on demonstrators in Mosul, killing seven and injuring dozens. Two weeks later, on 28 April, soldiers in Fallujah killed seventeen protesters and injured seventy-five others. A 2003 Human Rights Watch investigation into civilian killings by American soldiers found a pattern of "over-aggressive tactics, indiscriminate shooting in residential areas and a quick reliance on lethal force" (Abrahams 2003, 4). A 2007 congressional investigation uncovered a similar pattern among Blackwater mercenaries (House of Representatives Committee on Oversight and Government Reform 2007). To give a sense of the scale of this violence, the US Army recorded 4,492 "escalation of force" incidents between January 2005 and January 2006. Only sixty-seven instances (1.5 percent of the total) involved anti-occupation fighters; the remainder involved civilians (Rayburn et al. 2019, 548–49). This analysis implies that, in 2005 alone, American soldiers fired on civilians more than forty-four hundred times.

Sometimes US soldiers and mercenaries shot civilians by accident. On other occasions, however, they did so intentionally (Schmidt 2011). American forces have committed numerous murders and massacres since 2003 (ACLU 2007; Schofield 2011; Glantz 2017; Whitlock 2009; Kennard 2012; Chappell 2019b). Some events are well-known; for example, the 2005 massacre of twenty-four civilians in Haditha (Schmidt 2012) and the 2007 killing of fourteen in Baghdad's Nisour Square by Blackwater mercenaries (Neuman 2017). But there have been many other, less infamous, crimes. In May 2004, for example, US helicopters and soldiers attacked a wedding in the village of Mukaradeeb, killing between forty-two and forty-five people, including fifteen children (McCarthy 2004b). As witness and survivor Haleema Shihab told *The Guardian*, at 3 AM "the American soldiers started to shoot us. They were shooting low on the ground and targeting us one by one" (McCarthy 2004a). Consider as well, the "Iron Triangle Murders," one of multiple killings and attempted cover-ups.[8] On 9 May 2006, American soldiers killed four unarmed Iraqis during a raid on an island in Lake Tharthar. The soldiers first shot and killed a man and detained three others, all unarmed. The Americans then released the men and told them to run before shooting them, in an attempt to make it look like they had tried to escape (Zielbauer 2007a). In one of the most disturbing known crimes, on 12 March 2006, five American soldiers broke into the home of fourteen-year-old Abeer Qassim Hamza al-Janabi. The soldiers killed Abeer's mother, father, and younger sister before gang-raping, killing Abeer, and setting her body on fire (MacAskill and Howard 2007).

Although the killing of Abeer and her family was shocking in its brutality, US cruelty has been endemic to the post-2003 invasion. In the first year of the occupation, the American military arrested and detained thousands of individuals (Amnesty International 2004b), the overwhelming majority of whom (between 70 percent and 90 percent) were innocent of any crime (International Committee of the Red Cross [ICRC] 2004). US forces in Iraq also engaged in the widespread torture of prisoners (Brody 2004). The most well-known abuse took place at the US-run Abu Ghraib and Camp Bucca prisons at which American soldiers beat, sexually assaulted, and raped captives (Taguba 2004). Far from isolated incidents, American forces tortured Iraqis—sometimes to death (White 2005)—in numerous locations throughout the country (Brody 2004). For example, three American soldiers told Human Rights Watch (2005) that they and their comrades at Forward Operating Base Mercury near Fallujah routinely beat prisoners, forced them into "stress positions" until they passed out, and denied them food and water for their amusement. American forces also turned over captives to their Iraqi allies for interrogation, abuse, and torture (Leigh and O'Kane 2010). The American occupation officially ended in 2011. However, more than ten years later, US soldiers remain in the country, although at a much-reduced level.

In reaction to the violence committed by the American forces, the invasion and dismantling of the Iraqi state sparked legitimate armed anti-occupation resistance. It also opened space for intercommunal violence between the long politically dominant Sunni minority and the majority Shi'a population. Importantly, although there are significant theological differences between Sunnis and Shi'a, the intercommunal violence that has plagued Iraq in the past two decades is fundamentally politically driven, rather than religiously (Inhorn 2018). After 2003, sectarian militias formed and recruited Iraqis and foreign fighters to resist the American and other occupying forces (Cockburn 2016). Armed groups pursued their own goals and sought revenge against members of Iraqi society. The United States formed, trained, funded, and fought alongside Iraqi police and paramilitaries. Some of these groups, including the notorious special police commando Wolf Brigade, acted as death squads engaging in widespread torture and killings with US knowledge, if not approval and collaboration (Mahmood et al. 2013). Organizations such as al-Qa'ida in Iraq, and its later offshoot, ISIS, flourished in the chaos of the American war and launched campaigns of violence against occupation forces, the new US-imposed Iraqi government, and the population. As Wissam argued in our interview, before 2003 there were "certain people or certain red lines you didn't cross, and you stay safe. Now, you don't know who's your enemy. Your enemy is unseen. [You don't know] who is going to take your house, take your rights. So, it's very hard. . . . Every party has its own militia, and they fight all the civilians who are the victims. And they keep fighting with each other" (22 October 2017). Although the contours and intensity of the American war in Iraq have fluctuated since 1991, it continues. The Biden administration announced an end to the US "combat mission" in Iraq in December 2021 (Burns, Madhani, and Abdul-Zahra 2021). However, given the multiple previously declared ends to the conflict in 1991, 2003, 2011, and 2017, and the continued drone bombings, airstrikes, and special forces raids throughout the region, only time will tell whether the United States will ever fully end its war in Iraq. As explained in more detail below, several interviewees, including Abdullah, Tariq, and Wissam, noted that they had initially supported the idea of removing Saddam from power, only to become disillusioned with the seeming lack of a US postinvasion strategy and in light of the violence his regime's fall unleashed. Hashim alluded to opposition to the invasion, saying, "wars never solve anything. Actually, they make things worse. You saw after the Iraq war in 2003 until today . . . it's completely destroyed" (Hashim 1 October 2017). One individual, Walid, 39, living in Upstate New York, explicitly stated that he was against the war before it began. He said: "We like solving things without violence, without war. In a diplomatic way. We were tortured by Saddam Hussein, but I disagree about the war in Iraq. There's too many other ways. . . . There is no mercy in the war, unfortunately. There are going to be too many mistakes" (Walid 27 September 2017).

During our interview, Kasim, 45 from Baghdad, and now living in Maryland, discussed his view that the Bush administration's prosecution of the war was a "total failure." Bush "just went there and he couldn't do anything," Kasim said, "So, Obama pulled back, pulled out his troops. It made things worse" (27 February 2018). When we spoke in February 2018, he interpreted the Trump administration's renewed engagement as promising to "go back to Iraq, we'll solve the problems, and that's what he did" (Kasim 27 February 2018). Intense US bombing continued through late 2017 and began to taper off in early 2018. At the time of this writing, in mid-2022, airstrikes against ISIS in what is now a cross-border conflict in Iraq and neighboring Syria continue, although at a reduced rate. Approximately twenty-five hundred American soldiers and forty-five hundred Department of Defense Contractors remain in the country, supporting Iraqi forces as they continue to battle ISIS (Schmitt 2021; Deutsche Welle 2021).

Three individuals with whom I spoke, Hashim, Marwa, and Ali, said that Americans occasionally apologize to them for the harm caused by the war.

When this happens, Hashim observed, he responds, "it's not your fault, don't apologize . . . it's just politics. It's not the people" (1 October 2017). Marwa, 48, and now living in Upstate New York, explained: "Some people, they say sorry. They know what it's like there when they attacked, when the American army attacked Iraq and that's why we are here. Some people, and they are veterans, they say sorry. . . . I say no, don't say sorry. Saddam Hussein, he was very bad. I'm not a person who liked him. I'm happy when they took Saddam Hussein out. I was so happy" (25 November 2017). Ali said that when Americans find out he is from Iraq, "not all of them, but most of them," tell him they are sorry, "we ruined your country because of a false war" (14 January 2018). "I feel happy when I hear that," he said, "because if my country didn't have war . . . I wouldn't be here, you know?" (Ali 14 January 2018). The following section further explores the ways in which, according to many of those I interviewed, the 2003 invasion shattered Iraqi society.

The War's Corrosive Effects on Iraqi Society

The majority of those with whom I spoke described how the American invasion and toppling of the Iraqi government precipitated the social, economic, and political breakdown of Iraqi society. Chaos ensued in the wake of the invasion and overthrow of the Saddam Hussein regime. While life had been difficult under Ba'athist rule, toppling the Saddam regime left a vacuum of basic state services and eroded the minimal safety that had existed before. Trust between individuals and communities began to fracture, militia and paramilitary groups flourished, and foreign fighters entered the country. Militias fought against both the occupation of the country by foreign armies as well as other members of Iraqi society as intercommunal violence spread. These groups, most of which were unknown in Iraq before the invasion according to interviewees, terrorized the country's population.

Iraqi society is composed of individuals from myriad diverse religious and ethnic backgrounds. Many Iraqis lived in heterogeneous communities and coexisted relatively peacefully before the 2003 American-led invasion (Crane 2021). According to Marwa, for example, in Iraq before 2003, people of different religious backgrounds, such as Christians, Muslims, and Yazidi interacted with each other: "My neighbor, she was a Christian. . . . I celebrated with her, she celebrated with me" (25 November 2017). Sarah too noted that there were multiple communities living together in Iraq prior to the invasion, including Muslims and Christians. She said when she was in school, many of her friends were Christians. Tariq said that Americans are surprised when he tells them "We have Christians in Iraq" along with many other religious groups, some that do not exist in significant numbers in the

United States (2 November 2017). In Iraq, Tariq had friends from multiple religious backgrounds, and those differences were not a source of tension. For example, if he, a Muslim, invited his Christian friend to a religious celebration, his friend would "never tell me: 'No, Tariq, I can't. I'm Christian.'" Rather, he would respond, "I'm coming!" (November 2017). After the 2003 invasion, militia and other violent groups targeted minority populations, causing significant numbers of Iraqi Christians of various denominations to leave the country for refuge abroad (Sassoon 2009).

Moreover, Kasim offered the insight that although many different groups have lived together in Iraq for millennia, relations between them have not always been peaceful. Kurds in Iraq, for example, have long struggled for political and cultural autonomy and suffered from repeated military assaults during Ba'athist rule (Marr and Al-Marashi 2017). Kasim compared the situation in Iraq in 2018 to that of Iraqi Jews in the 1940s and 1950s. "Our parents or grandparents didn't talk about it, [but] now . . . we are suffering exactly what they suffered" (Kasim 27 February 2018). Jews were "part of society and they had all the rights, just like ours. And it's their country, they've been there for thousands of years. We should give them the opportunity to come back. We should prepare the society to accept them again" (Kasim 27 February 2018). In the early 1950s, the majority of Iraqi Jews, one of the world's oldest Jewish communities, emigrated under increasing threat by the Iraqi government in the wake of the 1948 creation of the State of Israel (Shiblak 2005).

Kasim went on to say, that Iraq "has to be a tolerant society to everybody. . . . It's a mosaic of different cultures" (27 February 2018). However, as he explained, successive minority groups have been "oppressed or pushed out" throughout Iraqi history (Kasim 27 February 2018). "And then the Christians now, the Yazidis. In every time period there've been one of the minorities being subject to some kind of discrimination," he said.

The American war did not create the cleavages and tensions in Iraqi society. However, its destruction of the Iraqi state created a situation that allowed sectarian violence to flourish. In addition to producing the conditions that led to violent conflict between Sunni and Shi'a militias (Marr and Al-Marashi 2017), ethnic cleansing of Iraqi Christians in the first decades of the twenty-first century, and ISIS genocide against Yazidis in the 2010s (United Nations 2021), the violence and instability created by the American war and its aftermath eroded education and employment opportunities and persistently threatened the personal safety of Iraqis of all backgrounds. Nearly all interviewees spoke at least briefly about their experiences during the conflict. Some expressed their views concerning the US invasion and ensuing occupation, offering a range of perspectives. A particularly salient thread that appeared across the interviews was the ways in which the 2003 invasion created instability and violence throughout the country.

Sarah, for example, spoke about the postinvasion intercommunal violence committed by Sunni against Shi'a and vice versa, based on group identity. As she explained, this ongoing violence had caused "Too many people from Iraq to escape to go to another state, because some people don't like this situation.... Many people, not just me" (Sarah 30 November 2017). She noted that common countries of resettlement included Australia, Sweden, and the United States.[9] Her brother left Iraq and went to Germany, while other relatives had resettled in Sweden and Turkey. Sarah and her sisters left Iraq to find a safer situation in Syria, remaining there for eight years before relocating first to Arizona and later to New York City. I asked her whether she had a choice of resettlement country when she applied with the United Nations in Syria and she said, "Actually, no. I told them we wanted to go to London because my uncle lives there. Maybe he could help me and my sisters. But the UN told me it doesn't work. It's very hard. [The UN sent] me and my sisters here, to America" (30 November 2017).

The ongoing war in Syria began while she was there, and she witnessed conflict unfold in her home country as well as her society of refuge. In Iraq, "Sometimes we see this situation in front of my eyes," she said, "some people died and me and my sister, when you see this, we'll be crying, and I can't sleep" (Sarah 30 November 2017). "We escaped from Iraq, we went to Syria," she continued: "I saw the bad situation there also when the war started.... I heard the warplanes, up in the air. We saw the school, high school near to my apartment, it exploded.... Many people were afraid and scared. We see the same situation, from Iraq to Syria. It's very hard.... It's still hard. We remember that and still, I am too afraid of the plane, the warplane. The sound, I can't sleep"(Sarah 30 November 2017). Sarah also explained that she believes both Iraqis and Americans have suffered because of the war: "The American people, some families, lost maybe the husband, the father, the brother or the son because of the war. I see on TV, too many American people that suffered from this. It's not good. The war, it's not good for any country" (30 November 2017).

Similarly, Nada explained how stressful the conditions in Iraq were before she and her family decided to leave. If her husband or children were late coming home from work or school, she worried they had been kidnapped. She said: "And I told you why we are coming here: for my husband and for my kids. I wanted to have more safety. And I wanted to sleep. Really" (Nada 1 November 2017). Nada's husband worked for an American company after the invasion and, at one point, she found a note in her garden at home that read: "You should go now. You should leave now" (1 November 2017). Those threatening her life because of her husband's work left a bullet with the letter. "What can we do?" she said, "Of course, my kids and my husband are very important for me, this is my family. So, we decided to come here [to New York City]" (Nada 1 November 2017).

Nora explained that she has a mixed background. "I'm coming from . . . Kurdish and Arabic," she said, "And then, part of my family is Sunni and part of my family is Shi'ite. That makes it harder for me to adjust to the whole conflict back home. That was one of the things that I got threatened because of. It's like, you cannot hate your own family" (6 February 2018). She continued to elaborate on the threat she and her family faced: "My whole family was threatened by the two parties, the Sunni and the Shi'ite. We got kidnapped, my brother got kidnapped twice. My dad got kidnapped. And I was threatened to be kidnapped, to get killed actually, to be honest with you. I'm quite sure. Because I was in two different families, Sunni and Shi'ite and I cannot support one of them against the other because they both are my family. Like my sisters, my aunts, and my brothers-in-law, so, I got rejected" (Nora 6 February 2018).

As Hashim argued in his succinct summary of the invasion that serves as the epigraph to this chapter: "Everyone knows . . . there were no good reasons to destroy the country and to make the people immigrants and . . . kill so many . . . people in Iraq just because of Saddam Hussein and his administration at that time. The country is completely destroyed. . . . I mean, the Iraqi people didn't deserve that. This is something that is just not fair" (1 October 2017). For Hashim, the consequences of the invasion began in 2003 and continued up to late 2017 when we spoke. In his words:

> You saw after the Iraq war in 2003 until today . . . it's completely destroyed. Everybody now, they want their parts. The country is becoming divided. . . . We have ISIS in Iraq. We never heard about these kinds of terrorist groups. We never had them in Iraq before. We used to live in Baghdad, we were really a very successful community. We have schools, we have universities. We studied, we had very good education, and we had very good entertainment places, everything we had. Now everything is destroyed. We have the worst education. We have the worst healthcare. . . . It's just not fair. (Hashim 1 October 2017)

Because of the invasion, Hashim said, "We were never able to plan for anything in Iraq. Even if I planned for two years or three years and then something happened in that city, either war or conflict or anything it will completely destroy all our plans" (1 October 2017). Hashim's parents still live in Baghdad, and he said: "I would really, really love to go back to them, to live with them." However, "at the same time . . . we cannot do anything there. It's just very hard to plan, to set a future for your kids" (Hashim 1 October 2017).

Tariq asserted, "In 2003 if you were there, and you saw how the United States, the Marines, and Army came, everybody welcomed them. You will say: 'We didn't know that Iraqis, they love the United States. They have no problem with us'" (2 November 2017). During the war, he joined the

American Marines as a translator because, as he argued, "we want to, people like me, they think that if the US they came to help us, we should help ourselves" (Tariq 2 November 2017). However, his attitude changed. "The turning point," he said, came when "you [the American government and military] left everything open to . . . al-Qa'ida. They moved into Iraq. This is the point that I started to believe the United States, they did a really bad job with us, and they killed us" (Tariq 2 November 2017).

Abdullah said it was difficult to determine whether Iraq would have been better off without the 2003 invasion. "Because," he said. "We had a problem with the regime. . . . He [Saddam] was a dictator. There is no question about that. . . . You had no freedom in Iraq. Ok, you were safe. You had basically, barely you had food. But you had no freedom of speech. You could not say anything about politics. So, I believe that the regime should have changed" (Abdullah 14 January 2018).

However, despite those conditions, Iraq was better off in some ways before the invasion, in his view. For example, echoing Wissam, he said, "Iraq was much stronger, our education was good. . . . We had a good reputation in the countries, we had our place within the countries of the world. . . . People respected us" (Abdullah 14 January 2018). Nevertheless, the negatives far outweighed these perceived positives for Abdullah, and he was convinced that the regime needed to change, although not in the way the United States accomplished it. As he observed:

> I would say that if there was something else other than the war . . . if you could have changed the regime without having all the circumstances that happened after, consequences, I think that would be a perfect solution. But the way the USA did it, I think it was a disaster. Because I believe that the people who were in charge at that time, the American administration, they had very poor knowledge about Iraq and the Iraqi people. (Abdullah 14 January 2018)

The American war "made Iraq a total mess," Abdullah said: "And it made Iraqis pay for that until this day. Like, it has been what? Fourteen years? And we still have violence, we still have a lot of corruption, a lot of killing in Iraq. If the people in charge had been aware of what's going on in Iraq, we could have avoided all of that" (14 January 2018). Considering his analysis of the repercussions of the war, he said:

> If you were [to ask me whether I was] with or against the war in Iraq based on the results that we are having right now, I would say 100 percent I'm against it. But maybe if you asked me . . . in 2003 if I was with or against the war in Iraq, I would say if you would bring knowledgeable people who were actually trying to help Iraq and who are trying to implement a system and they have a plan after the regime falls . . . I would say, yeah. I wouldn't say a war, because at the end of the day I don't like the facts of the war. But maybe there's another solution. So, unfortunately, that thing happened, and it was a huge

mess and I'm shocked, really to know that people who were in power at that time had this poor knowledge about Iraq. It was a complete mess. (Abdullah 14 January 2018)

As we continued our conversation on the American invasion, Abdullah added that there were a few positives after the war, although he did not name any specifically. He began to say "freedom of speech" before stopping himself and noting, "You can't say really freedom of speech because yeah, on paper, you have freedom of speech. But there are a lot of militias and if you say something, you know you are at risk" (Abdullah 14 January 2018). Therefore, Abdullah concluded, "some people they got advantages from the war. And others, which is the majority of the people, their lives completely got destroyed" (14 January 2018).

"I was one of the lucky ones," he said, "I think I got lucky to get a scholarship" (Abdullah 14 January 2018) to travel to the United States for college. (I describe this in more detail in the following section). He went on: "If it was during the Saddam regime, I wouldn't have got it. So, in terms of career-wise and education-wise, I got lucky to get it. And I feel, actually, guilty to get that thing, because there are millions of other people who cannot go to school. So, I got that good thing . . . from the war. But at the same time, I cannot see my family. So, it's half, half. But in general, it was bad. The war was bad for a lot of Iraqis. And there are thousands of people who got killed, completely innocent people. And I don't think people should support decisions that will lead to killing a lot of innocent people" (Abdullah 14 January 2018).

Wissam expressed similar views on the conflict. In the period leading up to the invasion, "we were really pro it," he said: "Because . . . I was born under the Saddam regime, and I was thinking of leaving even before he was thrown out. So, it wasn't that pleasant. But the problem was, we trusted the US government, they know what they're going to do after that. After that now everybody says: 'Oh we wish we could go back to Saddam's days'" (22 October 2017). Although there were no political freedoms under Saddam's rule, "to some extent it was peaceful," he said, "There was no ISIS, there was not that ethnic fighting. There was not this corruption. The infrastructure was really good. . . . It was very secure because nobody can even steal a car, or the government will kill him" (Wissam 22 October 2017). "We were safe at our houses," Wissam reiterated (22 October 2017). However, he said, "There was no money. That was the hard part. Because there were economic sanctions in Iraq. . . . Now, we got the money, you can't do anything with it. You don't feel safe at your house. You don't feel safe. There is corruption from the smallest employee in the government to, maybe, the Prime Minister" (Wissam 22 October 2017). Wissam concluded: "I left in 2005. I think it would be very hard for me to go back and adapt to that situation" (22 October 2017).

Finally, Ali related several stories about himself and his family to illustrate how dangerous it was after the 2003 invasion. Like many Iraqis his age, he worked as a translator with the US military during the occupation, which made his life in Iraq increasingly difficult (Campbell 2016). "We started to get threats at home," he said: "'You are helping the invaders. . . . Your brother is working with them.' Whatever. So, our life became difficult over there. Even our travel, our commute. Because . . . there were a lot of militia groups at that time on the ground. From different sides . . . from Sunni and from Shi'ite. I don't want to say only Shi'a or only Sunni. For me, I'm a Sunni person. But it happened a lot. And they started to kill interpreters and put a note on their chest. So, we decided to flee" (Ali 14 January 2018).

The incident that precipitated his decision to leave Iraq involved his brother's narrow escape from death. At the time of the incident, Ali's brother Abu Bakr was a college student studying to be a veterinarian. As Ali shared:

> So, he's going to his college and encountered a checkpoint. They are stopping cars and asking for IDs. The checkpoint was run by a Shi'a militia. So, they asked about his ID and he gave his ID. They said: "Abu Bakr? Okay Abu Bakr, step out of the car please." At that time, I have also newspaper reports, these militias used to kill according to names. Omar, Abu Othman, Abu Bakr. Those three names are top for them. They start to kill them and cut their head off and put their ID on their chests.[10] . . . So, my brother was smart. On the other side of the road . . . there was an [American] convoy coming, my brother speaks English. So, he stopped them. "Stop them! They are going to kill us according to our names. I'm seeking your help!" he shouted. (14 January 2018)

Because Ali and Abu Bakr's father held a position with the Iraqi Foreign Ministry under Saddam, Abu Bakr had spent time in the United States as a teenager. As Ali recounted:

> My brother . . . was here [in New York City] in 2001 and 2002. He had his ID from high school, from New York . . . so he showed the American soldier. He [the soldier] saw Manhattan . . . my brother explained to me, he said he felt like I am one of them; "They cannot abandon me." So, they went to the checkpoint, they stopped the line, they stopped the cars, they stopped the traffic. The checkpoint appeared that it wasn't authorized by the Ministry of Interior because they made calls. And then they put them down on the ground and they cuffed them, and they took them. And they stopped the car and they said to my brother and his two friends, "Go back, take them to the nearest point, to their home." After that, we said then "that's enough." I fled my country in 2006. (Ali 14 January 2018)

Ali left Iraq shortly after this incident, but his brother stayed. However, looters occupied their family home during the war, forcing Abu Bakr to move. Ali's father had collected antiques from around the world during his travels for work and had amassed a library of books. "This is his life," Ali said, "30 years of working and traveling" (Ali 14 January 2018). But, as Ali demonstrated with his fingers, all of this was gone in a snap.

Ali punctuated his description of the breakdown of Iraqi society after the invasion with a final example:

> A criminal used to go and steal cars, steal from homes and he was in prison for 3 years. That was before the war. . . . He got caught in one of my friend's houses. . . . After he went to prison. Then . . . during the war all of the prisons [had prison breaks]. . . . This guy started to take revenge on the people who made reports to the police. My friend was one of them. And he went to their house seeking money or their life. They had to choose. So, they gave the money. After two months, my friend got killed by the same person. (Ali 14 January 2018)

These incidents were illustrative for Ali. Reflecting on the war, he said: "When you remember what happened to you, to your sister, to your brother, to yourself. And then how people changed all of a sudden after that war. There was one person [Saddam Hussein] holding the law and holding everything together in one hand. When he was gone, everything went upside down. When you think about it, it's ruined. The country is gone. It's torn apart. There is no law to protect you. And you go to the police station [the officer would say]: 'What can we do? We can't do anything'" (Ali 14 January 2018). Ali left Iraq and first went to Jordan. "Jordan was too difficult," he said, and "then I went to Syria. In Syria, I opened a small translation office to help immigrants and refugees during the Iraqi crisis. . . . It went [approximately] two years and 7 months. After that, I went to Egypt, and I stayed in Egypt five years till I came here [to New York City]" (14 January 2018). Ali's comments provide a segue to the next section, which provides the principal reasons interviewees shared for why they chose to leave their homes and seek refuge in the United States.

Deciding to Leave: Seeking Refuge Abroad

Millions of Iraqis were displaced from their homes during the conflict because of US military action, fear of militia groups, and deteriorating living conditions. Sassoon (2009) has argued that the initial response by the United States government to growing violence in Iraq and concurrent displacement was to pretend the problem did not exist and hope it would go away. Fewer than one thousand Iraqis arrived in the United States as refugees between 2003 and 2006. The figures fluctuate widely by year thereafter, but between 2007 and September 2017 an average of 14,500 Iraqis immigrated to the United States each year (Refugee Processing Center 2019). The Trump administration drastically curtailed refugee resettlement. At the time of this writing, the Biden administration has promised a return to pre-Trump levels of admission, but full implementation of that policy is still pending.

While myriad factors contribute to leaving one's home, as interviewees explained, becoming a refugee entails a decision, and often a series of decisions, that together prompt a person to seek safer or more stable conditions elsewhere within their country or beyond. Many of those with whom I spoke indicated that they left Iraq in response to the deteriorating living conditions there. As described above, Nada, for example, explained that she and her family faced threats because of her husband's work with an American company in Baghdad. Life in Iraq after the invasion was "very, very difficult for us, for my family" (Nada 1 November 2017). She was afraid for her safety and that of her husband and children and, ultimately, that concern resulted in her decision to leave Iraq.

Many interviewees confronting similar conditions first fled to neighboring and nearby countries such as Jordan, Syria, Lebanon, and Egypt before immigrating to the United States. Some had applied for resettlement in multiple countries, including Australia, Canada, and Sweden, before deciding to go to the United States. For this reason, these decisions, which unfolded for individuals across months or years, are best conceived as processes, rather than discrete single-time events.

For example, Hashim's relocation choices entailed multiple stages. He lived originally in Baghdad and worked for both the United Nations, and later the United States Agency for International Development (USAID). In 2006, he decided to move from Baghdad to Erbil, a city in the north of the country in Iraqi Kurdistan. There, the physical danger was lower, and he found meaningful and well-compensated employment. Nonetheless, he decided to apply for the Special Immigrant Visa Program in 2014:

> The decision was very difficult to take. I applied for the SIV program. I traveled in less than a year, in ten months. And then it went very quick. I wasn't expecting that . . . because it takes years for many people. With me, it took only ten months until I received my visa . . . and it expired within three months, so I had to travel within 3 months of . . . when I received it. So, it was a really difficult decision to take. I had so many friends living in the United States, and everyone was telling me different things depending on their experiences and their backgrounds and everything. So, I didn't have a very clear understanding about life in the United States until I arrived and then we made the decision and we decided to travel. But now I would say it was one of the best decisions I've made in my life. (Hashim 1 October 2017)

Walid, who came to the United States through the United States Refugee Admissions Program, narrated his experiences leaving Iraq in the following way:

> I came to the US in 2008 as a refugee. I'm a US citizen now. . . . I was a middle school teacher in Iraq, a business owner in Iraq when the war started. I worked sometimes to interpret with coalition forces, the American army there. . . . Also, we established a nonprofit organization for human rights. We weren't successful at that because we did not have protection from the government. We lost family and friends because of that reason, which made me feel unsafe, so I moved to Syria before the war in Syria in 2006. We lived a very good life there. A Syrian family helped us and supported us. (27 September 2017)

Walid and his family were among the more than one million Iraqis to seek refuge in Syria before and after the US invasion (Harper 2008). Like his friend Walid, Mohammed, 38, and now living in Upstate New York, went to Syria and was displaced twice over. As he put it: "Before I came here, in Iraq, we had a civil war, and it was terrible. I lost my two brothers, my father, and a lot of friends because [of the conflict]. I decided to move to Syria and Syria started a civil war in 2011, so we came here. . . . When I had the interview with the UN, they asked me if you have friends in America. I gave Walid's name so they brought me here too . . . so Walid can help me" (Mohammed 2 November 2017).

Becoming a refugee can entail identifying and seeking out opportunities to change one's circumstances. Wissam left Iraq in 2005 to study in Jordan. When Barack Obama was elected president in 2008, replacing George W. Bush, Wissam heard acquaintances in the US Army say that the new government planned to withdraw its soldiers from Iraq to focus on the concurrent war in Afghanistan: "At first," he said, "we didn't believe that because they spent billions and billions of dollars there. But after that turned out to be true, things started to collapse there, so it was not safe for us to stay" (Wissam 22 October 2017). So, he and his family decided to emigrate. The university in Jordan where Wissam studied had an American campus, and he received a visa to go to the United States for his graduation ceremony. Originally, he intended to come for the commencement events and then return home. However, while in the United States, he decided to seek asylum.

Wissam's experiences also speak to the complexity of "refugeeness" and the overlapping legal regimes one might pursue to find a safer place to live. He and his parents received asylum, first coming to the United States and then making their request. His wife applied for and received a visa through the Special Immigrant Visa program. Several members of Wissam's family also resettled in different parts of the United States by leaving Iraq for a second country before applying for refugee status through the United Nations and the United States Refugee Admissions Program. Wissam's family's experiences illustrate that individuals apply for the programs for which they may qualify, and pursue whatever opportunities they can identify, to ensure their safety.

Like Wissam, Nora applied for asylum after arriving in the United States. In Baghdad, she had worked as a lawyer at a women's organization providing pro bono legal services. In what ended up as her final case, she represented the wife of a powerful militia leader as that woman sought a divorce and legal protection for herself and her son. As the case proceeded, the husband threatened Nora and her coworkers. Indeed, at one point, he came to Nora's home and handed her a bullet telling her he would kill her if she returned to court. Later, militia members came to her house looking for documents related to the case. As Nora explained: "He put papers on my door. They put a sign on my house like a red cross on my door. . . . They [militia] were everywhere, you know? And I had an incident before that. My dad got kidnapped and it's like they know us, somehow. I don't know. So, I said: 'There's no way to go back'" (6 February 2018). So, she "left everything, I left my office, I left this organization" (Nora 6 February 2018), and her home and moved in with a friend before applying for a visa to the United States to visit her brother in Ohio. After she arrived, she petitioned for asylum. Looking back at these events, she said, "I got past this whole thing, it was very horrible. . . . It was so hard to lose everything. To lose my house, everything in my life was there. I am starting all over here from zero and it is so hard" (Nora 6 February 2018).

In a final example, Abdullah first left Iraq for Syria and applied for and received refugee status there. While living in Syria, he heard about a nonprofit organization that facilitated a program that offered refugees the opportunity to come to the United States to pursue higher education. In late 2008 or early 2009, Abdullah applied to that program, even though he did not read, write, or speak English. He asked a friend to assist him with the application. He received a call from the program organizers, who told him, by way of his brother who could converse in English, that language proficiency was required. They asked Abdullah to sit for an English proficiency exam, on which he scored a "0." Thereafter, he decided to dedicate himself to learning English so that he could apply again: "I kept studying for three months straight from my room," he said (Abdullah 14 January 2018). His efforts led to scoring two levels higher than necessary for the program when he took the exam a second time. He applied to the scholarship again and was successful, receiving a visa to go to New York City to attend a local university in 2010. The examples explored in this section have demonstrated the multiple paths individuals take to resettle in the United States, weighing options and pursuing possible routes to safer conditions.

Conclusion

This chapter has outlined the destruction caused by the American war against Iraq and the displacement and resettlement of approximately 172,000 Iraqis in the United States that followed in its wake. As argued at the outset, the planners of this war must be made to face justice for their crimes, and Americans need to acknowledge and make reparations for the enormous harm the US government has inflicted on the people of Iraq. Unfortunately, evidence suggests that Americans have not developed a serious, critical recognition of the ramifications of this conflict. Consider an interaction Nora described with an American in Virginia, who could not clearly recall the 2003 invasion:

> I have met people who don't know where Iraq is. Literally, a lady . . . asked me about my accent . . . and she's like: "Where is that Iraq?" And I was very, very, very depressed and I was like: "Where is *that*?" I told her: "Do you know the Middle East?" She said: "No." "Do you remember 2003? George W. Bush had a war on a very, very small, dumb country claiming that they had a nuclear weapon?" She said: "Oh, I don't know why, but I remember there was a war, the United States was part of it." I was like: "I am that small dumb country. . . . So, do you know where that is?" And from there, that was the last time. I was like: I need to calm myself down and not be nervous about people asking me where I am from. Because I get very nervous, especially when I see the ignorance.[11] I was like: "Your country has been in two wars, and you don't know why these people are coming in?" We are coming in because we're fleeing the war. (6 February 2018)

This encounter is illustrative of a broader lack of adequate engagement and self-reflection among Americans concerning the devastation their military has caused in Iraq for three decades. A 2018 poll conducted by *HuffPost* and YouGov found, for example, that only 34 percent of respondents remembered the Bush administration's justifications for the invasion of Iraq "very well" (YouGov 2018). Twenty-eight percent of those surveyed reported that they "don't remember" whether they supported the war in 2003. Only 33 percent indicated that they had supported the war in 2003, despite contemporaneous polls suggesting that more than 60 percent of Americans supported invading Iraq.[12]

Much more work needs to be done to build broad recognition among US citizens that they have an urgent responsibility to make reparations for the war against Iraq. Considering the incredible harm caused to the people of Iraq, it is critical that Americans reject as fundamentally illegitimate asserted claims that the United States has a right to remake other societies through violence (Anderson 2014). Significant work must be performed by activists, scholars, and teachers to expand Americans' ethical and political imaginations beyond the deeply rooted notion that violence is necessary and well-intentioned when committed by the American military (Immerman 2010). By rejecting the assumed legitimacy of American geopolitical violence, it is possible to seek alternatives to war and conflict that can build more peaceful relations between people (Jackson 2019).

The next chapter examines interviewees' experiences living in the United States after resettling. It explores their interactions with Americans and perceptions of belonging in the society amid widely circulating discourses portraying Arabs and Muslims as irreconcilably different and dangerous. It also elaborates on the opportunities many have found to interact and exchange with native-born Americans and fellow newcomer friends, neighbors, and coworkers.

Notes

1. Portions of this chapter have been adapted from Keyel 2020.
2. The United States contributed the most forces to the conflict beginning in 1991. While other governments sent soldiers to Iraq in support of the 2003 invasion and occupation, the United States military and American private mercenary forces have led the war. Although the United Kingdom was the principal US ally and second-largest force in Iraq in 2003, the scale of its engagement peaked during the initial invasion in March 2003 with forty-six thousand troops, compared to 145,000 American soldiers. By May 2003, the UK troop level had fallen to eighteen thousand and continued to decline until British combat operations ended in 2009 (BBC 2011). Although the United States has caused the most harm, the UK and other countries that have attacked Iraq must also be held accountable for the harm they have caused.
3. American and British intelligence agencies anticipated the consequences of the conflict before the invasion. Declassified US National Intelligence Council documents written before the 2003 invasion outlining the anticipated consequences of a US military attack on Saddam Hussein's government estimated that a US-led war and occupation of Iraq would increase "popular sympathy" for terrorist objectives in the short term; groups like al-Qa'ida would attempt to exploit the war by ramping up their "anti-US operations"; and neighboring states would "jockey for influence" by fomenting strife among Iraq's multiple ethnic and religious communities (Pillar 2003b, 5–6). One million Iraqis had been internally displaced in conflicts in Iraq prior to 2003, and these intelligence reports included estimates by the UNHCR that an assault on Baghdad would displace nine hundred thousand persons internally and create 1.45 million more refugees (Pillar 2003a). The British Joint Intelligence Committee also predicted that launching a conflict against Iraq would increase the threat of terrorism and communicated its assessment directly to Prime Minister Tony Blair before the invasion (Chilcott 2016). All the predicted consequences, ignored by the Bush White House and Blair at the time, unfolded as forecast.
4. Until 2020, The Bureau of Investigative Journalism extensively tracked and kept an up-to-date count of American drone strikes and covert actions in Afghanistan, Pakistan, Somalia, and Yemen. That accounting can be found at https://www.thebureauinvestigates.com/projects/drone-war. The work of conflict tracking passed to *Airwars* in 2020: https://airwars.org/.

5. As the aggressor states, the United States and its allies are responsible for the immense human suffering caused by their war against Iraq, including the death and destruction directly committed by their militaries, the violent resistance to occupation, and the resultant rise of groups such as the Islamic State.
6. The United States extensively used cluster munitions during and after the 2003 invasion. Such weapons have been widely condemned, and in 2008 outlawed by 102 countries under an international treaty (Human Rights Watch 2017), because they cannot distinguish between combatant and civilian targets. When fired, cluster bombs release thousands of smaller munitions that litter the area of attack. A percentage of each payload fails to explode on contact, essentially leaving behind a minefield that can injure and kill for years after. As Human Rights Watch reported in December 2003, cluster munitions killed and injured hundreds of civilians in the first months of the conflict (Docherty and Garlasco 2003). For example, Dr. Sa'ad al-Falluji, director and chief surgeon at al-Hilla General Teaching Hospital, told HRW that 90 percent of war-related injuries treated at the hospital between March and May 2003 had been from cluster munitions. That experience was indicative of the form of injuries that occurred all over the country. According to HRW, the heavy use of cluster munitions in populated, residential areas by the United States and its allies "represented one of the leading causes of civilian casualties in the war" (Docherty and Garlasco 2003, 85).
7. For example, in January 2004, Army Sgt. 1st Class Tracy Perkins ordered soldiers under his command to throw two Iraqi men into the Tigris River as a deterrent against looting. One of the men drowned while the second was able to swim ashore and escape. Perkins was tried and sentenced to six months in military prison for this crime (Roberts 2005). Sergeant Perkins also faced charges for allegedly pushing another Iraqi off a bridge near Balad the previous month, in December 2003. According to testimony of a former Irish Guard Captain at an inquiry into Iraqi casualties, "wetting"–the practice of throwing Iraqis suspected of looting and other petty crimes into waterways, rivers, and canals–was commonplace among British occupying soldiers (Cobain 2016).
8. For example, American soldiers massacred eleven people in the town of Ishaqi on 15 March 2006. After a firefight, American soldiers entered the home from which they believed shooting had originated. They gathered eleven individuals, five children, four women, and two men, and executed all of them (Schofield 2011). A helicopter gunship then bombed the house, destroying the evidence. American soldiers were cleared of responsibility in this case (White 2006). However, documents released by *Wikileaks* in 2011 revealed that autopsies conducted after the attack indicate the victims were handcuffed and shot in the head (Schofield 2011). The following month, on 26 April 2006, American Marines entered the home of a fifty-two-year-old man with a disability, Hashim Ibrahim Awad, bound him, dragged him outside, and shot him in the head multiple times. Seven US Marines and one Navy medic were convicted and jailed for this crime (Glantz 2017). Navy medic Melson Bacos, who pleaded guilty to the crime, testified that after shooting Awad, a Marine planted a rifle and shovel to make it appear as if Awad had been involved in setting up a bomb when he was

killed (CNN 2007). A third incident with a similar modus operandi took place in spring 2007. American soldiers arrested four Iraqi men in Baghdad on suspicion that they had attacked occupation forces. The detained men were handcuffed and blindfolded before American soldiers shot all four in the back of the head and then dumped their bodies in a canal (Whitlock 2009).

9. Sweden accepted significant numbers of Iraqis for resettlement in the first five years after the 2003 invasion. By 2009, as many as forty thousand Iraqis had joined established Iraqi communities throughout Sweden (Sassoon 2009). Sweden, a country of ten million people, has proportionally resettled ten times as many Iraqis as the United States.

10. In 2006, *The Guardian* reported a rise among Sunni Iraqis in Baghdad changing their names to be less identifiable and forging identification indicating they were Shi'ite. In one incident, Baghdad police uncovered the bodies of fourteen young men all named Omar who had been shot in the head and left in a garbage heap by a militia (Beaumont 2006).

11. Reinforcing Nora's interpretation, in 2015, *Public Policy Polling* asked Americans whether they would support or oppose bombing Agrabah, the fictional Middle Eastern city from the Disney film *Aladdin*: 30 percent of Republican and 19 percent of Democratic voters said they supported bombing this fictional city. Trump supporters were the most likely to support, at 41 percent (Jensen 2015).

12. Similarly, a 2015 YouGov poll found only 38 percent of respondents reporting that they supported the war in 2003 (Frankovic 2015).

2

How Does it Feel to Be a Refugee?

Belonging, Precarity, and Cultural Exchange

> As a refugee, I'm doing . . . a lot of good things. And I'm doing a great job . . . for the community or for my work, you know? But, sometimes, if you make one single mistake . . . they will forget about all of the good things you have done the past five years.
>
> —Ali, 14 January 2018

Introduction

The preceding chapter explored the ongoing American war against Iraq, the effects that conflict has had on that country's society, and the decisions many Iraqis made to leave their homes and resettle in the United States. This chapter turns to the postresettlement experiences of belonging in American society of those with whom I spoke for this inquiry. To reiterate from the introduction, belonging, as conceptualized here, consists of the informal possibilities for individuals to exercise their rights substantively and to obtain acceptance as full members of American society (Brubaker 2010), should they choose to seek it, as well as the reciprocal feelings of acceptance and processes and possibilities for interviewees to identify and build relationships with members and institutions of American society at multiple levels.

Belonging is intertwined and co-constitutive with democratic membership and participation. Each factor can influence the others, and there was necessarily overlap among the feelings of belonging, understandings of democratic membership, and opportunities for participation among interviewees for this study. As a result, while I discuss these factors in separate chapters, I do so to ensure flow and clarity, rather than to indicate a sharp delineation between the concepts or how interviewees experienced them.

This chapter first briefly elaborates the process of resettling in the United States and interviewees' experiences with that process. It then explores interviewees' sense of belonging in their local communities and in the United States more broadly. Those with whom I spoke suggested that such attachments can be partial or unresolved in various ways. The chapter then focuses on the recurring theme of, as W. E. B. Du Bois (1903) framed it, the "strange experience" of being seen as a problem by many in society. For some interviewees, this strangeness was informed in no small part by widely circulating anti-Arab, anti-Muslim, and anti-refugee discourses and discriminatory policies in the United States. Thereafter, the chapter considers the precarity expressed by some interviewees, both long-standing and increased following the election of Donald Trump to the US presidency. Trump ran an overtly racist and xenophobic campaign and pursued and enacted policies aimed at making resettlement more difficult during his tenure (Johnson 2015; Newkirk II 2018).

The chapter concludes by exploring the role of diversity in interviewees' communities and cultural exchange between resettled Iraqis and their neighbors and friends in building and galvanizing a sense of belonging for them. Importantly, many of the individuals with whom I spoke cited perceptions of widespread resistance to newcomers from some native-born Americans even as they were able to create positive relationships with other neighbors and colleagues and develop possibilities for mutual exchange. I argue in this and the following chapters that a positive welcoming by American citizens in general—and in response to negative rhetoric and governmental policies— not only facilitated the resettlement process for those I interviewed, but also widened informal spaces for belonging and participation at all levels of society.

Refugee Resettlement in the United States

As described in the previous chapter, the individuals who participated in this research sought refuge in the United States through different programs and paths. Seven interviewees arrived in the United States through the United States Refugee Admissions Program. Established by the United States Refugee Act of 1980, this program systematized US policy related to refugee resettlement, which had until then been ad hoc. For Iraqis, resettlement through the USRAP involves leaving Iraq for a second country such as Jordan or Syria, registering with the United Nations High Commissioner for Refugees (UNHCR) as a refugee, and then applying for resettlement in a third country. Qualifying for refugee status requires that those applying demonstrate a "well-founded fear of persecution" because of their membership in a particular "race, religion, nationality, membership in a particular social group, or political opinion" (Bruno 2019, 9). This process involves extensive background checks and verification processes. The US government coordinates with UNHCR to process resettlement applications. The US government also contracts with nine nonprofit resettlement agencies, which provide support services to newly arriving refugees.

I also interviewed five Special Immigrant Visa recipients. The 2006 National Defense Authorization Act (NDAA) created a program to allow Afghans and Iraqis who worked with the United States military as translators and interpreters to apply for SIVs to resettle in the United States. This program was later expanded to include Afghans and Iraqis who worked in other capacities for the US government during the US wars in their countries (Bruno 2019, 9). There is significant overlap between refugee status and an SIV, and many individuals qualify for both programs. A major difference is that receiving an SIV does not require demonstrating persecution as does refugee status; however, the SIV program does require applicants to show they have experienced "ongoing serious threat" because of their work for the US government (Bruno 2019, 9).

In addition to resettling via the USRAP and SIV programs, two interviewees came to the United States and claimed asylum. Refugee status, SIV, and asylum also have some overlap. Unlike the USRAP or SIV program, asylum-seekers arrive in the United States through multiple means—for example, a tourist or student visa. They must apply for asylum within one year of arriving in the United States. Asylum status provides many of the same rights and protections as refugee status. Like refugee status, a successful asylum claim requires applicants to demonstrate that they have a well-founded fear of persecution in their home country. Like successfully receiving refugee status or an SIV, successfully receiving asylum often requires those seeking safety to narrate and reiterate the details of often-traumatic events that caused them to flee their home country (Bohmer and Shuman 2008).

In the United States, newly resettled refugees, Special Immigrant Visa recipients, and those granted asylum are eligible for public support directly through state and federal government programs and government-contracted, nonprofit resettlement agencies (Nelson et al. 2016). Nada related, "In the beginning, in the first six months, when we came here, of course, [the refugee resettlement agency] helped us with food stamps and health insurance until we got good jobs" (1 November 2017). Ahmed, too, spoke about his interaction with the resettlement agency in Chicago, saying it assisted him and his daughter for a short time:

> You need to be signed up to a resettlement agency . . . and I met the worker in the beginning. They gave me access to my first apartment. And, of course, they furnished the apartment a bit. And they helped with the registration of my daughter in the school. Also, they were very welcoming. They said: "Do you need us to help you go to the social security?" I said, "No, I want to try it

myself." "So, do you want help getting a driving license?" I said, "No, I want to try it myself." But they helped with the school registration. They also gave me an appointment to do the health screening and stuff. (2 October 2017)

Some individuals who resettle may also find an individual sponsor in the United States who agrees to assist them when they arrive. Kasim, said, for example: "I was living with the sponsor, but [the refugee resettlement agency] helped me with the food supplement program, and medical program for the few months. And then . . . I started working and I was able to work within my field of experience at the time. And, I was able to support myself and pay the rent and all that" (27 February 2018).

Although not officially sponsors of Marwa's resettlement, another Iraqi family that her husband knew provided support upon her arrival in the United States; she explained:

> I'm lucky I have this family here. They are a nice family, they are big family. They consider themselves like a family for my husband because my husband, he grew up with their kids. And, I didn't know them, but they heard about me from my husband or from my husband's family. I didn't meet them before. But they are so nice. They helped me. The [resettlement] agency they rented, an apartment for me but this family they took care of everything. Because when you came here, it's okay the agency they help you with something. But, the big [things], you need family. You need friends here. (2 October 2017)

The need for additional help in the resettlement process is due, in part, to the reality that much of the assistance provided by resettlement agencies is time-limited and means-tested, leaving those unable to find adequate employment quickly in difficult circumstances. Because cash assistance is time-limited and relatively small, many resettled refugees face economic hardship (Inhorn 2018). As Mohammed explained, the resettlement agency provided services for ninety days. "After three months you have to be responsible for yourself. Okay, I didn't speak English, how can I be responsible for myself? I didn't [even] know how to go shopping" (Mohammed 2 November 2017). Echoing Mohammed, Walid said: "When refugees arrive in the United States, there's a funding program, which is 90 days, three months. After 90 days the funding is stopped. And if they are eligible for social services they get the services, it depends on their medical, mental problems. If they are not, they have to find work. So, after three months just imagine yourself, you don't speak the language, you moved to another country, you don't know their culture, you don't know the mail that came to you, you have a family, it's very overwhelming" (27 September 2017).

Marwa said that the resettlement agency helped her with "basic things" but that in her experience resettled refugees need more support than the resettlement agencies provide. Refugees are expected to be "self-sufficient" within a few months of their arrival. Marwa explained:

[The resettlement agencies] are not a big help. I want to be honest. I had a bad experience with them. They didn't help that much. . . . When I called them, they didn't answer: "Oh we are busy like that. We've been busy like that." Yeah, they did for me the basic things. They help you with basics. They took me to the welfare [office]. They applied for food stamps for me and cash [assistance] because I was considered a single mom when I came. I was considered single with the three kids. And, they helped me with that. (25 November 2017)

However, Marwa implied that when the resettlement agency found out about the support she received from her husband's family friends, they stepped back from assisting her.

In addition to the nine resettlement agencies the US government contracts with, nonprofit and community organizations provide essential services to supplement those limited supports offered by publicly funded institutions and contracted resettlement agencies. These organizations may be formal or informal and include mutual aid societies and religious organizations. Some such organizations are dedicated to assisting particular immigrant groups, immigrants in general, or refugees. As explored in more detail in later chapters, several of the individuals I spoke with had volunteered with and, in some cases, founded community organizations dedicated to supporting immigrants in their areas.

Resettlement can be a difficult process. Interviewees discussed specific challenges they faced after arriving in the United States such as inadequate housing, the high cost of living, and frustration with the limits of the resettlement agencies charged with supporting them. Mohammed said: "The big thing in America [that makes] life difficult: the economy. Oh my god, it is really difficult. Not just for me, for all the people" (2 November 2017). Even with two incomes, his and his wife's, Mohammed said that paying the bills was a challenge. Paying everything every month left nothing extra to save. As he put it with a laugh: "You can take a breath for free. But nothing is free for you" (Mohammed 2 November 2017).

Sarah was surprised that the resettlement agency in Arizona, where she first arrived, placed many newly arrived refugees, even those with degrees from their home countries, in jobs in places such as warehouses. She said, "Me and my sister, we completed our education in Iraq. When you come here to start work, we were surprised [by] the kind of work here. In the beginning, it's not good actually. And some refugees suffered from this part" (Sarah 30 November 2017). Hashim discussed this issue as well, saying of his experience: "When I first arrived, I had my expectations regarding [my] career. I was expecting to find something that can serve my background, serve my experience, to continue this career. And then when I first came the only jobs being offered to me were only like survival jobs working in stores, working in department stores or warehouses and all of that. Factories" (1 October 2017). It took time for Hashim to find employment that he found fulfilling: "I would say we started to think more seriously about life and about establishing ourselves in the country. So, I'd say that happened a year after I arrived. Actually, no, like a year and a half maybe. I would say that the first year was the hardest for us. After that, we were able to fit in. Because during the first year, during the whole first year we both had the same idea of traveling back to Iraq. To leave everything and travel back to Iraq because it was very hard. It was very difficult" (1 October 2017).

Only after he and his wife secured full-time work did Hashim begin to feel settled. He went on to describe feeling that he had adjusted to life in the United States relatively quickly compared to other Iraqis he knew. Nonetheless, he explained:

> It's been hard. It's been very long [and] difficult. We had many difficult days at the beginning. It was really hard to adjust with the community, to adjust with my career. For me being a graduate from Iraq with a master's degree and I used to work for, like, 10 years in Iraq with experience working with many healthcare organizations, many nonprofit organizations. I worked for the United Nations in Iraq. I worked for the USAID. It's one of the biggest nonprofit agencies working in Iraq. So, when I first arrived I had so many expectations about life in the United States, which turned out that it's not really that easy. (Hashim 1 October 2017)

Hashim and several others said that knowing English had made their transition easier. Those who had worked with the United States in Iraq as translators and interpreters, for example, could engage more quickly with the day-to-day aspects of life after resettling such as completing government paperwork, applying for jobs, and meeting new people. Others, like Nada, endeavored to become proficient in English as soon as they could. She said:

> I started to learn English after just one month. When I finished all my paperwork. So, I started to learn English [at a nonprofit] and I took two levels at the same time. I started from literacy. And then my teacher really saw I can do something because I learned very quickly. So, they encouraged me to take more classes in college. And I took evening classes, at [a local college] at the same time. I studied in the morning at the [nonprofit] and I took an evening class [at the college]. I finished all these classes during about 9 months. . . . Then my teacher encouraged me to help them in summer classes [at the nonprofit], to teach the students. (Nada 1 November 2017)

Resettling requires navigating new economic, social, cultural, and political structures and processes. As a result, interviewees' experiences with resettlement are further explored and woven throughout the rest of the text. The next section begins to examine resettled Iraqis' perceptions of belonging and engagement in American society and politics.

Between Here and There: Complexities of Belonging in American Society

The interviews were in-depth explorations of individuals' experiences of belonging in their local resettlement contexts–Upstate New York, New York City, Chicagoland, the Shenandoah Valley of Virginia, and the Washington, DC, metro area–as well as in broader American society. Overwhelmingly, individuals with whom I spoke envisioned remaining in the United States to live, work, and raise their families. Some were certain, while others expressed a lack of control concerning whether they would–or could–stay. Both Ahmed and Tariq said, "I hope so" about the possibility of remaining permanently in the United States. Some with whom I spoke, including Omar and Ali, attributed their intention to stay to the roots they had put down and the opportunities available for themselves, their children, and their families in the United States.

Omar explained this process in the following way: "This question [Do you plan on staying in the United States permanently?], if you asked me when I came here, I would say no. But now, every year, my roots in this country become stronger and stronger. So, imagine, 9 years. The roots are now bigger. Because we went back [to Iraq] this year in August. . . . I missed all the places, I missed everything. But still, the country was not ready to welcome us. Still, it's in chaos" (14 December 2017). Others, such as Nora and Zaid, 35, now living in the Washington, DC, area, indicated they would likely remain. However, if they could not, they would not return to Iraq because of the ongoing danger and instability in their home country.

Interviewees often described their feelings of belonging in the United States, the society in which they were rebuilding their lives. Many of those with whom I spoke were "claiming and creating the social spaces of belonging" (Crane 2021, 56). For some, including Ahmed, a sense of attachment began to develop immediately upon arrival, while for others, including Nora and Marwa, becoming comfortable in their new home was still an unfolding process. Similarly, for Tariq, that evolution remained unfinished or constrained. As I elaborate below, some of those with whom I spoke articulated a sense of being "betwixt and between" Iraqi and American cultures and societies (Campbell 2016). For some, this feeling meant "keeping certain stuff" (Crane 2021, 45) from their Iraqi heritage and background and amalgamating it with elements of American cultural practices. As multiple interviewees explained, Americans' reactions to them, positive and negative, played a substantial role in this evolution of attachment and belonging.

Ahmed explained that he immediately had a sense of connection to the United States. As he described it: "I always say, if asked by any of my American friends, actually it started from the moment I arrived. The first words I heard here in the US were: 'Welcome Home' from the immigration officer, right before any other word she said. She just said, 'Welcome home,' and at that moment I really felt connected" (Ahmed 2 October 2017). Despite what he called Chicago's "bad reputation," he had been comfortable upon his arrival. In his experience, "People here are really friendly, supportive. They care for the community. Everyone was supportive around me. So yeah, I feel connected, and I think there was not really a process" (Ahmed 2 October 2017). He gave the example of an interaction he had on the first day his daughter started at her new school. According to Ahmed, staff members "immediately came and asked me if there is any religion or anything related to your tradition, we want to include that in her teaching. I said no, let her be like other kids. . . . So, from that moment on, I think we were really connected" (2 October 2017).

For his part, Hashim explained that in Chicago, he was able to live with diverse members of the community: "I am not feeling in any way that I am different here. And this is what I like about Chicago, especially. So many communities, everybody's living together peacefully without any problems or conflicts . . . like what we had in the Middle East. So, that's why I really love this place and this city" (1 October 2017). Hashim's in-laws had also moved to Chicago and two of his brothers now live in Texas. As a result, he said, "I feel like we have been building community, building connections, building everything. At the same time, we are receiving the same rights, we are following the same policies and rules as US citizens, so I feel . . . 100 percent comfortable with being a US resident" (Hashim 1 October 2017).

Nada said, "*in sha' Allah* [God willing], why not?" (1 November 2017) about the possibilities of belonging in American society. She continued, "Because, after one year, we will be citizens. . . . When we came here, after five years, we can become a citizen" (Nada 1 November 2017). Nada and her family's arrival in the United States via the Special Immigrant Visa program provided them with a path from legal residence to citizenship. She said of her feelings when she first arrived in New York: "Really, I was afraid. Because, the first thing, we are old, me and my husband. We built everything in our country. We studied there. We worked there. . . . So, when we decided to come here, I felt at that time—of course now, I'm comfortable—but, that means I will face many challenges. I will face a new life. I don't know about the people there. But, *khalas* [enough], this is our decision. . . . And when we came here, really, all the people were very, very nice" (Nada 1 November 2017).

Nora expressed a strong sense of belonging in her city in the Shenandoah Valley of Virginia, saying, "I do feel very, very strong belonging to this community, this society. . . . It's very local" (6 February 2018). She explained that meeting others and volunteering with local organizations had been integral to her development of belonging:

It was a process. The first year I was like: "No, I don't belong here. I don't have friends, I don't know how they make friends, everyone is living by himself. There are no family bonds." And I was like, "No, this is not what I am used to, so I cannot do it." But then, I tried volunteering. . . . When we came to the Shenandoah Valley Region, the man who rented us the house became very close to us. So, he brought his wife, we asked them to come for dinner. And his wife met me and said: "I know a lady in the community, she is very nice, and she always tries to meet new people." So, I met her. (Nora 6 February 2018)

The woman Nora met served as the chair of an activist coalition with branches throughout Virginia. Nora began volunteering with the organization's Shenandoah Valley Region group and met many other community members through that work. She also learned about and became active with, refugee-serving organizations in the Shenandoah Valley Region. She described this experience and the individuals she met and with whom she became friends: "I met two women that have changed my outlook about the United States. . . . It's like, they were the turning point in my life and I'm not alone in this" (Nora 6 February 2018).

Using an example, Nora illustrated the process of increasingly perceiving herself as a member of the community. Nora's city holds an international festival that Nora has attended every year since she arrived. As she explained:

The first year we came to the Shenandoah Valley, and I came to this festival, I felt so, so down that I didn't know anybody. I'm just walking and seeing booths and stuff. The second year, when I walked [through the festival] I was like: "Hi! Hi!" People started to know me. The third year . . . people knew me all the way down. This year, I was standing in the refugee office booth and then I went to another booth, and I was like, people know me, and I've been talking and talking, and this made me feel very, very connected to this place. Like, I know everyone here. Like I am from here. I feel that. Like I belong. (Nora 6 February 2018)

Similarly, Walid observed, "I feel that this is my country now, because it is the place that gives you respect, love and probably support. I consider this my country now" (September 17, 2017). Importantly, for Walid, this feeling of belonging meant learning about and incorporating aspects of American culture into his life while retaining his Iraqi heritage–a dynamic I explore in more detail below. Abdullah, likewise, indicated that he felt a sense of belonging in US society, yet was still Iraqi: "I feel that I'm both in between, you know? I still am proud of my Iraqi heritage, my Iraqi culture and that is part of me that never changed. Since I was born, I am always proud of that" (14 January 2018). Later in our conversation, he said:

I think the USA is a great country. I really believe that. I just don't like some of the regimes that come here, and they affect other people's lives. You know? But as a country, as an idea, the USA is a very interesting and unique country.... I don't feel it's just a country. It's basically, I don't know what to call it.... I feel it's like an organization or a club. Really, it could feel that way, people from everywhere in the world they come here and try to contribute to make it more successful. So, I really don't think these people who are coming here are causing problems. If you look at it most of these people are actually helping the country. (Abdullah 14 January 2018)

Also speaking to the complexity of belonging, Zaid said: "I came from a Sunni/Shi'ite family. So, I'm neither Sunni nor Shi'ite. I'm just a typical Iraqi citizen. I used to be. Now I'm American.... I'm still both" (27 February 2018). Despite retaining his Iraqi identity, Zaid said there was "no way" he would return to Iraq. He left the country in 2007 and spent three years in Jordan before coming to the United States. He had returned to Iraq in the summer of 2017 to visit his family still living in Baghdad. He said, "It was really hard for me. I couldn't even recognize anything when I went back.... I mean, it was really bad when I left the country.... When I came back last summer, it was even worse.... It was really bad. But, for some reason, people are just adapting to that way of life" (27 February 2018).

Like Ahmed, Zaid described the point at which he viewed himself as an American. He explained: "The day that I really felt that I was an American citizen is the day when I came back from Iraq [after a recent trip] and the border agent officer told me: 'Welcome home.' I really felt that, yes, this is my home now and I really felt that I just wanted to come back, even though I only spent about a week outside this country" (Zaid 27 February 2018). However, Zaid continued, "to be completely honest with you, I still feel that I am Iraqi because I cannot deny that even talking to you now, I know that you're looking at me thinking: 'You have citizenship, you ... speak good English ... but he is not from here" (27 February 2018). He apologized to me for saying this and added: "I see this like in every, in most, of the people that I interact with. Although no one has, almost no one, has ever shown me this kind of feeling. But, maybe it's just the way I feel" (Zaid 27 February 2018). Despite the perception that many native-born Americans with whom he interacts view him as an outsider even though he is a citizen, Zaid explained: "But, still, it's much better than the way that I felt in my home country, Iraq. At least, I'm dealing with people who respect me, just because of me ... not because of my background.... Maybe I'm ... giving you mixed information, but it's ... the way I feel. It's complicated. It's really complicated" (27 February 2018).

Mohammed offered that the question of belonging for him was unresolved as well. He remarked, "I have good communication with the American people.... The people in Upstate New York are really friendly" (Mohammed

2 November 2017). However, when I asked him "do you feel like the US is your country?" he said, "Right now, yeah. Like 75 percent, yes. But you know, if you go to Iraq right now, you will miss your country. It's difficult, do you know what I mean? I was born there. All my life was there. Yeah. So, yeah. But it's not 100 percent" (Mohammed 2 November 2017).

For Marwa, belonging was a process. The "first time is hard," she said, "I came here and already I knew English. But, the accent, the dialect, it's different. But let me tell you: it depends on your personality; if you accept it or if you adapt. I feel I am flexible, I adapted" (Marwa 25 November 2017). She attributed this successful outcome to her outgoing personality. In her words: "I like to talk with the people. I like to ask a lot of questions. I didn't feel shy" (Marwa 25 November 2017). Now a US citizen, Marwa considered herself both American and Iraqi, "I love my country [Iraq] because my family is there," she said (25 November 2017). The week after our interview, Marwa traveled to visit her family in Baghdad for the first time since 2011.

Unlike Marwa, "I'm a citizen, but I don't feel I'm a citizen," Tariq said. He continued: "It's hard because . . . some groups, you will see yourself as a member, based on them and how they treat you. When you go to other groups, you can tell, you're not part of it. You can't be part of it. So, it's difficult. Maybe in the future, this is what we hope. . . . So, unfortunately, I don't want to lie, I am not a member [of American society]. But we hope in the future, maybe" (Tariq 2 November 2017).

Finally, Kasim was the only individual with whom I spoke to pointedly say no, belonging in American society was not fully open to him. "There will be barriers," he said. He continued: "I tried, but I felt some kind of prejudice especially when I apply to jobs. When I go to places where the employers mostly are white, they think I'm different. When I go places where employers mostly are black Americans, they think I'm different. So, it's always this problem, that's what I felt. I don't know to what degree it's correct, but that's what I felt" (Kasim 27 February 2018). Despite this feeling, Kasim said it was not difficult to "assimilate" into American culture. He continued: "I know what the Americans want. And, probably that's part of me, I cannot give it" (Kasim 27 February 2018). By way of example, he explained, "I'm not an American football fan. If I was, it would be different. Yeah. Like, my brother, he's a fan, so he was able to communicate more. My other brother, he drinks alcohol. . . . Also, his wife is American, so he doesn't have a problem. He's very much into the culture. Whereas I'm different, I stopped drinking two years ago. . . . So, I feel like I'm more distant, like there's some kind of barrier" (Kasim 27 February 2018). Moreover, Kasim argued that the United States is a "very much divided society. . . . Each community has their own, basically their own micro-culture. . . . Here, everybody has their own ways of adjusting to society. So, they create their own communities . . . as they obey the law and go by the rules. . . . There are shared aspects, but generally, it all depends. . . . But, American culture, it's a big word. It can accommodate or incorporate any culture, that's the beauty of it. As long as you just go by the rules . . . you can make it (Kasim 27 February 2018).

Within this context, Kasim described the levels of what he called "assimilation" for himself and other Iraqis he knew. In his words:

> From my interactions with Iraqis . . . they range differently in terms of assimilating to the culture, the American culture. Some of them are very well attached or connected to the American culture. And some of them are more distant. I would put myself at out of ten, I would put myself at six in terms of assimilation to the culture. I know people who are way further into that process. Like my brother, he got married to an American girl and he's, he cannot be ten out of ten, he's like nine or eight out of ten. My other brother is probably seven. So, I would consider myself five or six. (Kasim 27 February 2018)

Beyond himself and his family members, Kasim said, "I've seen some people, some of them . . . cannot integrate with the culture. They still have this barrier. Some of them, they went back home. . . . They couldn't take it" (27 February 2018).

Kasim also linked these experiences in the United States to his native country of Iraq, saying "We want to be seen just like how the US is. You know, everybody lives happily, doing their own thing. Nobody's restricting them . . . as long as they don't affect anybody adversely. . . . This nation, it wasn't a nation. It just came from different people who came from different places in the world, and they created a big society, a very tolerant society" (27 February 2018). He reiterated his argument that "each community operates separately but at the same time they follow the rules . . . and that's fine. It's a nice thing to see how people [Iraqis] have changed, but hopefully they will be able to go back, and in a way that they can educate others" (Kasim 27 February 2018).

Kasim's explanation of the challenges he encountered to "assimilation" was emblematic of several interviewees' nuanced feelings of belonging. The following section elaborates on the sense for individuals, including Ali, Hashim, Omar, Tariq, and Zaid, of the otherness that can simultaneously exist with a sense of belonging.

The "Strange Experience" of Being a Problem

This chapter's title paraphrases W. E. B. Du Bois's famous formulation of the implicit, hesitant, and unasked question on the lips of many white Americans toward African Americans: "How does it feel to be a problem?" Describing this experience at the turn of the twentieth century, Du Bois (1903) offered the trenchant observation that it entails a "double consciousness" of always comprehending oneself through the eyes of another who looks at you with pity and contempt. For some African Americans, addressing this tension meant accommodating the society that scorned them, while for others it entailed rejecting that society. Du Bois argued that African Americans wanted simply to "make it possible for a man to be both a Negro and an American, without being cursed and spit upon by his fellows, without having the doors of Opportunity closed roughly in his face" (1903, 2). As I examine below, Tariq explicitly compared the experiences of Iraqis in 2017 to the historical experience of African Americans and described his own desire to belong to the society in starkly similar terms to those articulated by Du Bois.

The historical and contemporary contexts and experiences of African Americans and Iraqi refugees are not completely analogous; however, members of both groups experience the intersecting effects of prejudice, discrimination, and negative stereotyping (Inhorn 2018). Both groups have attempted to enact belonging in the face of active hostility (Crane 2021). There is a long history of arbitrary exclusions targeting Arabs and Muslims in US institutions and culture. Khaled Beydoun argues that "The Orientalist views of Arabs as inassimilable people who would threaten Christianity and undermine American civilization were firmly established before the first immigrant from the Arab World petitioned for citizenship" (2013, 48).

Moreover, Arabs (individuals who claim membership in an ethnolinguistic group originating in the Arabian Peninsula) and Muslims (adherents from myriad cultural, ethnic, and geographic backgrounds to Islam, a heterogeneous set of religious traditions and practices) have long been conflated in American discourses and law. The two groups have often been treated as a single, racialized amalgam Arab/Muslim, even though the population of Arabs and later Arab Americans living in the United States has always been overwhelmingly Christian, and most Muslims living in the country are non-Arab. Muslims of any background were legally barred from gaining US citizenship until 1944, and Arabs could only overcome their racialized exclusion as "nonwhite" by demonstrating the sincerity of their Christian faith to naturalization judges (Beydoun 2013, 48). Therefore, even though in the early twentieth century Christian Arab immigrants in the United States opened a path to gain citizenship, and thereby status as "marginally white" (Cainkar 2008), the "conflation of Arabs as inassimilable Muslims continues to limit the 'substantive citizenship' held by Arab American Muslims today" (Beydoun 2013, 36–37).

With this in mind, strangeness and apartness pervaded the experiences of living in the United States described by some interviewees, including Hashim, Ali, and Tariq. The construction of the "Oriental" other as inherently different from "the Westerner" is deeply rooted (Said 2003), as is the reductive and ahistorical notion of an unbroken and ongoing "clash of civilizations" between monolithic formations of Islam and Christianity (Kumar 2012). Moreover, negative portrayals of Arabs, Muslims, and refugees as incompatible with American society have long been staples in US media, government propaganda (Beydoun 2013), popular culture (Shaheen 2003, 1984), and political discourse (Muslim Advocates 2018). The particular stereotyped image of the Middle East has evolved with time and changing historical and economic contexts. Common stereotypes of Arabs and Arab Americans may rely on assumptions of difference and alienness while others are premised on the notion that Arabs are inherently violent and dangerous (Mango 2012).

In the aftermath of the 11 September 2001 terror attacks, for example, US president George W. Bush declared that a "war on terrorism" that targeted multiple Arab and/or Muslim majority countries was a "crusade" against "evil-doers" (Bush 2001), a rhetorical construction that draws on deep historical assumptions of a fundamental conflict between the so-called East and West (Kumar 2012). More recently, former president Donald Trump and other Republican Party (especially but not exclusively) elected leaders have promoted discourses of danger and otherness regarding individuals from many other parts of the world, particularly the Middle East (Johnson 2015; Muslim Advocates 2018).

As noted in the introduction, nativist and xenophobic discourses circulate alongside the grand narrative within the American popular imagination that the United States is an "immigrant country" that has been exceptionally welcoming of immigrants (Alba and Foner 2015). This trope was familiar to several of the individuals I spoke with. Echoing the immigrant country narrative, Abdullah commented that "a lot of people, including myself, we came here to follow our dreams and to contribute to [the United States]" (14 January 2018). Mohammed, too, said, "When I came to the United States, I thought that it was a big dream, really. Because I see the United States on the TV so, I'm always hearing United States, United States" (2 November 2017). However, he soon discovered many challenges related to life in America: "When I came here [to Upstate New York], I came in February so there was a lot of snow. . . . The weather was very bad. . . . The apartment I lived there in, it's a very bad area. So, I just sat in my apartment, I don't know where I'm going for three months. I said: 'What is going on here?' I can't go outside, I don't know how I can use the bus, everything is difficult. Everything is difficult. So, I decided to come back to Iraq" (Mohammed 2 November 2017).

Mohammed did not go back to Iraq and eventually built a social network and found fulfilling employment. However, his experience speaks to the reality that neither a completely negative nor fully positive grand narrative describes or accounts for the experiences interviewees shared. This section continues to illustrate both the nuances and subtleties of participants' experiences as refugees and former refugees.

Some interlocutors, including Ali and Tariq, expressed a sense of irreconcilability with American society and a conviction that no matter how hard they tried, they would remain, as Tariq phrased it, "second class" residents or citizens, or in a precarious position. This sense of uncertainty led Nada and Zaid to suggest that even with legal rights as residents or citizens, they might still face potential penalties for exercising them. Hashim and Tariq expressed a desire to live and be treated like everyone else, something that they did not perceive they were fully experiencing at the time of their interviews. Finally, during our conversations, Tariq and Kasim pushed back against the notion that Islamic religious commitments or a culturally transferred Muslim background were inherently dangerous and violent, and Omar and Nora discussed their fear that speaking their first language, or a language other than English, publicly would put them at risk of opprobrium or worse.

As Ali explained in his observation cited for the epigraph to this chapter, he perceived a stringent standard to which he and other resettled refugees were held. And, as he argued, if someone like himself makes one mistake, or if others perceive his actions as wrong, the work he had done to live up to that standard would be erased. "As a refugee, I'm doing . . . a lot of good things. And I'm doing a great job . . . for the community or for my work, you know? But, sometimes, if you make one single mistake–if it was a mistake, sometimes it was interpreted like a mistake–they will forget about all of the good things you have done the past five years. And they will catch only these single things" (Ali 14 January 2018).

Tariq contextualized his comments about his life in Upstate New York by describing his expectations of the United States before he left Iraq. Because of the new and often expensive equipment that the American occupation forces brought to Iraq during the war, Tariq assumed that life in the United States would be materially comfortable and that everyone would "live in peace," which he desired for himself and his family. As he put it:

> So, I was thinking when I moved to the US, it's the homeland for them. If . . . people overseas have the offices, the lifestyle everything, that means the US will be better. Right? This is what you think. If you see me overseas with all the fancy stuff and all the degrees that I have, the lifestyle that I have. You think: "Oh, what about his home country? Probably it will be better then." . . . And when you go to the US embassy in Iraq, it's heaven. You walk the gardens, and the landscaping is beautiful. . . . If you go there, you don't want to come back. It's beautiful. So, we think, people like me: "Oh my god, if it's overseas and they have all that beautiful stuff, so definitely in the US it will be better." So, I was thinking we will be better. And we will live in peace. This is what I want. So, we moved. (Tariq 2 November 2017)

However, when he arrived in the United States, the reality did not meet his expectations. "I was surprised by all the nonsense. Like, there is still [racism between] white and black. And [it is assumed] immigrants and refugees, they don't work or whatever. They all moved here for benefits. All nonsense. And I said, 'Oh my god, really?' And then drugs, a lot of issues. A lot of poverty. A lot of poverty. So, this is what surprised us" (Tariq 2 November 2017).

Consequently, Tariq suggested that he must work twice as hard as Americans do to prove that he has the right to be in the United States: "We work double. So, we want to work and show them that we are just normal people and . . . you made the right decision by letting us in" (2 November 2017). As noted, he compared his experience as an Iraqi, a refugee, and a Muslim to the historical experience of African Americans: "Now, it's our era, unfortunately. It used to be black Americans before and now it's Muslims. . . . This is what I think. It's my opinion" (Tariq 2 November 2017). Moreover, he pointed out that despite centuries of struggle, there are still significant unresolved issues between black and white Americans: "For us, it will be tough too" (Tariq 2 November 2017). Tariq regarded his social position as one of living with a feeling of persistent suspicion, a sense that he was viewed by many as untrustworthy and somehow guilty of an unstated transgression. Tariq attributed this perception to his background as a refugee from the Middle East. As he put it, "Because if you are a refugee from Europe, who cares? Probably they . . . are white, who cares? They don't know you. Even if you have an accent, if you say I'm Italian, you're good. If you say I'm from England, you're fine. You're white, you're fine. But, when they know you are from the Middle East, they are a little bit concerned. . . . It's profiling" (Tariq 2 November 2017). "You're not trusted," he continued, and "If some Muslim did something, it's all over the news for the next month" (Tariq 2 November 2017). Indeed, Kearns, Betus, and Lemieux (2018) have found that terrorist attacks committed by individuals identified as Muslims receive between 1.81 to 4.93 times more media coverage than those perpetrated by those of other backgrounds.

Tariq argued as well that such reports emphasize the perpetrator's Muslim background, even if tenuous, and that the complexity of identities is flattened with anyone from the Middle East or with an Arab background assumed to be Muslim, an identification believed to be dangerous and violent. He pointed to the inconsistency or double standard in the way media have often portrayed crimes committed by white Americans and Muslims. When a "white guy" commits murder, he is portrayed as mentally ill. "When we do it, we're terrorists" (Tariq 2 November 2017). He mentioned several examples–including the 2015 murder of three Muslim students in Chapel Hill, North Carolina, by their white neighbor (Blanford 2017)–in which white Americans shot and killed multiple people, and many media outlets attributed the shooter's motive to mental health issues with no mention of terrorism. A 2019 YouGov poll found a similar double standard among respondents' interpretations of such events. In general, respondents labeled violent attacks committed by Muslims as terrorism and similar violent acts committed by white Americans as hate crimes (Frankovic 2019).

Considering this inconsistency, when he learns of a mass shooting or bombing, Tariq's first reaction is to hope the perpetrator is not a Muslim:

> Every time when I hear somebody [committed a shooting], really, I say: 'Oh my god, I don't want to know if it's a Muslim.' This is reality for a lot of us. When I hear about a shooting, mass shooting and bombing. . . . Don't say . . . Muslims did it because this is what is killing us. Like, oh my god, then it will be on the news, and you go to the store. Boom! And his face is looking at my face. . . . People see us as a terrorist. They don't see us as people. (2 November 2017)

Terror attacks committed in the United States are exceedingly rare compared to other violent crimes, and Muslim perpetrators have been responsible for a minority of this small number of incidents (Neiwert et al. 2017). However, despite this reality, the fear that Muslims will face backlash if an attacker is identified as Muslim is both well-founded and persistent (All Things Considered 2013).

In less stark terms than Tariq, Zaid experienced a sense of difference "because I am a foreigner" (27 February 2018). As he put it, "I am not an American citizen, I am a *naturalized* citizen. . . . Not an American-born citizen" (Zaid 27 February 2018). Elaborating, he indicated that he especially had this sense when he visited the state of Kentucky with a friend. "It was like everyone was just staring at you" (Zaid 27 February 2018). As Zaid recounted, his friend, who is white but originally from Russia, shared this perception: "She's Russian. I mean, she's white. But you can tell that she's not from here. And she got the same feeling. You know?" (27 February 2018). I asked Zaid whether he believed that this feeling would change in the future, to which he said: "No, I think not. With everything going on now, with unfortunately having a racist president [Donald Trump]. This is my feeling. This is the way I feel now" (27 February 2018).

Nora, too, speculated that perhaps she had had interpersonal issues in the Shenandoah Valley Region of Virginia because she was "different." I asked her whether her background as an Iraqi had created any challenges for her in the United States. She responded: "No. I think people have challenges, no matter where they are from. It depends on the person that you're dealing with, right? I don't think it is because I am from Iraq. I don't look at it this way. But I think because, I don't know, maybe because I'm different than [other city residents]. Like, I don't have the southern accent, with the blonde hair" (Nora 6 February 2018). She asserted that some Americans would always treat her differently based on her country of origin: "No matter what your language is, even if you don't have an accent but, people always treat you as where you're from, even if you get citizenship" (Nora 6 February 2018). However, she continued with a laugh, only a minority might treat her that way: "Not all of them, but one in twenty will. So, it's okay, it's only one. You have nineteen more that welcome you and that's okay" (Nora 6 February 2018).

I asked Omar the same question concerning whether his background as an Iraqi had created any challenges for him. He argued that rather than proving a hindrance, his Iraqi origin provided a justification for his presence in the United States: "If you are being asked 'why are you here?', for example, I would definitely say: 'I came here because of the war that I didn't create.' So, it's kind of a justification to help me justify my presence here" (Omar 14 December 2017). He explained how this aspect of his background could be used to assert his right to live in the United States: "As an aid, I would use it, definitely. . . . Because I worked as an interpreter for the US troops. And for that reason, my father was killed. And, I have sacrificed a lot for the US, more than anyone who's asking this question or other citizens. Easily I can ask him: 'What did you give to your country, other than the taxes that you are giving? Did you give your son? Your father?' So, the war actually it's not challenging here for me. But, I mean, challenging back home" (Omar 14 December 2017).

As a follow-up, I asked Omar whether he felt the need to justify himself to Americans or whether anyone had asked him to do so: "The problem is because they think that they have the right. And to be honest with you: They don't because they are immigrants like us. And, we all should justify our presence here to the Native Americans" (14 December 2017). In his view, Americans who asked him to explain his presence would do so because they had been affected by propaganda: "To justify, I mean, it's something that has propaganda for it, everywhere. So, people believe it" (Omar 14 December 2017).

More explicitly than asking why he was in the United States, individuals told Mohammed to leave the country. At one point, he held a job at a local airport that involved enforcing traffic and parking rules and preventing cars from approaching the security entrance. Occasionally, while enforcing the rules, individuals had yelled at him, "Go back to your country!" He noted that he laughs this sort of remark off and observed, "I don't care about it. I just told them: 'I respect that, just move your car'" (Mohammed 2 November 2017). He interpreted this aggression as a type of interaction that could occur in any society. As he explained: "I think this is normal and happens in each country . . . they have bad and good people. But 75 percent of the people are good. So, this does not mean . . . this country is not good. . . . Anywhere you can find good people and bad people, but I think the people here are really good people, really friendly. Yeah. No issues from racists" (Mohammed 2 November 2017).

However, Mohammed had encountered the opinion that he should accept his circumstances without question. Soon after arriving, his resettlement organization caseworker told him the only available employment involved cleaning cages at the local zoo. As Mohammed narrated:

> I told them: "I don't have any issue with this job. But I can't do that. I worked with the government in Iraq. So how can I go to the Zoo? I'm sorry, I graduated with a [technical degree] in Iraq." So, he told me: "Okay go back to your country if you want to." This made me very, very, very upset. . . . I told him: "Okay, you can fix up my country and I will go back tomorrow morning. You brought me here. I had a civil war." . . . So, I told him I don't need cash, I don't need food stamps. I decided to work. (2 November 2017)

Thereafter, Mohammed declined any further services from the resettlement agency and set out to find employment on his own. He first found employment delivering pizza and then at a Walmart before securing the job in airport security. At the time of our interview, he was working as a caseworker at a social services organization.

In addition to markers of difference like those noted by Nora above, such as speaking English with an accent, physical features or hair color, a particularly visible sign of Islamic faith are the various head coverings some Muslim women wear. Only one of the women I interviewed, Marwa, wore a hijab. The other women with whom I spoke did not. Marwa did not express any concern about covering her hair in Upstate New York. Rather, she said: "Sometimes when I'm at an event with my community, like for a wedding party or funeral, [friends may ask]: 'You wear a scarf, you are *muḥajiba* [a woman who wears hijab]. Do you find a hard time?' I say: 'No, absolutely no.' . . . They respect that. I didn't find any disrespect. From my experience, no" (Marwa 25 November 2017).

However, several men with whom I spoke discussed women they know who, they believed, were facing prejudice or harassment, or may in the future. Tariq, for example, expressed fear of walking in public and a particular concern for his wife because she covers her hair and therefore is visibly Muslim. He said: "My wife wears a headscarf, and I am afraid somebody will kill her or hit her. This is a big mess. You know, this is what we think all the time about. . . . You can identify [Muslim women] easily" (Tariq 2 November 2017).

Ali worried as well about incidents targeting women who cover their hair, including his mother. "What I am hearing from friends," he said, is "if they wear hijab, they pull the hijab from them, they spit on them. They curse them. . . . I have my mother, she wears a hijab and I'm afraid for her when she goes out. She doesn't speak the language. So, maybe she doesn't understand when someone curses at her . . . or someone spits on her" (Ali 14 January 2018).

At the time of our interview, such an incident had not occurred to Ali's mother. However, a 2018 New York City Commission on Human Rights report found that similar incidents are common in New York City, where Ali lives. In a survey of more than three thousand Muslim, Arab, South Asian, Jewish, and Sikh New Yorkers, the Commission found that 38.7 percent had experienced "verbal harassment, threats or taunting referring to race, ethnicity or religion" (The New York City Commission on Human Rights, Frazer, and Howe 2018, 9), and 27.4 percent of Muslim Arab women wearing a hijab reporting being intentionally pushed or shoved on a subway platform.

Ali continued, arguing that members of the government had failed to speak against such actions: "In the past, you used to hear of one, two [such incidents] in different states. Some happened here. . . . Now, it's increasing a lot . . . and increasing in a dangerous path.[1] No one is doing anything. No one [such as President Trump] is going out and speaking saying: 'This is not acceptable. This is not what we do. This is not what the Constitution says.' These are my fears, you know? These are what I'm thinking of" (Ali 14 January 2018).

Walid, who has founded and leads several organizations serving refugees, used a part of his interview to share his experience working with the Iraqi and Muslim communities in Upstate New York. Drawing from these interactions, he spoke about women encountering problems because they cover their hair: "Others don't know I'm a Muslim from my face, probably. But they know the woman with her scarf. These women [pointing to two women wearing brightly colored headscarves sitting on a nearby park bench], I know are probably from Somalia or Sudan. Having this scarf, my perception, they are Muslim. . . . I have had some families mention they use the metro, and somebody tried to say bad words about that and make these women feel unsafe and uncomfortable" (Walid 27 September 2017).

Walid and fellow organization members encouraged women to voice safety concerns to the police: "We told them if something like this happens call 911 [the US emergency services phone number] and tell them I'm not feeling safe somebody is saying something. Also, we try to educate and tell them what they are supposed to do if something like this happens. Some women start to think about taking off the hijab because they are not feeling safe. I found this concerning. It's kind of a shame the society [is not educated about practices such as wearing a head covering]" (27 September 2017).

We Want to Be Like Everyone Else

Echoing findings from earlier studies of resettled Iraqis (Inhorn and Volk 2021; Crane 2021; Campbell 2016), Hashim and Tariq stressed that they had resettled in the United States to pursue building lives exactly as native-born

Americans do. They desired safety from conflict for themselves and their families, economic opportunities, and engagement in their communities. In this way, they desired to live like "everyone else." Both Hashim and Tariq put it in the same language, saying resettled Iraqis are not "aliens." At the end of our interview, Hashim emphasized his shared humanity with Americans, laughingly saying: "We are not coming from a different world. . . . We are not aliens" (1 October 2017). In remarkably similar language Tariq said: "We're not aliens . . . from a different universe. We're just people" (2 November 2017).

Hashim argued, "We are here because we escaped from there. We escaped from everything happening there. . . . We are not going to do anything bad in this country" (1 October 2017). Reacting to the rhetoric and policies originating in the Trump White House, he observed, "Maybe I agree . . . with setting stricter rules on people that did bad things, . . . let's say the bad people. I really agree on that, to go after them. To try to set stricter rules on them. But, not on everyone. This is very unacceptable" (Hashim 1 October 2017). He continued, rejecting the idea of barring Muslims or other groups from entering the United States:

> You cannot just say that we ban Muslims from entering the country. This is completely not fair, you know? The Muslim community or the Iraqi community or any other community, they have been here for many years, and they did something. They participated in the community. . . . Many of them, I am not saying that everyone is bad, or everyone is good, but many they have been here for many years and all of them they have their goals in life. They want to just be safe, to just get a good education, to just get good healthcare for their families. We are just trying to be safe here and plan for our future. . . . The majority of immigrants, 90 percent of them, are here for a better life. (Hashim 1 October 2017)

Later in our conversation, Hashim reiterated this point, saying: "I'm not asking for us to be treated differently, I'm just asking for us to be treated just like everyone else. . . . Everything now is against Muslims, Arabs, and Iraqis, all the media and all of the officials. I think this is very wrong. . . . We're just like Europeans here. Just like Chinese here. Just like everyone else in this world. So . . . it's just difficult for us to be treated this way. We're not asking to be treated in a different way" (1 October 2017).

Tariq also indicated that he wants to "live like anybody else" as a member of the community: "Me and my family, and I have a lot of friends who all come with degrees. And we want to . . . live in the US, be part of the US community and live like anybody else. You know, live next to everybody and you wake up in the morning, say hi to everybody, live in peace" (2 November 2017). He reiterated this point later in our conversation, saying, "We came here to be like anybody else. We work and we want to be like anybody . . . and we live our lives. We love the US, that's why we moved here" (Tariq 2 November 2017). Moreover, like Omar, Ali, and others, Tariq worked with the US military after the 2003 invasion of Iraq. As in Omar's account, he noted his service with the American Marines as a justification for having the opportunity to live like others in the United States. He explained:

> I put my life in danger, probably a lot of people they didn't do anything, even here. I served with the Marines. Probably, there's a lot of people, they served. But there is still a huge number, they didn't even serve. . . . So, this should really demonstrate to people that: Come on, people they put their life at risk, they helped you see your father back home safe, see your son, see your wife, see your daughter back safe and he's never been to the US before. So why did they do that? For fun? Nobody joins the Marines or army in general for fun. There's no fun there. And then, so they just want [Americans to] give us an opportunity. (Tariq 2 November 2017)

Assumptions of Islam and Muslims as Uniquely Violent

The portrayal of Islam as essentially irrational, violent, and dangerous is pervasive in American cultural (Shaheen 2003, 1984) and political discourse. For example, Michael Flynn, retired US Army Lt. General, former Defense Intelligence Agency director under President Barack Obama, and former National Security Advisor to Donald Trump, has a long history of inflammatory rhetoric about Islam. Flynn is an advisor to the board of directors for the anti-Muslim group ACT for America (SPLC n.d.). In a 2016 speech, he declared "We are facing another 'ism,' just like we faced Nazism, and fascism. . . . This is Islamism, it is a vicious cancer inside the body of 1.7 billion people on this planet and it has to be excised" (Kaczynski 2016). In the mid-2000s, the term "Islamofascism" came into vogue among some cultural commentators, liberal and conservative, to describe America's supposed enemies in "The War on Terror" (Judt 2006; Hitchens 2007).

The endurance of such discourses led Ahmed, for example, to say, "You get accustomed, especially after all the events in the last twenty years that have happened, you get a certain stereotyped image about the Middle East" (2 October 2017). Abdullah similarly argued that it is important to be willing to recognize and encourage nuance "because there are a lot of people from the West who [assert that] all Arabs and Muslims are attacking everybody" (14 January 2018).

It was important to Nada to preface our conversation by stating: "Of course, my religion is Muslim and really, I am proud of this. I want to show everyone here what it means to be Muslim. I know they have the wrong idea about Muslims. But I'm a Muslim and I love all the religions here, . . . everyone here, really because they respect me, so I respect them. And when I came here, they helped me so much and helped my family. So, I love all the people here. Everyone here. . . . Just, I want to say that" (1 November 2017). I understood Nada's insistence as pushing back against the widespread trope in this country that Islam is inherently and uniquely violent among religions and cultures of the world and that she was taking the opportunity of our interview to voice an alternative, more accurate, understanding.

Other participants also pushed back, arguing that groups such as ISIS claiming to act in the name of Islam were violating, rather than upholding, Islamic principles. Unlike some American commentators or politicians who assert the uniquely violent character of Islam, but who have little knowledge of its tenets or traditions, these interviewees rejected that claim from within the faith. In this way, they set and (re)interpreted boundaries around what qualifies as authentic and inauthentic Islam. In characterizing the intercommunal violence in Iraq after 2003, for example, Sarah said that Sunni would kill Shi'a and Shi'a would kill Sunni. However, those who killed based upon this division within Islam were not genuine Muslims, in her view: "These people, we think, they are not Muslims. . . . Bad people, yes, that's why so many people from Iraq escaped" (Sarah 30 November 2017). Like Nada, Sarah emphasized that she respected everyone, regardless of their religion or race. She too stressed that "Muslim people, in general, are peaceful people. . . . In general, the Muslim people don't . . . hurt others. I think that and I see all the Muslim people like that. And, I respect my religion and I don't have any problem with any other religion" (Sarah 30 November 2017).

Walid put it in similar terms: "In every religion, in every society, there are good people and bad people, and some of these bad people, they use religion as a tool to justify their criminal acts. And they are not Muslim. . . . I consider them criminal people because Islam teaches me how to love people, how to help. . . . We give to charity, the same as Christianity. There is no difference. We never heard about these bad people who attacked the United States on 9/11 and it's all related to politics. They use religion to justify their political opinions" (27 September 2017).

He framed the motivations for such acts as reacting to US violence in the Middle East. In his estimation, the perpetrators followed the logic, "Why did you attack the Middle East? We want to attack you" (Walid 27 September 2017).[2] He continued: "And this is not about religion. This is a war between countries, not religion" (Walid 27 September 2017). In Walid's view, and as polling data suggest (Poushter 2015), "many people disagree about this kind of criminal behavior of some people who consider themselves . . . Muslim" (27 September 2017). Indeed, a 2011 Gallup poll of 131 countries found no correlation between religiosity and support for attacking civilians, and that respondents living in Organisation of Islamic Cooperation (OIC) member states were less likely to justify military attacks on civilians (18 percent) than non-OIC member state respondents (24 percent). Americans were the most likely to justify violence against civilians (49 percent) of any country surveyed. Only 8 percent of Iraqis said targeting and killing civilians is sometimes justified (Gallup 2011). Finally, as explained in more detail in the following chapter, Wissam highlighted the Islamic injunction to protect Christian and Jewish houses of worship, arguing, "What they're doing is all false" (22 October 2017), when ISIS and similar groups that claim to act in the name of religion attack such sites in Iraq.

In strikingly similar language, Kasim and Tariq pushed back at the persistent stereotype of Islam as inherently violent. Tariq strongly refuted the notion that Islam is "bad," and that Muslims are raised to hate and kill. One example of such a stereotype emerged in 2015, when Donald Trump declared that "Without looking at the various polling data, it is obvious to anybody the [Muslim] hatred is beyond comprehension" and that the United States should not allow Muslims who "have no sense of reason or respect for human life" to enter this country (Johnson 2015).

Reacting to rhetoric like this, Tariq explained:

> You have to understand that when somebody shoots, it doesn't mean all of us want to shoot. I keep telling them, if it's our religion that's bad, we are a billion and a half. So, if we are raised to kill people, a billion and a half, . . . we will fight everybody. Probably there will be war, from a long time ago, because we're raised to kill people, right? So, why if I was raised to kill people, I'm here and we should fight all the time. . . . Fighting everybody because we hate everybody. This is what you guys think. No! If we were raised to kill everyone, I told you, we are a billion and a half! We are going to have a Third World War . . . or . . . you know, the First World War would have been us against everybody. (2 November 2017)

Tariq continued by saying that if these assumptions were true, he and I would not have been sitting in his living room and talking. In similar terms, Kasim articulated the view that many Americans already know this, and that they understand that the problem is not Islam, per se. As he argued: "I remember when 9/11 happened, there were a lot of incidents against Muslims. . . . When we came here, we didn't find that. That sentiment was gone already. And, people have come to realize after all these years that the problem is not Muslims. The problem is . . . terrorists.[3] If you think it's the Muslims, there are over a billion Muslims in this world. If they do the same thing [commit acts of terrorism], the world would be like hell for everybody. So that's not the case" (Kasim 27 February 2018). He went on to attribute the notion that all Muslims are violent to "propaganda." He said: "This is propaganda some people use against Muslims, and we know who they are. But the general public has now come to its senses: 'These people are just like us.' You know? And we find terrorists everywhere, in every culture, in every time. You find sick people anywhere, everywhere in any community. So . . . it's a good thing, I think society probably realized that to a big extent" (Kasim 27 February 2018). Kasim did not clarify whom he meant when he said that "some people" use propaganda against Muslims. However, even though he is a Donald Trump supporter, later in our discussion, Kasim called Trump's rhetoric racist and characterized it as propaganda.

Arabic as Dangerous Speech

Not only did some of those with whom I spoke perceive their religious background, or that attributed to them, as problematic in terms of how they were viewed by other Americans, but several interviewees also shared that they were sometimes uncomfortable speaking their native language, Arabic, in public spaces. Tariq said, for example, "At the airport, if I speak my language, they could kick me out easily" (2 November 2017). Although he did not reference any incidents of this happening to himself or others, there have been multiple cases in recent years of individuals interrogated by airport security for carrying Arabic flashcards (N. George 2015), detained before boarding a flight after passengers complained about overhearing Arabic (CBS News 2015), and removed from flights for speaking Arabic on the plane (Hassan and Shoichet 2016).[4] Moreover, various agencies such as the NYPD and FBI have targeted and profiled those of Arab descent or Muslim religious background for increased surveillance and scrutiny in airports, Mosques, and community organizations for many years (Kumar 2012).

The experience of airports as a site of discrimination against Arabs, Muslims, and those assumed to fall into such categories is widespread. The Council on American-Islamic Relations (CAIR) has called the phenomenon "Flying while Muslim" (CAIR 2017). A play on the term "Driving while Black," which describes increased police suspicion and racial profiling of African American motorists, Flying while Muslim highlights the analogous situation in which those outwardly appearing Muslim and/or of Middle Eastern origin are targeted and assumed to be dangerous. In the years since the 11 September 2001 attacks, airlines have subjected such passengers to discrimination, profiling, and arbitrary denial of access to, and removal from, flights (CAIR 2017). Speaking Arabic is one marker used by fearful travelers and airport security to profile individuals arbitrarily as threatening to the safety of other travelers.

Omar suggested that those overhearing Arabic spoken in public spaces might deem it inappropriate and that he might be disliked simply for speaking it. As he explained: "In a public café, we do not try to speak Arabic loudly. . . . You know, it's also not appropriate in terms of being liked by others. They may think, 'Oh hey, these people are speaking Arabic? Oh man, we'd rather not have this.' Usually, if you are going for enjoyment or entertainment . . . we'd rather not. Sometimes, we socialize in an Arabic café. But other places, no. Yeah, we'd rather not [speak Arabic]" (Omar 14 December 2017).

Nora, too, perceived spaces in which speaking her native Arabic had proven problematic: "Sometimes just people look at you [for speaking Arabic], but I don't care. If this is the way my mom [who does not speak English] will understand me, no, my mom is way more important than the public" (6 February 2018).

Unease and Uncertainty: Long-Standing and Newly Piqued

In addition to the tensions between belonging and strangeness, and othering by some members of American society, various interviewees indicated that they or others they knew experienced a sense of precarity living in the United States. For Nada, this was a long-standing sense, while for others, like Abdullah, Omar, and Nora, it first arose within the context of the 2016 election and Donald Trump's xenophobic and anti-refugee election campaign. Multiple interviewees identified a sense of growing unease since the 2016 presidential election and executive actions such as the 2017 travel ban, which sought to bar refugees from seven countries, including Iraq, initially, from entering the United States: "I don't know what he's going to do or what his next step will be," Ali said, for example (14 January 2018). Although not everyone indicated that they opposed the Trump administration's policies, Nada, Abdullah, and Omar, for example, discussed how executive actions and immigration policies had contributed to a sense of foreboding for themselves or for others they knew.

Nada discussed how, as a Green Card holder, she knew she had a legal right to travel within the United States as well as outside of the country. Nevertheless, she was afraid to exercise that right. She said: "I want to visit some other countries. Really, but I am afraid. I want to visit Canada. I want to see it. . . . But, I am afraid, because I have a Green Card, just a Green Card. I know I can do it. The rules allow me to do that. But, I am scared, because sometimes, for example, Trump . . . decided the rules, I can't come back again. Because I have just the Green Card. This is my fear" (Nada 1 November 2017).

Although Nada did not directly connect this fear to the travel ban, when it initially went into effect, thousands of individuals were detained at airports, some for multiple days (Cheng 2017). Media reports indicate that, in some cases, legal permanent residents were among those detained, including Iraqi SIV recipients (Macguire, Gostanian, and Ortiz 2017; Darweesh 2017). Hundreds of others with "legal visas or refugee status" were prevented from boarding flights bound for the United States at foreign points of origin (Gomez 2017). Nada's fear increased under Trump, but she was also nervous to travel under his predecessor, Barack Obama. As an SIV recipient, she said "I know that Iraq compared with another country, they give us more chances to come [to the United States]. But I am afraid. I want to protect myself and my family" (Nada 1 November 2017). Fortunately, at the time of our interview, Nada had only one more year until she could apply for citizenship, after which time, she believed, this concern would dissipate.

Abdullah also expressed an increased feeling of uncertainty: "I feel less protected. Any decision that president [Trump] might make could directly affect me. And, I'm living on the edge right now" (14 January 2018). As he continued to explain: "Honestly, since he got elected until now, every day he comes up with some order and I'm basically freaking out. Am I staying here or not?" (Abdullah 14 January 2018). At the time of our interview, Abdullah had been granted Optional Practical Training (OPT) status, which allowed him to remain temporarily in the United States for up to three years to work after he had concluded his studies in engineering. This program was among the immigration policies that Trump said he would seek to reduce or eliminate (Fu 2018). As Abdullah put it, "I'm on OPT status and he is pushing to change that. So . . . basically, I have a right [to live in the United States], he might basically be able to take it, to take my right" (14 January 2018).

Abdullah suggested that this insecurity was the primary challenge he faced in his daily life: "So that part is the main thing that is annoying me right now. If you asked me: 'What is the biggest struggle right now?' It would be that because I'm going to work and doing everything fine. I'm moving up in the company and all of that could change in one day" (14 January 2018). He continued to explain: "So, right now, I don't feel as protected as before. For sure. It is very stressful . . . because in that case, you feel like you have no rights. Because even if your papers are fine and if you have the right to stay here, you feel, not safe" (Abdullah 14 January 2018).

During our conversation, Omar returned to one of the first questions I asked him; whether he planned to remain in the United States permanently, saying: "Back to your question about if I'm going home or staying, that also has something to do with whether the community will keep accepting me or not. Recently there are some signals that: 'Oh, you guys, you are bad.' Even though we were productive. We were clean. We were educated. We were paying taxes. But still, if someone did something, that will be counted for all people from that country or ethnicity or religion" (14 December 2017).

Omar saw a change in the way he and others like him were being treated in his community since the election of Donald Trump. That shift emanating from Washington would "impact the whole nation, whether it is negative or positive," he said (Omar 14 December 2017). Omar also noted the effects the president's rhetoric and actions were having on children, including his own, in his community. He related a story about a recent incident in which classmates bullied his fourth-grade son, calling him names such as "terrorist." Despite this episode, and his overall sense that there was less support coming from the national government, he perceived his local context, the city in which he lived in Virginia, as overall supportive of immigrants and refugees: "In [my city] people are, I would say 90 percent of them, very good. Yeah. That is what made me live here nine years. It's a unique city" (Omar 14 December 2017).

Nora described the day after Trump's election in 2016 and the way in which one of her American friends reacted:

> When he got elected, I remember the second day, I couldn't sleep, so I woke up at 7 o'clock. I was going to my job and then my friend, she's American, called me and her son was crying, and was like: "Are you going to leave the United States because Trump is going to make you leave?" And I was like: "No, I'm not going to leave. I need you to be there for me. Okay?" And, my friend's like: "I'm sorry, I want to apologize to your mom. I know she's waiting for your brother to come . . . but, we're here for you" (6 February 2018).

Mohammed spoke of others' fear saying "Some people are scared of the president right now. I will be clear with you. . . . We don't know what the government will be deciding in the future" (2 November 2017). "But," he continued, "I'm sure the American Congress and American people, in my small experience, they won't accept anything racist or anything like this. They will support us, and I think that because I read about the American people in history and . . . the American people don't accept racism" (Mohammed 2 November 2017).

Although Trump appeared on TV and threatened refugees with harmful policies that would "push the people outside America," Mohammed was confident Trump would be prevented from enacting them: "It will never happen because the Constitution, I think, the Constitution protects the people. Not just the refugees, all the people in America" (2 November 2017). Mohammed was especially convinced that community members and the local government in his city in Upstate New York would protect the rights of people like himself.

Speaking to the environment in Upstate New York as well, Walid said that Trump's election in 2016 created difficulties for his work with refugee communities in the area. This was particularly true because many of those with whom he interacts have family members abroad awaiting resettlement: "It does create challenges. We still have many families overseas. They are waiting to join their family members here. And all the process is now a mess. They don't know what's going to happen" (Walid 27 September 2017). At the time Walid and I spoke, significant uncertainty remained as to the legality of the travel ban. He received a phone call during our conversation from a Green Card holder living in Upstate New York whose wife was in Lebanon. Her visa application had been pending for three years before the Trump administration entered office, and that process was suspended after Trump's election. According to Walid, the pair was considering divorce because the husband wished to remain in the United States, but after waiting three years without resolution, the wife wanted him to return to Lebanon. Walid said similar uncertainty had created difficulties for other families with which he works: "We see some people waiting for their mom, some people for their daughter and it's causing emotional difficulties for many family members with the new policies of the administration" (27 September 2017).

Because of a profound sense of insecurity, Tariq said many individuals from the Middle East would avoid confrontation, even if they believe they are in the right because they are afraid that American society and government are predisposed against them. He said, "This is the toughest part. And this is what the people are living with now in the Trump era. . . . [Trump] said it: 'If you do anything, you're out!'" (Tariq 2 November 2017). With such constraints, he questioned what he should or could do. As a hypothetical example, Tariq said that even if he were physically assaulted, he felt he could not assert his right to safety: "If I walk in the alley and somebody hits me, I can't say anything, you know?" (2 November 2017).

He went on to suggest that as someone in a precarious position, he empathized with those individuals affected by Hurricane Harvey, a severe storm that struck the state of Texas in the months before our interview: "I was really touched," he said, "if you are in my position, probably you feel this situation a little bit" (Tariq 2 November 2017). As he explained, and media reported at the time, many of the people displaced by the storm were undocumented migrants who were afraid of calling the police or emergency services for help or seeking recovery assistance after the storm because they could be arrested and/or deported (Capps and Soto 2018). As a result, they faced danger and even risked death. Police representatives and officials in some areas made public calls that those affected could seek help without fear of US Immigration and Customs Enforcement, but many storm victims remained fearful (Owen 2018).

Tariq said that this situation was the same for him:

> I am legally here, but I'm scared to do it because no matter what . . . I'm not from here. I don't speak the language fluently that they speak. Maybe they [police or judges] would use a term I don't understand . . . against me. And he [Trump] makes this one [police and judges] very strong now. If you hit somebody, immigrants, they just walk away. So, he is going to create a massive . . . disaster. It's a dictatorship. This is how they built a dictatorship in Iraq. This is how we had Saddam Hussein. If you say something: Boom! Done, you're gone. And your family. (2 November 2017)

He then described what he viewed as the process by which government can move toward authoritarianism and highlighted signs in American society that such a shift was occurring. As he argued:

> This is how it starts. You say something, you get kicked. Or they put [a negative mark] on you when you apply for a job. They know you are bad; you are from this family, you are done. And then day after day, he has more power because people gave him power. Nobody says no to him. So, he gains more power, starting now. Not kick you from the house or deny you a job; now he can kill you. He killed one, two, and everybody. Oh, it's fine. Nobody says anything, okay let me take his family. Then you say something, and they take your family. This is how life in Iraq was. (Tariq 2 November 2017)

Although Tariq's fears luckily did not come to pass and the Trump administration was voted out of office in 2020, his concerns were well founded. Trump, members of his government, and some of his supporters did attempt to overturn the results of the 2020 presidential election. These actions culminated on 6 January 2021, when a mob of Trump supporters stormed the US Capitol building, breached its security, and barricaded themselves inside in an effort to disrupt the final electoral vote count confirming Joe Biden's victory over Trump (Blake 2021).

Consequences of Demonization

Tariq, Nora, Ali, and Zaid all discussed the potential ramifications for individuals when the president and other elected and appointed officials rhetorically attack Muslims, refugees, and other immigrants, and enact restrictive policies. Such actions by government officials intersect with disproportionate media coverage of acts of terrorism committed by Muslims compared to those perpetrated by others and narratives in popular culture that portray Islam as dangerous and violent, as described above. Tariq and Nora spoke of the radicalizing effects this scenario can have on those so targeted. Ali and Zaid suggested that perceived government support for demonization gives license to racists to act in aggressive and violent ways toward refugees.

In Tariq's experience, many immigrants believed they did not need to worry about policies that would make it more difficult for others to enter the United States because they had already successfully immigrated: "A lot of people think: 'Oh yeah, because I'm here, I'm good'" (2 November 2017). In fact, Kasim, expressed this exact view, as I describe in more detail in the discussion of the travel ban in Chapter 4. This was a mistaken understanding, according to Tariq, because such policies can radicalize those targeted:

> Because there are a lot of people who want to be here. What about if I'm there, and I'm waiting desperately to move. And I have a death threat. And

now, for example, I believe a lot of people have the same thing. Like I have a death threat and now Trump banned me from going. What should I do? Get killed? And that's it? What are you going to do when you have this situation? Probably, you will join ISIS and fight the US. Why did they do that? I helped you and now you kick me out? You don't want to have my family and me. So, we shouldn't underestimate these things. (2 November 2017)

Tariq argued that Trump does not care about the long-term consequences of his actions. "How long are you going to be president?" he asked, "Four more years? And then what? You're gone. You are going to create something, a massive problem elsewhere, they are going to fight" (Tariq 2 November 2017). Conversely, he said this situation could change "if we had support from people, from the White House, from Washington and the news stopped [perpetuating anti-Muslim discourses]" (Tariq 2 November 2017). He hoped to see less division in the future in the United States.

The assumption of danger targeting those already in the United States has far-reaching ramifications, Tariq argued. "It's not going to affect me," he said, "because of how I was born and raised, I'm strong. I know that's not us" (2 November 2017). However, the danger, according to Tariq, is that children of Muslim backgrounds born in the United States will "grow up on hate. Watch the news: 'Muslim, Muslim, Muslim.' And he's Muslim and he's a kid. And he's not going to understand. So, you created that beast and then he grows up a little bit, he now wanted to be a Muslim. But he went to the wrong side. People like ISIS, they say: 'We are Muslims'" (2 November 2017).

As Tariq pointed out, reviewing the small number of terrorist plots or attacks in the United States involving Muslims, the overwhelming majority involved American-born, rather than foreign-born, individuals (Neiwert 2017). Despite this reality, as noted above, in the United States, news media disproportionately cover terrorism committed by Muslims compared to attacks perpetrated by those of other backgrounds. Moreover, Islam, particularly as represented by predominately Arab societies in the Middle East, has long been conflated with terrorism in popular culture (Shaheen 2003, 1984). Tariq observed that this conflation is incorrect: "This is the mistake that people make to consider Muslims terrorists. We're not. . . . One crazy guy gets mad, not because he's a Muslim. He gets mad probably because of the behavior that you guys show him. And that's why I keep telling friends, teachers: 'Don't blame me in the future when one of my kids, because of you, you feed him hate and you tell him you're different.' Because when the kids are born, they don't know black and white. We teach them black and white" (Tariq 2 November 2017).

Forcefully continuing to frame this problem in personal terms, Tariq said: "In our homes, we feed them that stuff. So, don't blame me when he does something stupid in the future. He was born and raised here [in the United States]" (2 November 2017). Therefore, Tariq argued: "If he did something stupid, don't say he's a Muslim, because of his religion. No! Because you made him do that. This is how you do it: 'You're green, your black, you have an accent. You are from there.' This is what makes him angry. This is why he wants his revenge" (2 November 2017).

Nora, too, highlighted the effects of demonization and targeting by the government. For example, policies such as the separation of child migrants from their parents and imprisonment by immigration authorities create anger, she argued.[5] "Why are you making people angry because when you take somebody's father, how is his son going to feel? This anger inside of him, how will you deal with that?" she asked rhetorically directed at those who implement such policies, "Because you created that in the first place" (Nora 6 February 2018).

In such a context, the concern for Nora was ensuring that the individual, such as the angry son, does not go in a "bad" or "wrong" direction. As she put it, "I lived in a situation like that. Sometimes people do the wrong stuff by choice. They just think: 'Okay, I have to do it because I feel I'm not treated fairly.' . . . And they develop a way of thinking and living that's some kind of a way that it might end up badly" (Nora 6 February 2018). Nora argued that one way to ameliorate such a situation is to reach out to those who exclude or perpetuate alienation and explain that there are long-lasting effects of exclusionary rhetoric and policies.

Ali and Zaid pointed out that when it is not only members of society who demonize the other, but also the most visible leader of the country, in this case Donald Trump, it gives license to those who would harm targeted groups to carry out discrimination and violence. As Ali explained:

> If I am a racist and if I see a lot of people going and . . . protecting other religions, protecting other communities, probably I will change my mind a little bit. [The racist individual will think]: "Hey listen, this is just only me and look how a lot of people, and some of them, this is my cousin, and this is my neighbor," they will change. But, if you see, like a [person in a position of authority] . . . if I'm a racist I'll do whatever I want to do. I don't care. (14 January 2018)

Supporting Ali's argument, Trump's words have been cited in multiple incidents of violence since 2015. In August 2015, for example, two men were arrested in Boston for allegedly attacking a man with a pipe and urinating on him. At the time of their arrest, they told police: "Donald Trump was right. All these illegals need to be deported" (Ferrigno 2015). One of the men later told police he had attacked the man because he appeared to be "Hispanic" and an "illegal immigrant." The influence of Trump's rhetoric reached far beyond the United States. In November 2018, the Nigerian Army justified the killing of forty protestors, some of whom threw stones at soldiers, by specifically citing Donald Trump's assertion that US soldiers would shoot migrants who attempted to throw rocks at American military members patrolling the southern US border (Searcey and Akinwotu 2018). The alleged perpetrator of the 14 March 2019 terror attack on two mosques in Christchurch, New Zealand, in which more than fifty people were killed, wrote in a "manifesto" that Donald Trump was a "symbol of renewed white identity and common purpose" (Smith et al. 2019).

Zaid pointed out that Trump, whom he called racist as noted above, received a significant share of votes in 2016. As he argued: "Almost half of the people [who voted], voted for him and I think they voted for him for that reason. I wouldn't blame . . . people for being afraid of change and adapting to new things. Maybe that's why people here are more open-minded because they have seen with their eyes, they have interacted with people from different backgrounds. But to have the head of the country kind of adopting or encouraging this kind of racist behavior, I don't think that these things will fade away any time soon, unfortunately" (Zaid 27 February 2018). Still, Zaid was hopeful that the situation would improve in the future. This was in part because, as he maintained, even though many Americans seemed to support racist views, "there are even more people who are against these ideas, and they are fighting on our behalf" (Zaid 27 February 2018).

Diversity and Cultural Exchange

Strangeness, unease, and uncertainty exist together with many interviewees' experiences of engaging with American friends, neighbors, and coworkers on a daily basis. Multiple individuals described their interactions with acquaintances and colleagues as a positive aspect of life in the United States, particularly when they involved those of diverse backgrounds coming together to exchange points of view and learn from one another. Some likened life in the type of multicultural society they experienced in the United States to their lives in Iraq before 2003. Many interviewees expressed a desire to have opportunities to give opinions about practices in the United States as well as to share their culture with friends, neighbors, and co-workers and to enjoy similar occasions to learn from native-born Americans.

Importantly, routine and mundane contact between members of "different human groups" does not guarantee that they will develop the viewpoint that all human beings are "equally entitled to certain rights" (Benhabib 2006, 153). Those with whom I spoke described both routine interactions with diverse others as well as many experiences of intentionally seeking to build such a cosmopolitan point of view. Fostering such contact requires, as explained by interviewees, purposeful interactions and a willingness on the part of both native-born Americans and newcomers to change, learn, and grow.

Diversity in Daily Life

An important factor in developing a lived experience of inclusion and belonging is the possibility of building relationships across cultural, religious, and ethnic backgrounds (Crane 2021). Multiple interviewees pointed out that individuals of backgrounds different from their own had assisted them with their resettlement. For example, Nada explained that when she first arrived in New York City, members of the Jewish community helped her and her family to settle into their new surroundings. She elaborated on the diversity she experienced: "New York City has different cultures. So, of course, each culture has many things. Maybe, for me, I don't like it. And maybe for another, they like it. So, because we have law here, they protect me, and the law protects them. So, for this reason, all the people can live here and feel very comfortable. And, I say it again: I respect them, and they respect me. This is normal" (Nada 1 November 2017). Nada continued, "America has a lot of cultures because we have law. Of course, any law has many mistakes, but we can change that" (1 November 2017). She indicated she believed this situation was better than in Iraq where "we don't have good government, we don't have law, we don't . . . respect each other. This is our problem" (Nada 1 November 2017).

Ali, too, described the everyday diversity he experienced in New York. When he first arrived, a Christian woman living in Manhattan hosted him for several weeks: "She kept me with her for fifteen days with no charge. This is huge. . . . And I don't know her personally. I know her through Facebook, through a person. The first time we saw her, was when we came from the airport to her place. . . . It's a big thing, you know?" (Ali 14 January 2018). His host also invited him to parties to meet people. Additionally, a volunteer, whom Ali noted was Jewish, took his daughter to a children's activity club. He said: "She's Jewish. Okay. And my host is Christian. And I am Muslim. . . . So, I like that. I like the diversity of people, living together in peace. I love that here. I cannot explain how much I like that" (Ali 14 January 2018). Later in our conversation, Ali said again about New York: "You can practice whatever religion you want. No one will ask you what you're doing. When the mosque here on the corner has an event for Ramadan or in Eid, three police cars protect them. The same thing when Hindus have an event, three cars to protect them. When a temple, a Jewish temple, [does so], they have protection too" (14 January 2018).

We met in a café in New York City and Ali pointed to the other customers, saying he could see Muslims, non-Muslim Americans, and people of different backgrounds living together and shopping at each other's businesses. Near to the location of our interview, for example, was a restaurant that advertised halal [prepared in accordance with Islamic prescriptions] Chinese food with signage in English, Arabic, and Chinese. During our interview, I noticed several other patrons speaking Arabic in the café as well. Ali compared this experience to Baghdad's atmosphere before the 2003 war.

Ali explained that, before 2003, Baghdad had been lively with shops open and residents on the streets until 3:00 AM. However, after the invasion, shops closed early in the evening and the city became "dead." The interaction of Iraqis of diverse backgrounds ended as well. After 2003, Shi'a did not enter Sunni districts, and vice versa, for fear of violence. Individuals would be asked to produce identification to prove their group belonging and trust between individuals broke down. Ali suggested that "This was all because of the war. It wasn't like that before. It was just like here [New York City]" (14 January 2018).

Like what he had experienced in Baghdad before the war, Ali said, in New York, "I feel safe and I feel in the United States, people from different backgrounds and religions are living together" (14 January 2018). In his view, protection by the law facilitated this situation: "Why there, do they fight? Outside the United States. This is the question. Because of the law! If the law is gone from any country, it will be chaos. I'm not talking about my country. I'm talking in general" (Ali 14 January 2018).

For Sarah, too, an aspect of life in New York that she liked was that so many people from varied backgrounds lived there: "Many people here live together. Different kinds of people, from the world . . . with different religions, with different citizenships, with different colors. It's good. This part for me, I like that. It's good for America, it's good to live together. . . . And also, they have to respect each other" (30 November 2017). Earlier in our conversation, Sarah said it can be challenging for newcomers like herself to interact with others from so many different backgrounds: "It's really difficult for new people. . . . Iraqis, when you come here to see these people, different cultures, different religions, different traditions or different languages" (30 November 2017). However, in her experience, overall this diversity has been positive.

Walid chose to resettle in the United States specifically because of its diversity. He had the choice to immigrate to Canada or Germany, too, where some of his family members had already settled. Nevertheless, he chose to raise his family in the United States because in his view it is a "country of diversity." "I can raise my family," he said, "In terms of discrimination, I know that country [the United States] has an experience working well with different races (Walid 27 September 2017). He compared the United States to Germany, saying, "When I speak with my sister-in-law, she says there's always only Germans. They don't have this kind of diversity" (Walid 27 September 2017). Moreover, Walid said, the United States is an "immigrant country, so that's why I felt more comfortable" (27 September 2017). Walid also noted that his city in Upstate New York has a significant resettled refugee population, which creates a diverse community. He said, "We have migration from Europe, from Africa, Asia, so we are a diverse community here in Upstate New York" (Walid 27 September 2017).

Like Walid, Wissam said, "The good thing about the US is the different backgrounds and cultures you have here" (22 October 2017). As he observed, "Even if you have an accent, even if you want to learn, you see lots of people are going through the same thing and you don't feel different from anybody else, . . . especially in Chicago" (Wissam 22 October 2017). He mentioned that Chicago does not have a dominant group; rather, "It's very mixed, very culturally welcoming, people are very nice here and I don't feel singled out," he said, and "I fit in right away" (Wissam 22 October 2017).

In Wissam's view, the experience of "people here [in the United States] living in harmony, from all different backgrounds, all different cultures is very big" (22 October 2017) and should be emphasized more. He noted that his own mixed background had created challenges in Iraq: "I'm from Iraq . . . I lived in Baghdad, but originally, I'm from Sulaymaniyah [a city in Iraqi Kurdistan]. So, I have a mixed background . . . Kurdish . . . my grandmother is Turkman, and my mom is Arab" (Wissam 22 October 2017). As a result, "Maybe you'll find I am the most neutral person because I have all these different backgrounds and so I have cousins from all ethnicities. . . . I have to listen to everybody" (Wissam 22 October 2017). He concluded that Americans "tend to take it for granted" (Wissam 22 October 2017) how relatively well members of distinct groups can live together. For Wissam, focusing on these positive experiences makes people more willing to learn about other cultures and accept other points of view: "After all, we all have the same goal: to improve this country to make it the best country that we can live in. And, in the end, all our lives will be better together" (Wissam 22 October 2017).

Building Community through Exchange

Related to the substantial discussions about the positive role of diversity and difference I had with many interviewees was the notion that individuals from disparate backgrounds could not only live in proximity to different cultures or practices, but also could and should interact, form relationships, and learn from one another. As several interviewees explained, such processes often entailed finding and creating spaces to voice their views concerning social and cultural norms and practices. The experiences and activities described in this section involved the (re)iteration of such norms among newcomers and native-born citizens to ponder, alter and expand their understandings of belonging.

Importantly, and in view of the preceding sections describing widespread assumptions of the fundamental "otherness" of Islam by a significant share of the American population, I preface this discussion by noting that the distance between cultures is often less wide and the differences less stark than asserted by those opposed to immigration. Monolithic ideological constructs such as "the West" and "the East"–and a supposed intractable conflict between them–present a world of discrete, homogeneous cultures that does not correspond to social reality or history. For example, there are and have been cooperative and conflictual contacts, exchanges, and syncretism among the heterogeneous practices of what we now think of as Judaism, Christianity, and Islam for centuries all over the world (Kumar 2012; Asad 2011). Moreover, as Rogers Brubaker argues, "Migration is as old as human history" (2010, 76). People of diverse and disparate backgrounds, cultures, languages, and so forth have been interacting and influencing each other for millennia. Therefore, it is important to challenge assertions of uncrossed and uncrossable social, cultural, and/or political boundaries among human communities. As multiple interviewees explained, and as noted in the previous chapter, Iraq, like the United States, is a diverse society with many ethnic and religious communities including Muslims, Christians, Jews, Yazidi, Kurds, Arabs, and others. For example, as Nora observed, important Christian figures such as Jesus and Mary are central to Islamic tradition as well. Although she is Muslim, she said in her city in Virginia: "I've been invited to go to churches. I've been going to lots of Sundays. I've also been going to services on Christmas eve" (Nora 6 February 2018). With this in mind, I turn to the issue of exchange among interviewees and their friends, neighbors, and coworkers.

"When I was in Iraq," Abdullah explained, "we were under sanctions basically all my childhood. And we were not in touch with people from different countries. We were a very closed country. So, my mentality was constrained... in that way" (14 January 2018). He continued, "I didn't have a good image about the USA when I was in Iraq. Because I told you, we had almost zero interaction with people. And, the only interaction we had with foreign people were the American soldiers" (Abdullah 14 January 2018). As he noted, and as Chapter 1 explored in greater detail, when a soldier interacts with civilians, "they are unlikely to act nice" (Abdullah 14 January 2018). However, when Abdullah left Iraq to seek safer conditions abroad, he began to think differently about those of non-Iraqi backgrounds, "Once I went to Syria, I met people from America, from other countries. It changed my view," he said (14 January 2018). As he detailed: "As soon as I traveled, I came here to one of the most diverse places in the world. My mentality completely changed and even my way of thinking became a combination of American mentality and also my school, engineering. They usually make you think in a logical way, you know? Use more of a problem solving, critical thinking. So, I think a combination of all that affected my mentality" (Abdullah 14 January 2018).

Later in the conversation, he elaborated:

> When I came here [to the United States], it completely changed my views. And I was able to distinguish between good people, bad people, government actions, people's actions. So, right now, if I see someone saying something negative about the West, I will try to defend it. Because this is not right, you cannot generalize. Because there are a lot of people from the West who are talking just like that about all Arabs and Muslims, that those groups attack everybody. So, it really goes both ways. . . . I believe if you generalize, religion, countries, race, whatever, I believe this is wrong. (Abdullah 14 January 2018)

Abdullah suggested that he understood learning about difference to be a two-way process. He argued that Iraqis have responsibilities to educate themselves about the United States, and Americans have a responsibility to meet and learn about Iraqis and challenge negative stereotypes concerning them:

> When we were back home, we always had a bad image about the West because our media was controlled by the regime and it always [portrayed Americans as] bad. And then when I met other people, that changed my views. So, I think the same thing should happen for Americans. They should go meet other people, they cannot just trust the media because most of the media are controlled by bigger people than us and they have agendas. . . . I think it's 50/50. . . . I think the best way to learn is you actually go there and learn . . . and build human connections. If you are staying far away from a person, you cannot really have that connection with them, even if you hear stories. The extremists are not really helping people from the Middle East, our reputation, but if you actually go there or read more or just interact with people here in the country, I think it would be a surprise how people are different from whatever the media is showing. (Abdullah 14 January 2018)

Hashim, too, viewed deep interaction as essential to changing the views of others: "If someone decided not to think about something, it's very hard to change opinions by going through discussions with them. I don't think that will change that much. Because with all the media, with all the things happening now in Iraq they just think that we are enemies, anyway" (1 October 2017). As noted in the introduction, significant percentages of Americans believe that Iraq is an enemy of the United States. However, Hashim argued that protracted interaction and relationship building between himself and native-born citizens could potentially change such views: "For people that I know, when they know me better, when they see, when I get them to my house and then they see my family, when they see how we are living and how we are hard workers and how we are studying and how we are raising our kids. I think they will change their opinions. So, I will be, just an example of an Iraqi person living and working in the United States to set a good example. That's the only way to maybe participate in changing their opinions" (1 October 2017).

To illustrate this point and process, Hashim discussed several individuals who began as coworkers and whom he now considered friends: "In my work, I have many friends now. But let's say, last year when we first met them, they had different opinions. So, I think I just set a good example of the Iraqis, that's the only way, you know? Just to show them that: Hey, we are just like you. We are just doing exactly what you are doing, we don't hate, we don't hate you. I don't know you to hate you. So, it's just: Try to set a good example I think" (1 October 2017).

Through these efforts, he has constructed friendships, changing his friends' initially wary perceptions of Iraqis in the process. Describing the challenges and need for such processes as well, Walid related his experience raising children in Upstate New York: "In Iraq, the way of raising children is totally different than here. So, sometimes I'm thinking about how my kids grow up here, and my 15-year-old daughter she has started to tell me: 'Daddy you are not understanding me.' Even I'm a social worker, I'm a counselor . . . but, she thinks I'm only from Iraq. So, I told her: 'Please teach me how this happened'" (27 September 2017).

Walid remarked that teenagers, both newcomers and Americans, face difficulties. Nonetheless, "it's kind of a challenge raising kids here in both cultures. It's very difficult. Sometimes people feel that they are losing their culture. . . . They're becoming more American" (Walid 27 September 2017). He described as well how a friend's son told his mother he did not want her to go to his school because she wears a hijab, an outward sign of her, and by extension the son's, "different culture" (Walid 27 September 2017). Walid said about this situation: "We found it very important to address this issue with the school: 'Why don't you have an international day? Or have different flags in the school? Or have presentations? Or the students from different countries teach the kids where you come from and show the students about Iraq?' We have 5,000 years of history and we want to learn about your history. To make these kids feel proud of where they come from, rather than [experience] shame or guilt because of their different culture" (27 September 2017).

In Walid's view, the negative feelings he noted had led immigrant children to "want to be just American. They want to lose their identity and culture because they want to belong to the community. . . . Many families have a lot of pressure [because of this]" (27 September 2017). Walid also described his own personal experience of belonging to multiple communities, observing "I can't say I'm only Iraqi. I can't say I'm only American. I'm Iraqi-American" (27 September 2017). He continued: "So, half of me is Iraqi, half of me is American. Part of why I see this is because I feel this society changed a lot of my views for the future. For example, if I'm in Iraq, maybe my wife will stay home and take care of the kids. Now, my wife she's working in a chemical dependency program, she's helping me with the kids.

It's totally different. . . . So, we see many families now they are learning. It depends on if there's enough exposure to US families" (Walid 27 September 2017).

Immediately following these comments, Walid said that local religious organizations had facilitated such processes:

> What helped me a lot is when I met with the church, and the church helped me to adjust to the life and also integrate into the society very quickly. I'm a very curious person and to learn I went to a temple, I went to a church, I went to a Hindu temple, to a Jewish temple, I want to learn, understand this society. It is part of my curiosity. Maybe, the other people just want to stay home. . . . I want to make sure I'm raising my family in a healthy way, keep both cultures and try to support them. There's also bad parts of the American culture in terms of drugs, alcohol. . . . But many families learn from this culture, the good part of this culture (27 September 2017).

Finally, Walid described how he has also attended interfaith meetings that engage Jews, Christians, and Muslims in the area in dialogue about their particular experiences:

> They come together; they meet monthly. And they have like a conference, invite the community. And they discuss different topics. For example, one of the people said: "I grew up in [a nearby suburb]," which is 45 minutes from here. He said, "All my friends are Yemenis, they are Muslims." . . . The other person, he's Jewish, they started to share their experiences. He said, "I grew up in [another suburb], I never have met a Muslim, but please go and try and do something to teach us. We don't know how to find you." So, you need to raise awareness. (27 September 2017)

Walid said of such programs: "So try these kinds of [activities]. There's a lot of education, interfaith organizations try to invite people to discuss different topics. What are their concerns, what are the most important things?" (27 September 2017).

Mohammed, too, occasionally attends church services in Upstate New York, even though he is Muslim. A good friend attends this church, and he enjoys the company of the other parishioners. As he put it, "I like the people there. I have a friend in the church and so, I like to mix with another religion to [have a] good experience, to see what's going on" (Mohammed 2 November 2017). "But," he said, "I never go to the Mosque [in my city]. Maybe one time" (Mohammed 2 November 2017). Mohammed went on to describe the process of cultural exchange, comparing life in Upstate New York to his life in Iraq: "I feel the people are not very social. It's difficult to know your neighbor. . . . But in our country, we have good social ties with the community. All your neighbors, when they cook, they bring the food for your house. When you cook, you send the food to your neighbor. But here, no. You don't know the name of your neighbors, so . . . it's difficult a little bit" (2 November 2017).

Mohammed had worked against this insularity, attempting to build community with friends. He spoke about an American family, friends of his family with whom he "mixed" cultures:

> We have two families, [mine and an] American family. We mix the cultures between us. My friend . . . and his family [come to] our house. We stay together, eat together and we go to his house . . . he has been my friend for three or four years. And I asked him: "Why do you like our culture?" He said: "Mohammed, actually, in America, we are losing the culture." . . . So, he said: "I need to mix with your family." And I told him, "I need to mix with your family to understand the American culture." So, we work together and sometimes we discuss together how we can, like, help my daughter and his daughter because they are teenagers. (2 November 2017)

In general, however, Mohammed indicated that he perceived crosscultural communication as difficult. In his view, connecting on a personal level can be challenging: "If you ask him [an American] about his job, it's difficult. If you ask him about his family, it's difficult. If you ask him, everything is difficult here. It's difficult to make communication with the people a little bit. He's your friend, it's difficult to enter his life, or to discuss with him about anything personal with him. It's very difficult" (Mohammed 2 November 2017).

In an early attempt to break through what he felt was a barrier, and move beyond pleasantries, Mohammed began bringing coffee and Iraqi food to his coworkers at the airport. He told his colleagues that in Iraq it was a normal part of social interaction and that he enjoyed doing so. After he began this practice, his relations with his fellow employees started to change. His coworkers, who became friends, also began to bring food to share: "So, I changed it a little bit. My friends, they do the same thing. They go to Tim Hortons [a Canadian coffee and donut chain commonly found in Upstate New York], they bring you food, share with us. . . . They change it a little bit. It's not a hundred percent, but they change it" (Mohammed 2 November 2017).

Mohammed also explained that he had incorporated aspects of American culture into his daily life. "The American culture changed something good for me," he said (Mohammed 2 November 2017). As he explained, "In our culture, when I go to your house, I didn't call you first. . . . I just knock on your door" (2 November 2017). However, Americans, in his experience, approach such a visit differently and are more likely to ask before arriving. "Because maybe you're busy," Mohammed said, and he appreciated this norm. Americans have "borders" in their social interactions, he said, which Mohammed also liked: "So, I learned some culture and . . . I give the people some of our culture. . . . A little bit" (2 November 2017).

Marwa explained that in Upstate New York she now has a diverse social network: "I have a lot of friends who are Nepali, Burmese and Somali.... It's nice in the United States ... it's mixed. I like it.... I have a lot of friends from different countries. Yes. That's so great" (25 November 2017). Marwa said that when she first arrived in the United States, she and her husband often discussed issues she felt should change in American society: "They should change that, no I don't like that.... But now ... I accept it more when I became involved with the people ... and after learning more" (25 November 2017). She went on to say: "Some families, they didn't adapt to the culture here. They still want their kids to keep, like it's okay, it's nice to keep your culture.... It's okay, I have now, I keep some. But I want my kids to be involved. Some families, they didn't become involved with the community here and they want their kids the same.... They didn't know how to mix" (Marwa 25 November 2017).

Moreover, Marwa explained how drawing on her own background and parenting accordingly, she could lead by example and influence American culture and the actions of those around her indirectly. She said: "They are going to see a successful family, what they do with their kids. They are going to see. First, they are going to say: 'No, no, no.' But after when they are in trouble or have problems with their kids, they are going to say: 'Oh, you are right'" (Marwa 25 November 2017). I asked the clarifying question: "So you're setting an example?" to which Marwa replied: "Living an example" (25 November 2017).

Exchange and cooperation are not only a function of newcomers and Americans interacting as individuals, but also occur among members of various communities and representatives of institutions within American society. For example, as Sarah told me, it was the responsibility of both the American people and government to create welcoming feelings and environments for newcomers. Hashim too argued that the government had a responsibility to unite and not divide different communities. This role was important for Hashim, because he said, "The job of the government is to keep the communities united, to keep them more united, not to divide people because once you have this division ... you might start seeing some communities hate other communities and problems will happen. They will always happen. So, the government's job is ... to help or to set rules: 'Hey these people are just like you or just like other people'" (1 October 2017).

On this topic, Omar said, "In our city [in Shenandoah Valley], everything looks good" (14 December 2017). The local Islamic center has close cooperation with area churches and works to demonstrate its willingness to assist the entire community. For example, the Islamic center opens space to shelter members of the city's homeless population during Christmas because the churches that typically do so are unable to on that day.

Omar is personally involved with several projects aimed at creating a welcoming and multicultural atmosphere in his city and, those, he observed,

"Are a lot of work. But, for the long run. I think we will see something different. Different than other places" (14 December 2017). Indeed, "We can feel that," he said, adding, "We see new people all the time, and especially the businesses, they were very grateful that we are here. Very grateful. And they are enjoying the food, they are enjoying the culture. So, it's different. The city is different also. . . . It is developing faster and faster in just five years" (Omar 14 December 2017). Omar continued to elaborate that the effects of immigration on the city were not only economic, but also attitudinal: "The impact was not only on us but on the city itself in economic terms and in terms of the attitudes of people towards others. When they are introduced to the families, the refugees, they hear more stories, and everyone was impacted" (14 December 2017).

He saw the recent approval by the city council of his city as a "Welcoming City" as a sign of that fact. Such a designation is a project of the nonprofit organization Welcoming America, which indicates a commitment to working, "across multiple sectors, such as government, business, and nonprofit, to create inclusive policies and practices. . . . Welcoming Cities are guided by the principles of inclusion and creating communities that prosper because everyone feels welcome, including immigrants and refugees" (Welcoming America 2019). Over the course of several years, Omar worked with a community group to garner support and convince the city council to seek this designation. I examine the role of activist, nonprofit, and community organizations in fostering exchange among individuals of different backgrounds and advocating for the rights of refugees for which Omar and others have volunteered and worked in more detail in Chapter 4.

Finally, the processes of interpersonal exchange and communication can move in many directions. As Kasim explained in detail, he believed that the Iraqis who learned how to interact with diverse others in the United States could bring what he saw as newly developed openness and tolerance back to Iraq if they decide to return. Kasim first described his experiences living in Iraq:

> It was hard for me back home. . . . I didn't feel the freedom to say whatever I wanted. Not politically, even culturally. . . . When I was there, there was no cultural openness. If you believed in something, you will find somebody who really aggressively wants to deny your beliefs. In that way, there's no freedom. It's not because of government, it's because of the culture. There's no tolerance. . . . And it has nothing to do with the religion, it's just to do with the culture. It became so backward that they don't tolerate anything. (27 February 2018)

With this background established, Kasim went on to say of the experience of Iraqis interacting with diverse cultures after resettling in the United States: "So, now the Iraqis here [in the United States] know how societies work. How culture works. They have a bigger picture now. They're more tolerant, they're more open-minded. I wouldn't say they're Americanized, but they know how the world works now. . . . And, everybody here . . . they're an asset if they go back home or try to teach people. This is how societies work. If you want to move to the next step, you have to be tolerant to everybody" (27 February 2018).

Conclusion

The experiences shared by interviewees in this chapter challenge assertions that refugee resettlement poses a threat to the United States and that Muslim refugees, in particular, present a special danger because Islam is irreconcilable with so-called Western culture and societies. Culture is not a static object that is passively transmitted; it is actively created by people (Crane 2021). The individuals with whom I spoke sought to engage with their neighbors, coworkers, and fellow community members. Many of them desired both to learn about American society and to share their Iraqi culture with others. As these interviewees' experiences demonstrate, processes of engagement and exchange between newcomers and the native-born population are an empirical reality and a normative good. Mutual commitment to reasonable adjustment in practices and views is required for people of diverse backgrounds to live together in the same place (Carens 2013).

Overall, interviewee experiences point to three interconnected insights about resettlement processes. First, belonging is not necessarily a binary state that one experiences or does not. For some interviewees, it was a strong feeling, while, for others, it was partial or constrained, at least at the time of their interview. Others expressed a sense that they could never fully belong to American society. Importantly, these interviews suggest that it is possible to develop an attachment to a community even as challenges and barriers complicate that connection. These processes require an attitude of openness and welcoming on the part of both native-born Americans and newcomers.

Second, the anti-Arab, anti-Muslim, and anti-refugee discourses that circulate in American society can negatively affect members of those populations. Members of targeted groups are acutely aware of prejudices held by segments of American society, and this knowledge can create feelings of precarity and unease. Moreover, the existence of a national leader, in this case Donald Trump, who espouses such views and attacks newcomers in his rhetoric and policies can threaten individuals' safety and shape their perceptions of belonging.

Third, contact, exchange, and finding opportunities to share views and judgments on norms and practices among those of different backgrounds can be a fruitful process of building bonds and community among newcomers and the native members of their host society. Results require intentional exchange and are not guaranteed. As interviewees described them, these processes are multidirectional, and their character is the shared responsibility of immigrants, host society members, community initiatives, and governments at all scales. Individuals, religious groups, other nonprofit organizations, and government institutions and programs all have roles to play in these processes.

Finally, resettlement processes can be difficult, but the fact that they are challenging is not a reason not to attempt them. The alternative—as interviewees suggested has been true in their native Iraq after 2003—is social mistrust, fragmentation, and violence. The discussion in this chapter concerning perceptions of belonging flows into the following two chapters, which delve into democratic membership in the United States and the practices and engagement interviewees witnessed, participated in, and in some cases led, even as they encountered social, economic, and political barriers to doing so.

Notes

1. FBI hate crime data, likely an undercount of such incidents, show an uptick in reported incidents in 2015, the year the 2016 presidential election campaign began, from 154 in 2014 to 257. Reported hate crimes increased again in 2016 to 307 before falling to 273 in 2017. Despite the drop in such incidents in the most recent available data, the 2017 number remains significantly higher than that for 2014 (FBI 2015, 2016, 2017, 2018).
2. Indeed, Osama bin Laden, who claimed responsibility for the 11 September 2001 attacks, justified them in part on these grounds. In his "Letter to America," he answered the question "why are we fighting and opposing you" directly: "Because you attacked us and continue to attack us" in Palestine, Somalia, and Kashmir and elsewhere. In his letter, he specifically mentioned the starving of 1.5 million Muslim children in Iraq under sanctions to justify the attacks (bin Laden 2002).
3. Interestingly, Pew Research Center polling indicated that, in March 2002, six months after the 11 September 2001 attacks, only 25 percent of respondents reported believing that Islam encouraged violence among its adherents (Pew 2017b). That figure peaked at 50 percent in 2014 and fell to 41 percent in 2017—still significantly higher than in the aftermath of 9/11.
4. Similarly, in January 2019, two women, both American citizens, were detained for forty minutes by a United States Customs and Border Protection agent simply for speaking Spanish. The women recorded the agent saying, "The reason I asked you for your ID is because I came in here and I saw that you guys are speaking Spanish, which is very unheard of up here" (Chappell 2019a).
5. In 2017, the Trump administration implemented a policy of separating families who crossed the southern US border without a visa, including those seeking asylum, detaining parents and children in different locations (Seville and

Rappleye 2018). The policy was designed to "deter" mothers from migrating with their children (Ainsley 2017). Reports indicated that at least 2,737 children were separated from their parents in 2017 and 2018, but the actual number is likely significantly higher (Long and Alonso-Zaldivar 2019). Children who were separated from their parents and children who arrived alone, so-called unaccompanied minors, are typically placed in foster homes or shelters. Reports emerged throughout 2018 that the Trump administration was detaining separated children in cages in makeshift facilities (BBC 2018). In late 2018, the Trump administration began removing children from shelters around the country and concentrating them in tent camps in Texas near the Mexico/US border (Dickerson 2018). Importantly, the policy of child separation was met with significant public outrage as photographs of children in cages appeared in news reports. Trump took limited steps to end and reverse the policy after the backlash and the Biden administration has worked to reunite children with their parents. However, in some cases, the new administration has found it difficult to do so due to poor and incomplete record keeping during the Trump years.

3

Enacting Democratic Membership

Finding Time, (Re)Distributing Resources, Building Knowledge, and Protecting Rights

> We came here for safety, of course. And also, to practice democracy. . . . It was amazing to participate. To feel that you have a voice. . . . I was happy every time I did it.
>
> —Omar, 14 December 2018

Introduction

This chapter examines how this study's interviewees understood democratic membership in the United States as resettled refugees, residents, and, in some cases, citizens. As suggested in the introduction, democracy entails processes and mechanisms that facilitate opportunities for members of a political community to participate in making the decisions that affect their lives (Benhabib 2006; Pateman 2012). Hashim's description of his life in the United States captured democracy well: "I can set up rules that work for me in the things that I experience" (1 October 2017).

As I also argued in the introduction, democracies require porous borders–literal, physical, and territorial as well as social, cultural, and political–that grant newcomers entry and allow those formerly excluded to gain membership and engage in decision-making processes. Moreover, I assume that contestations concerning the character and content of democratic arrangements that include those who do not necessarily "share the dominant culture's memories and morals" are the mark of a strong "culture of democracy" rather than a threat to its existence (Benhabib 2006, 69). That is, there is no a priori reason to believe that newcomers are any more likely to present a challenge to a culture of democracy than those born into a social or political community. And essential to such a culture are deliberations by existing members about how to incorporate newcomers. The central analytical questions at issue in such discussions are how a democratic ethos and habits can be strengthened, how the boundaries of those beliefs and mores can be enlarged, discerning where substantive opportunities exist for newcomers to do so, and identifying what factors mediate or, in some instances, constrain such processes.

This chapter first problematizes the degree to which American institutions, and US society more broadly, qualify as democratic. I then explore several interviewees' views that there are reasons to be circumspect about the degree to which American institutions can be expected to provide the mechanisms to help them form and carry out their goals. As several interviewees explained, existing participation mechanisms in the United States cannot always create change in government policy or action, fundamentally calling into question those institutions' democratic character. I then explore individuals' understandings of democratic membership in the United States.

I examine whether and in what ways they understood themselves to have the same or equal rights as native-born Americans to participate in democratic decision-making processes. I then elaborate on four of the barriers and requirements interviewees identified to their engagement in such processes. The first is that participation in the decisions that affect one's life requires time, which is not always available amid the need to work long hours to support oneself and/or one's family. Second, the substantive exercise of democracy requires that members of a political community have a right to public provision of resources and opportunities to decide how those resources are distributed. Third, helping to shape the laws, policies, and rules that govern one's life requires adequate information and knowledge of the processes, institutions, and choices shaping one's environment; building such understanding also requires time. Fourth, a recurring theme in the interviews I undertook was that my interlocutors had lived much or most of their lives in a country governed by an authoritarian regime. For those with whom I spoke, it is necessary to address and reduce lingering suspicions of agents of the state and government officials more broadly to trust that political engagement is safe; some reported that they chose to abstain from democratic engagement and/or interaction with state representatives as a result.

The Character of Democracy in the United States

Before exploring barriers to its exercise in the United States, it is important to assess the democratic character of American society and institutions. One must interrogate the degree to which interrelated spaces such as US electoral political institutions, civil society, and workplaces are democratic in substantive ways, for newcomers and native-born citizens alike. The formal institutions of American representative democracy were designed by white men, most of them slave masters, to perpetuate a white supremacist state that subjugated and excluded most of the country's population from participation and perpetuated a political economy sustained by forced labor. White supremacy is inseparable from American conceptions and practices of freedom and democracy (Beltrán 2020). As a result, there has been and remains a fundamental contradiction and persistent tension between the universalist ideals articulated in the country's founding documents and their realization for many people who live in the country. Only through significant and sustained struggle in the face of state and vigilante violence have women, African Americans, and many other formerly excluded groups gained enfranchisement.

Moreover, reactionary segments of American society have reacted to democratic gains by these groups by devoting significant resources to attempts to roll them back (MacLean 2017). Efforts continue, particularly although not exclusively by the modern Republican Party, to gain and keep political power by preventing members of ethnic and racial minority groups from voting (Vandewalker and Bentele 2015). Importantly, as Bonnie Honig notes, even with the iterative expansion of rights for those formerly excluded, these groups "have still never come to bear those rights in the same way as their original bearers" (in Benhabib 2006, 112). Various forms of social, economic, and political exclusion continue despite ongoing activism by and on behalf of women, African Americans, Indigenous peoples, immigrants, and other marginalized groups. Additionally, despite these struggles, as Martin Gilens and Benjamin I. Page argue about the formal institutions of American government: "The majority does not rule—at least not in the causal sense of actually determining policy outcomes. When a majority of citizens disagrees with economic elites or with organized interests, they generally lose. Moreover, because of the strong status quo bias built into the US political system, even when fairly large majorities of Americans favor policy change, they generally do not get it" (2014, 576).

As I write this book, the US Supreme Court, an unelected body of nine individuals with lifetime appointments, is poised to roll back the seminal *Roe v. Wade* ruling. This precedent, supported by 69 percent of Americans (Yi and Thomson-DeVeaux 2022), has protected the right to bodily autonomy and necessary reproductive healthcare for millions of Americans for the last fifty years.

Importantly as well, decades of violent antisocialist and anticommunist campaigns, both domestically and around the world (Bevins 2020), have actively sought to purge economic democracy from American conceptions of a democratic society. In short, there is a significant need to protect and expand existing democratic rights and institutions that a reactionary minority seeks to undermine, and to continue the work of democratizing American society.

With this in mind, interviewees expressed varying levels of confidence that actions they could take would allow them to exert meaningful influence over the decisions that govern their lives, particularly in relation to the existing institutions of representative democracy. Sarah, for example, questioned the efficacy of discussion with government representatives. She queried: "When we are talking with this person from the government about a problem, can he do something good? Solve this problem? Or just talk and that's it?" (Sarah 30 November 2017). Sarah went on to express that if the government has been unable to solve issues such as affordable housing for Americans, it would be even less able to do so for newcomers like herself: "So, the American people, it is hard for them to get [affordable housing] and what about me and the Arab people? It's hard, doubly hard" (Sarah 30 November 2017). Hashim and Mohammed each expressed doubt about the potential that protests have to shape or reshape policies. As Mohammed put it, even "if a million people go to the street, nobody in government will change policies or laws" (2 November 2017).

In prefacing his critique of American electoral democracy, Kasim said "voting is important. You have to use your rights to make change. . . . I went there, I voted" (27 February 2018). Nevertheless, he went on to say, "I knew my vote wouldn't count, but if everybody doesn't vote . . . how can you participate? How can you make a difference?" (Kasim 27 February 2018). Kasim voted for Donald Trump in 2016 and continued to support him at the time of our interview in early 2018. "Many people disagree with me," he said, "but from day one I was like, I knew this guy. The minute I listened to his speeches; he just was in the same line of my understanding of how things work" (Kasim 27 February 2018). He continued to explain:

> I lived here in Obama's time. Obama is a very great guy. He's very intellectual and he's probably one of the best presidents. But, when it comes to implementing things, he had a hard time because that's not how the US [government functions]. . . . For Democrats, it's always hard to pass legislation because the power is with people who have money, and they are Republicans mostly. The power's always on the Republican side. Even if they are not in power, still. So, it's hard to pass legislation [for Democrats]. Whereas this guy [Trump], is a Republican. And whenever he says something, he can do it. Because they have the power. (Kasim 27 February 2018)

Wissam, too, pointed to this sort of corruption in our conversation. As he put it, "You have, maybe, not as much corruption as other countries. But you do have it. You have billionaires who want to use power" (Wissam 22 October 2017).[1] However, he understood the structure of American government to mediate this situation. He was more confident than Kasim that existing

American institutions could effectively address the issue of wealth translating into political influence. As he put it, "You have, maybe, the most billionaires in the world who want to use power. . . . Still, the Constitution is protecting this country from it. . . . We are currently seeing a lot of people abuse power. But at least there are checks and balances" (Wissam 22 October 2017). Wissam went on to say he had been reading about the American system of government. "I think it's very, very creative," he said, "They really predicted the right formula on how to create a democracy. But, it's very hard to stay consistent with it and that's what we are seeing here" (Wissam 22 October 2017).

Wissam works in the dining and restaurant business and discussed food safety laws in the United States as an example of the negative role of money in political processes. He said: "I want to really affect the laws about the standards of food here. It is all controlled by big corporations, it's very hard to fight them. . . . Not all the laws are for the best interests of the consumer and that's what I'd like to see changed" (Wissam 22 October 2017). To change such laws, he argued that lobbying was essential. "Mostly it's about lobbying," he said. "I don't know if there's any other way. Maybe you have a chance to speak with a reasonable government official and show them benefits [of a particular policy]. But if not, you have to go through lobbying. There [in Iraq], it's kind of illegal. But here, it's all legal. So, it is easier, of course, if you have the money. But in a way, those officials need to weigh the benefits versus what the lobbyists want. There has to be a balance so, I don't know" (Wissam 22 October 2017).

Ahmed, too, pointed to corruption as a concern, and like Wissam, he stated that it was perhaps not an insurmountable problem. During our conversation on taxes in Chicago, for example, Ahmed remarked: "I know there is . . . corruption, that's everywhere. But I would rather have corruption and services provided to me than no taxes with 100 percent corruption and no accountability [as was the situation in Iraq]. Here, even with the corruption, politicians still need to be accountable to the people who voted" (2 October 2017). Ahmed, like Wissam, argued that despite the corruption he perceived, US officials were accountable to citizens in ways they were not in Iraq.

Democratic Membership

With the forgoing critiques in mind, I move next to consider interviewees' understandings of their membership in democratic institutions and processes in the United States. As I illustrate below, their conceptions of substantive membership varied. Some, including Walid and Omar, were very positive about their opportunities for democratic membership while others, including Zaid and Tariq, were significantly less enthusiastic.

Nora, whose asylum application was pending at the time of our interview, said that in the future, she could be a member of formal democratic processes in the United States, but not currently. "I don't have citizenship to vote," she said:

> I cannot express my opinion about more political stuff, but I do . . . feel the democracy and I belong here because I talk about whatever I want to talk about. And I say that this is right and this is wrong. I should not be treated like this because I am different. So, I do practice . . . democracy here. . . . Like, I just used my rights and was like, even though I'm not American I do have the right to say or I do have the right to be treated differently. But . . . I cannot do any elections when it comes to this city council. . . . I cannot do anything. But I can express my opinion. (Nora 6 February 2018)

Nora's comments illustrate the different legal rights citizens and non-citizens have in the United States. Citizens can vote in local, state, and federal elections, while permanent residents or those with other immigration statuses typically cannot vote except in municipal elections in a handful of cities. However, all residents, including non-citizens, are formally protected by constitutional rights such as the freedom of speech that allow them to advocate for control of the conditions of their lives.

Walid observed, "I am very attached" to American democracy (27 September 2017). He said of his volunteer work with immigrants in his community: "We try to encourage people to get US citizenship. And we do have a lot of people, they reach five years of residency, so we encourage them to get naturalized and try to practice their rights because we came from the Middle East [where] maybe people they don't learn how to practice their rights and here we tell them it's really important. We have a congressman, a Congress. We can go and talk to [our representative]" (Walid 27 September 2017).

As an example of the types of activities he encourages community members to undertake, Walid described how many Iraqi families living in Upstate New York worried about relatives still in Iraq after an attack in the north of the country: "They said 'Walid, tell us what we do? We want to do something.' So, to raise awareness [about Yazidi women kidnapped by ISIS], we decided to use our democratic rights to contact the city council member, to invite some faith-based organizations to light candles . . . to express our feelings. We wanted them to not keep this anger and sit home because you are going to be very depressed and very tired if you do. We want to bring the community and teach them how to practice their rights" (27 September 2017).

Ahmed indicated that he had democratic membership "to a certain extent" (2 October 2017). As a resident, he could not vote in 2016. However, he remarked: "I watched the election. I did not participate in the election. Actually, I watched the election with popcorn. It was super exciting. I know for other people, they don't feel this way. . . . I met with a few friends after the election and obviously, we have like 50 percent of the population who feel downbeat about it. That's in any normal election or democratic process" (Ahmed 2 October 2017).

Ahmed counseled his friends to be optimistic, telling them, "No, you don't need to [be hopeless]. In four years or in two years, you still have the power to change it" (2 October 2017). "For me personally," he said, "I waited almost more than twenty years of my life to see another country forcing democracy [in Iraq]. I think it will be a super exciting moment for me just to participate" (Ahmed 2 October 2017).

I asked Ahmed whether he viewed it as his right to help decide what the laws are in the United States, to which he replied: "I think so. Not helping with the laws like going and writing them, but having an opinion about something, yes. Because in the end it will affect me and affect my family, it will affect my friends, it will affect the community I live in. I think so, yeah" (2 October 2017). He continued: "I look forward to being part of making a decision in the community, within the small group that I'm interacting with, maybe, if I can give an added value to their discussion. In terms of government? I think that would not be my role. I don't have, never had, any sort of [desire to go] into that direction I would say. . . . I don't have political aspirations" (Ahmed 2 October 2017).

Elaborating on how he understood decision making in the realm of government, he discussed the possibilities of changing a law or policy with which he disagreed: "I can voice my opinion, but I will not be in a position to . . . make a different decision. Because again, I don't think the government here works [in that way]. There will be other people factoring in their voices and their concerns. So, me being the decision maker? I don't think so" (Ahmed 2 October 2017).

For his part, Omar noted, "We came here for safety . . . and also to practice democracy. Democracy is very important" (14 December 2017). Describing his experience engaging in democratic processes such as voting, he said, "It was amazing to participate. To feel that you have a voice. And I was happy every time I did it" (Omar 14 December 2017). As described in more detail in the following chapter, Omar has been involved in establishing and working with several organizations engaged in a range of activities including education, civic engagement, community organizing, and coalition building since arriving in the Shenandoah Valley Region of Virginia.

On a personal level, separate from the community work he does, Omar noted that private gun ownership laws were a potential issue in which he desired to have input. He said,

If there is something to change, really, I would change the gun policy. That's very problematic, let me say. I am surprised that we see [such policies] here. Like in our community, the gun should only be restricted to the government. In our country [Iraq], even though it is not sophisticated like here . . . but we never have someone handling the guns. . . . So, it should be restricted. You see from time to time, crazy people. . . . So, why do you give them the opportunity to take these weapons and kill us? So, it is something that hopefully will be gone, so all will live in peace. (Omar 14 December 2017)

Omar proceeded to call gun ownership by private individuals a larger issue than many others, but one he wished could be changed because, in his words: "I love this nation. So, I want it to live in peace. That's the reason why I'm interested. Yeah, others they have the same opinion, but again they don't have the power, or they don't have the means. . . . It's bigger than us. It's business, it's everything" (14 December 2017). To make the change he wished to see, he argued that it had to emanate: "From people. No one can do it by power. When everyone, you and me, and everyone is convinced that my neighbor, why should I be scared of my neighbor? I'm living with my neighbor long, long years. That gun will not protect me from my neighbor. And then that's it. It starts from a member and then the community. And then city, state, that's it. . . . We need peace. Yeah. And the government is very strong, so it can protect anyone" (Omar 14 December 2017).

Like Omar, Kasim also asserted that an issue on which he wanted to have a say in deciding laws in the United States revolved around private ownership of firearms. He took a very different tack. He cited the rise in school shootings in the United States (Walker 2019) saying: "Nowadays, this problem with the shootings in schools. Definitely, I would love to try to push some kind of legislation that protects schools because it's really alarming what's happening. I mean I see my kids' school, they lock the schools, I cannot get in. How come people can get in and kill the kids? Something is wrong. I listened to a speech by someone who had his kid killed. And then he was saying that you cannot get a bottle of water inside a plane, and you can get a rifle inside a school" (Kasim 27 February 2018).

Coming to the opposite conclusion as Omar, Kasim said: "We have to do something about that. It's not about controlling guns. . . . They can come in with knives and kill kids. It's not about guns. Not about gun control. It's definitely not the case. It's about securing the schools from those maniacs. Crazy people. Terrorists, whoever. So yeah. That's really alarming" (27 February 2018).

Hashim, too, wanted to be involved in decisions that affect him and his family. As noted at the opening of this chapter, he said, "I can give my opinion and I can set up rules that work for me in the things that I experience" (Hashim 1 October 2017). However, he said:

Of course, I cannot give an opinion . . . [on subjects] I don't know about. But I can give an opinion on, for example, education for my kids in the community schools, if they have suggestions, if they decided to make some changes to the schedule or on the education guidelines and all of that. So, I really want to be involved in my community, involved in things affecting my family. So, I would really be happy to make, not make decisions because I'm not the decision maker, but at least to participate in the community and participate in decision making. (Hashim 1 October 2017)

Wissam expressed optimism that he was in a position to participate in decisions that affect his life: "I really hope it is my right to change the US in positive ways. . . . What's good about the US is you have all these . . . people from all different backgrounds and it's the most successful model because people are living here peacefully, they are working together peacefully, everything is working" (22 October 2017).

He proceeded to describe democratic membership as providing him "peace of mind." As he elaborated:

There are certain things you don't do, that will keep you safe. If you know what's right, what's wrong, then you are on the safe side to some extent. And being able to petition the government or talk with the politicians, I have never experienced that. But these things are very hard in Iraq and other countries because it's very hard to see someone who is in power, even if he works in the city or is just a manager, something like that. It's very hard, but now [in the United States], it's different. The whole system is different. (Wissam 22 October 2017)

Moreover, Wissam argued that he had an equal ability to give his opinion as Americans "to some extent, in certain areas" (22 October 2017). However, he said about private gun ownership, for example: "I can't speak for everybody who . . . was born with different values, different experiences. . . . Some things I'll feel strongly about but . . . don't control. I can't [control such issues] because people here have it since day one. We didn't back there, so we are not used to having guns at home or using them unless you are in the army [for example]. So, it depends on the topic" (Wissam 22 October 2017).

On issues such as gun control, even though he argued he was not necessarily able to effect change because he had not lived his entire life in the United States, Wissam said he could affect decisions by:

Letting them hear my side of the story. Because, again, they didn't live or go through what I went through. So, they need to listen to my story, what I went through. . . . And the good thing [is that] people here are open-minded, they understand. They understand we are equal. They understand: "Okay, let me listen to what he says," before they just shut you out. . . . But, again, am I the best person to explain it to them? Or convince them? Maybe not. So, it depends on who can speak [about such issues] well, you know? It's tricky. (22 October 2017)

Like Wissam, Ali suggested that his capacity to participate, and to engage equally, would be stronger if he had been born in the United States: "If I was born here, and an American, [the possibilities to participate would be] stronger. But, my situation, I was not born here . . . and I will remain as a refugee, you know? It's not forever, but this feeling inside you remains, even if you want to be an American" (14 January 2018).

In addition to the internal perception Ali described, he pointed out the distinctions government officials may draw between native-born and naturalized citizens. As an example, he pointed to the potential for scrutiny when interacting with airport security: "Whenever you want to go, especially during this time, if you want to travel, you are going to get questions, even if you have a US passport. You are going to get questions. Especially when it shows country of birth: Iraq. [If it reads] country [and city] of birth: New York City, USA it would be different. This is something that has happened in the past year, 2016. They are taking their phones, they are asking questions, which is not good" (Ali 14 January 2018).

However, Ali also argued that the law in the United States protected everyone living there. Therefore, for example, one could practice their religion freely. Ali stressed that if this legal protection were to change: "I will give my voice. I'll give my opinion. I believe this [equal legal protection] is better because from my experience, what I had back years ago in my country [the breakdown of law and institutions after 2003], this is what happened. So, I don't want this country to go through the same thing that my country went through. I'm talking about civil war, something like that. I don't want that to happen here in the United States" (14 January 2018).

Zaid stated that although he was an American citizen and had a legal right to engage in democratic processes, he did not believe he had earned the right to take part in decisions about laws and policies in the United States. As he explained: "I think it's not my right. No . . . I don't want to be a hypocrite. I have just been living here for seven years. I don't think I gained that right. Yes, I mean, I have the citizenship, but I can't decide for people who were born here, this is just my opinion. I know it's my right . . . but I believe that it's not really my right" (Zaid 27 February 2018).

When I asked Tariq, "Do you feel like you're a part of the democracy in the United States?" he responded:

This is a good question. Part of it, probably yes. . . . But we are a second level. You know China? China has levels, classes. Class one, class two, class three.[2] . . . So, when you are guilty and you have a bad record and you go to the judge and you say: "No, I didn't do it!" They're not going to trust you. This is what I feel here. We have a democracy, yes. But we can't say anything. We can't use it. What are you going to do? Everybody is against you, the news, the government. . . . So, you're weak . . . because you're not trusted. . . . So, it's not democracy. (2 November 2017)

He went on to argue that Trump had effectively authorized Americans to treat refugees badly: "We cannot practice our democracy, it's difficult when the government [is led by someone] like Trump, he's against us already, we're done. Now he has legalized people to do whatever they want with us. Right? Because he said: 'If you do anything, you're out!'" (Tariq 2 November 2017).

Tariq allowed that Trump ostensibly took this approach to keep people safe; however, he explained: "He was thinking it's going to be good to keep people away from problems, but you say that for people who make a problem, which is very few of us. Not every immigrant" (2 November 2017). This targeting of all immigrants led Tariq to ask rhetorically: "Is that freedom? Is that a democracy? It's not. It gives you a right to do it again and again and again, because it worked" (2 November 2017).

More broadly than the president's actions, for Tariq, life in the United States is difficult because a segment of the society does not support refugees. He is a US citizen now but still thinks of himself as a refugee. Tariq labeled the lingering tension and antagonism he felt from American society the "taxes" he and other newcomers must pay to live in that society. He said:

Why do I still think I'm a refugee or I'm an immigrant? Because no matter what, this is our taxes. This is how the first generation who moves to the US, I feel, this is our taxes. My kids probably will be better because they have the American accent, so it's hard for you to recognize them in the future. But for us, this is how we pay taxes. We still feel, from the community, from the news, from the politics, or from politicians when they do something against us, you feel like: "Oh, why did they do that against me?" So, you are not a full citizen. US citizen. . . . Why? Because we just moved, no matter what I'm still a foreigner because of my accent, my color, maybe. My whatever. So, still, you will struggle. (Tariq 2 November 2017)

Tariq went on to say that even if he were able to build a sense of belonging and democratic membership, one event could set all of that backward: "It's not going to be easy. . . . When you say something or you live your democracy very well because no matter what, on the news . . . one day if it's a whole year with no problems, people start to do better and you know, forget. And then boom! A shooting happens and they say: 'Muslim, Muslim, Muslim!'" (2 November 2017).

He was certain it would be impossible to have a right to participate equal to that of a native-born American. "That will take time," Tariq said, "it will probably be after I die. My kids at least [may have it]. Maybe, yes. But, no, no we're far behind" (2 November 2017). Moreover, he argued that the exercise of his democratic rights may place him in jeopardy: "For me, definitely you think you can say it, but I keep reminding you that for us to practice those things, it's a little for me at least, it's difficult. I don't want to put myself in a spot and then you will get hurt by the government. I know, probably, freedom of speech nobody is going to hurt me but, who knows? Probably they will consider it against me down the road. 'Oh yeah, you have been doing this and now you are a terrorist.' They can do that, easily" (Tariq 2 November 2017).

This was especially true under Trump, in his view. As he argued, Trump had, for example, directed ICE to take "people from their homes and moms from their kids, without mercy" (Tariq 2 November 2017). During the Trump administration, ICE increased mass raids that "terrorize[d] communities" by "indiscriminately rounding up, detaining, and deporting migrants" (Beltrán 2020, 102). Tariq compared these actions to the situation under Saddam Hussein, saying: "It's like Saddam Hussein. This is what he did after 1991, after the Gulf War. He sent his army to every house, and he took people from their houses. I almost lost my dad because of that. It's the same thing. ICE, same thing. They have the right, they have the power, to take anybody. So, it's easy for them to consider me, I'm the bad guy, easily" (2 November 2017).

Around the time of my interview with Tariq, the Trump administration had directed agencies, including ICE and the United States Border Patrol, to increase arrests, imprisonment, and deportation of immigrants. In June 2017, several months before interviews began, ICE ramped up efforts specifically to target Iraqis. Most of these individuals were Chaldean Christians who left Iraq before and after 2003 to seek refuge from violence directed at their community. A legal petition brought by the American Civil Liberties Union (ACLU) in July 2017 successfully halted the immediate deportation of fourteen hundred Iraqis who had been detained, allowing time for individuals to reopen their immigration cases (Kitaba-Gaviglio and Andrade 2017).

Tariq argued that if he were to exercise his freedom of speech by posting something critical about the government on social media, he could be arrested. He stated that immigrants who participated in protests against Trump took the same risk. As he explained, he believed that the government could arbitrarily exercise its authority over those engaged in legal activities because he had personally experienced this reality: "I was born and raised in this same situation," he said, and the government "can turn easily against you. So, for me, we have to always think ahead" (Tariq 2 November 2017).

Religious practice, too, is constrained, in Tariq's view: "We practice in a small place, and we don't go every time because I was scared to. Who knows? They come and they [will ask], 'What are you guys doing here?' Or they are watching us already. Maybe they're watching us already and they think that we're doing something they don't like" (2 November 2017).

"Maybe I'm wrong," he said. However, he continued: "it was true before . . . in the country that I come from. . . . You get killed for that. You get arrested for that" (Tariq 2 November 2017). Moreover, Tariq pointed out that the US government maintains watchlists of those targeted for suspicion. As noted in the introduction and Chapter 2, state authorities already disproportionately cast suspicion upon and surveil Muslims, mosques, and Islamic community organizations in the United States. Tariq observed, "Even if it's not true, this is what I feel" (2 November 2017). He went on to say: "I wish I'm wrong. . . . But, based on the data and [what I] see in the news, I have to be aware of that. Keep away from all the problems. Even if I'm a US citizen now, always keep away from anything because I just want to live my life. I don't want to do anything. I don't want anybody [to do] bad things to me and I'm never going to do anything to anybody" (Tariq 2 November 2017). Given these experiences and assessments of his position in American society, Tariq said: "So, it is just the democracy that we are looking for. We hope we'll be more like anybody else and that our voice can be heard, and they believe us when we say [something] because . . . they don't believe us" (2 November 2017).

Barriers to Democratic Participation

With these experiences of democratic membership in mind, those I interviewed also highlighted specific barriers as well as requirements to engage with democratic processes in the United States. Their insights on these topics accord strongly with Irene Bloemraad and S. Karthick Ramakrishnan's argument that: "Beyond language, immigrants may also face cultural gaps in understanding their new country's political institutions, its taken-for-granted norms about politics and civic activity, and the very ways that politics and civic engagement are understood and discussed. Immigrants must learn the ropes, so to speak, of their host country, and research indicates that those from authoritarian regimes are less prepared to participate in politics" (2008, 5).

Multiple interviewees identified four such fundamental themes. The first was that locating opportunities to participate requires time. Second, substantive exercise of democracy requires public provision of resources. Third, participation requires knowledge of processes and preferences. Fourth, interviewees' experiences living under an authoritarian regime left some suspicious of political engagement and skeptical that their formal legal rights would protect them in practice.

Additionally, several individuals identified language as an important factor, and in some cases, a precondition, to engagement. Many interviewees described how their knowledge of English facilitated both resettlement processes broadly and opportunities for involvement. In addition to enabling everyday interactions and the pursuit of daily activities, knowledge of English allowed them to advocate for themselves and to interact with state authorities, neighbors, and others in their communities. I turn next to a discussion of the four barriers/requirements to civic engagement as identified by interviewees.

Participation Requires Time

The majority of those with whom I spoke argued that they lacked sufficient time to participate in democratic processes or activities. Many individuals, including Ahmed, Mohammed, Ali, and Sarah, discussed how the need to work long hours left little time to see family and friends—let alone become involved in broader-scale discussion, debate, or activism. Marwa, for example, told me that voting was the extent to which she wished to engage in democratic activities. I asked her whether she had done so already, and she said: "I didn't have time. I already registered . . . but I didn't get [to do so]. I was busy working" (Marwa 25 November 2017).

Ali observed that he worked long hours during the week, occasionally not seeing his children or wife because he returns home late, "So, yeah, the weekend is fully booked for my family. Because the whole week, sometimes . . . I don't see them because I come late. Sometimes I see them like for half an hour and they have to go to sleep" (14 January 2018).

As Hashim explained, comparing his experience in Chicago to that in Iraq: "We had so many Iraqi friends at the beginning and then, you know, everyone is busy here in their lives. Back in Iraq, we had a lot of time to spend time with family and friends but right here we are so busy so we're just seeing the closer families and from time to time we can maybe meet with friends" (1 October 2017).

Between work and family, Ahmed, too, had little time to engage in additional activities: "Because I used to live [on Chicago's Northside] and it's basically between work and going back and family duties I was not really able to go into the community and talk" (2 October 2017). He said that he discusses important concerns with coworkers and friends, but not in other forums. Ahmed was interested in becoming more politically engaged, "if the opportunity comes my way" and he reiterated "with the time constraints I need to think about" (2 October 2017).

Similarly, Mohammed argued: "There's no time for American people to go out to talk with the government. Everybody goes to the job and comes back from the job. With this circle, who is thinking about the government? What are they doing? Nobody. Fifty percent of the American people, if you ask them about the name of the [Secretary of Defense] . . . they don't know" (2 November 2017).

Polls of Americans' knowledge of their government support Mohammed's assertion. For example, a 2014 poll found that fewer than half of respondents could correctly identify which party, Democrats or Republicans, controlled the House of Representatives or Senate at the time of the survey (Rozansky 2014). A 2018 poll found that 57 percent of respondents could not identify how many justices sit on the US Supreme Court (National Survey 2018).

Mohammed went on to argue that "the government puts the people in this situation. Just work, work, work, and don't think about politics. Don't think. Don't talk about politics. Just go to the job and come back home" (2 November 2017). In this way, he concluded, even if someone were interested in engaging politically, "There's no time. Who's going outside to lose his check for a week?" he asked (Mohammed 2 November 2017).[3]

Although Mohammed argued that he was too busy to engage, such involvement was something he was interested in undertaking, nevertheless. He said that he often speaks with his twenty-three-year-old cousin who graduated from college with a political science degree and moved to Washington, DC, to work for the Democratic Party, imploring her to work for positive change. Mohammed has also prioritized supporting his high school–aged daughter's civic engagement. He supported her participation in a two-week leadership program offered in Washington, DC, where she had the opportunity to meet with members of the government. He said of his hope for his daughter's future: "My plan in the future, I will send my daughter to study political science to do something for the people, not just for refugees, no, swear to God. For the American people, too, to change something in the future" (Mohammed 2 November 2017).

Wissam, too, said, "the problem here is people don't have time, they live in a bubble and life here is very fast. . . . People don't have time here to research" (22 October 2017). As a result of these constraints, Wissam argued: "So, they just trust the government. Whatever those decisions made for them, they don't have the time. I mean, even the elections . . . most people when they vote for senators or representatives, they are going to decide in a few seconds, depends on the picture, which picture is better. . . . They're not going to spend the time to research what this guy's plan is, which is unfortunate. So, people are relying heavily on government to make decisions for them" (22 October 2017).

Moreover, Wissam explained, the United States "is not a small country, it's a continent. So, even the government has limited resources to fight back against all the bad guys or all the lobbyists, everything" (22 October 2017). This situation "makes you lose hope and believe there is no way you can change that" he said with a laugh (Wissam 22 October 2017). For himself, "I just stay busy with . . . my business, and I don't care about anything else"

(Wissam 22 October 2017). Later in our conversation, Wissam said: "Not many Americans are engaged in political life. . . . Maybe now there are more. But I didn't see that many people care about what's going on. . . . So, they don't care, we don't care what's going on outside. And I'm busy with my life and my kids, things like that" (22 October 2017).

Kasim, too, contended that Americans he encountered were generally preoccupied with daily concerns: "When you are talking to an ordinary American person, he lives his daily life routine. He doesn't look outside the box" (27 February 2018). In more personal terms, Sarah said that she would participate in democratic activities in the future, but her work now kept her too busy to do so. For example, the resettlement agency that assisted Sarah and her sister when they first arrived in Arizona held workshops on various topics and, as she explained, "Some people went to the resettlement agency, but me and my sister we go just two weeks and then we started to work. And all my time is busy, we can't go there. Some people went to the organization to get more information about America. But, me and my sister we are busy all the time working ten hours per day. [Activities were held at] the same times we wanted to go to complete my education as well, but I can't. No time. No time" (November 2017).

Nora, who has been involved in several different nonprofit and activist organizations said that she had to step away from some of this work because she was caring for her mother, commuting between the Shenandoah Valley and Washington, DC, to complete a master's degree and working ten-hour shifts at her job four days a week. At one point, Tariq, too, was involved as a volunteer with an organization that assists Special Immigrant Visa recipients in the Upstate New York region. But, because he, too, was busy with work, he had reduced his time spent volunteering at the time of our interview.

Walid, who is very involved with multiple activities, said he knew five to ten people who were "donating their time to the community" in Upstate New York (27 September 2017). However, by and large, most members of the community, he opined, are "focusing on their own needs at this time" (Walid 27 September 2017). As he explained: "For individuals, I know many families in the community who help each other. Reading their mail, calling the doctor to schedule an appointment, we have this kind of help, supporting the community, in some way. But, in terms of taking issues to governmental or local agencies, they don't have time or ability probably to do that because they are very busy in this life" (Walid 27 September 2017).

Nada expressed a strong desire to be active in her community; however, she said she, too, was not involved in any activities at the time of our interview because: "All of my time [is spent] in my job or studying. Yeah. I don't have time. Especially my daughter, this year has the SAT. So, this is very important for me. I prepare everything for her to feel very comfortable, to study . . . and really on the weekend, I have one day to spend with her. . . .

Now, all my time is spent for my job and . . . studying and with my family" (1 November 2017). When I asked Nada whether she thought this busy schedule would change in the future or whether she would like it to, she said, "Yeah. Really, now I stopped everything to engage with any community because that means I need time. And, I explained to you, I don't have time now" (1 November 2017).

Zaid said his daily life entailed "working and working." He followed up by laughing and reiterating "and working" (Zaid 27 February 2018). "Seriously," he continued, "this is what I'm doing. Since the day I arrived until now . . . you are struggling against all the needs and demands. I didn't even get the time to have a life" (Zaid 27 February 2018). As he reminded me with a laugh, Zaid had come directly from work to conduct our interview. He was also caring for his parents who live with him in the Washington, DC, area. So, he said, "unfortunately I didn't have the free time. I mean, since the day I came here until now" (Zaid 27 February 2018).

Democracy Requires (Re)Distribution of Resources

The substantive exercise of democracy requires that members of a political community have a right to public provision of the individual and collective material resources needed to live full and meaningful lives as well as opportunities to decide how those resources are produced and distributed (Pateman 2012; Wolff 2012). As several individuals such as Tariq and Mohammed pointed out, part of the reason many in the United States must work long hours that limit their opportunities for democratic participation is due to limited social-democratic programs such as universal tax-funded healthcare or postsecondary education provided to residents or citizens in the United States.

According to Tariq and Hashim, in Iraq many essential services such as healthcare and education had been free at the point of service. In the United States, however, the cost of living is high, and one cannot depend upon social supports or public provision to fulfill needs. For that reason, the compulsion to work long hours constrains possibilities for democratic participation. As Mohammed put it: "The US government, they didn't give the American people anything for free. Nothing is free for you" (2 November 2017). Tariq addressed the trope that refugees come to the United States seeking public benefits, saying: "People think that we come for fun to the United States and to live for free" (2 November 2017). He continued: "What free life are you talking about? Healthcare, free? You got to pay for it. . . . You will struggle with a lot of things. I had it free in my third world country. It's a developing country [and] I had my healthcare free. I got my bachelor's degree for free. And we are a developing country. We got my health and school, free. It's mandated by government. We have to teach everybody, and we have to give healthcare to everybody" (Tariq 2 November 2017).

Hashim, too, discussed the high cost of healthcare in the United States and the fact that many other countries, including Iraq, have public programs that provide universal healthcare as a right to their citizens:

> [Healthcare] services are very expensive. It's too much. This is one of the highest in the world, actually. So, I think we need to reconsider about finding solutions, about how we can provide better services at the same time more affordable to people. When I first came, when I was reviewing healthcare bills I was receiving, like the clinic visits like emergency visits, it's just too much. For us in Iraq, for example, and most countries in the world, healthcare is free for people, right? So, we never thought about this to be part of our daily life, or our daily experiences. There must be a way. The government [should] be responsible for the healthcare services because this is a right. This is one of the human rights to receive the service, right? It's not something I [should] have to worry about.... If, for example, I got sick, one of my family members had any kind of disease or long-term treatment I was unable to afford so, what should I do? This is not something I have to worry about, this is my right to receive healthcare from the government, just like many countries like Canada, like I think Australia also. The government is responsible for their payments for the healthcare services. It's not something people worry about. (1 October 2017)

Moreover, substantive democracy requires that members of a political community have a say in how resources are distributed to meet needs and fulfill individual and collective aspirations. Both Wissam and Mohammed argued that a portion of the vast US military budget could be reallocated to civic projects and social-democratic programs, including healthcare and education. Wissam said of the military budget, "You spend trillions on the defense budget" (22 October 2017),[4] to the detriment of civilian infrastructure. He pointed to the poor quality of American infrastructure (ASCE 2021), suggesting: "If you spend maybe 10 percent of that for the infrastructure of the US, bullet trains ... or better airports, better roads or maybe to have a cleaner environment like electric cars, things like that and focusing on these kinds of things. It's better than spending all this money on the military. Especially ... the problem is, we are, the United States, spending trillions of dollars on our bases outside the country. So, money is coming out of our pockets to those countries" (22 October 2017).

Similarly, Mohammed said, "the government has to think about the American community.... Really, this is always my opinion: Why didn't they support the American community? Why?" (2 November 2017). As evidence, Mohammed also pointed to the vast sums of public resources spent on the military. He noted the then-recent congressional votes to increase the already-large US military budget by tens of billions of dollars for fiscal year 2018 (Stolberg 2017), asking, "Why? Nobody can tell me" (Mohammed 2

November 2017). He continued: "I promise you . . . not after 1,000 years, America is America. It has such a strong military; nobody can seriously threaten it. Be comfortable. So, if you want to spend like $55bn [roughly the proposed budget increase], you can spend it for the American people. Why are you spending it on the military? Why?" (Mohammed 2 November 2017).

Emphasizing the point, he questioned why the United States had spent billions–or trillions–of dollars fighting against Afghanistan, Iraq, and Libya.[5] "Why did you spend all this money?" he asked, "This is from the American people. These people work, pay taxes, and make the government strong. . . . But, the government, they didn't help the American people" (Mohammed 2 November 2017). He pointed to the economic hardships many Americans face, such as the high cost of healthcare, which only a few miles across the border from where he lives, Canada provides at much lower cost to all its citizens. As he remarked: "It can't be like this way always. You spend money, spend money on war, the money will run out in the future. So, the people will be angry, and there will be trouble. So, the government should change its mind to help the people, enough war, enough weapons. If you spend these billion, billion, billion dollars for the American people, everybody will be happy, and their lives will be changed. Right?" (Mohammed 2 November 2017).[6]

Programs such as universal tax-funded and government run healthcare and tuition-free higher education are supported by majorities of the US population (Hartig 2021; Galvin 2021). However, public support has not translated into policy. The lack of meaningful mechanisms to ensure that popular social-democratic and redistributive programs can be enacted demonstrates the lack of substantively democratic institutions in the United States (Gilens and Page 2014).

Decision Making Requires Knowledge

In addition to sufficient time and resources, information is required to engage in democratic processes. Many interviewees pointed to the need to make informed decisions as well as noted that they may not have enough information or knowledge of US structures, institutions, or processes to participate productively in authoring laws, policies, or rules affecting their lives. When I asked Nora whether she thought she could discuss her views on laws in the United States, she said, "I cannot do that. Not yet. I'm not knowledgeable about everything, such as what the laws have missed . . . and I have never been in a situation to say that, honestly" (6 February 2018). However, in the future, she was confident she could. "Why not?" she said, "If I cannot change it, at least I will highlight the issues to people who can change it, the policy makers" (Nora 6 February 2018).

Nora went on to say that possibilities for her to engage in democratic decision making existed in some policy areas but not others: "It depends also on what type of law you are talking about. Like, I cannot change, as an example, immigration law. No, I'm not going to change that mostly because they have the right to protect the country" (6 February 2018). But she continued: "If there is some stuff like why are you making people's lives more complicated and miserable, why not just try to talk about it, try to say something" (Nora 6 February 2018).

Ahmed expressed hope that he would be taken as seriously as native-born Americans when articulating his views: "I still hope so, but honestly speaking, I don't think so" (2 October 2017). The reason, he elaborated, is that "Americans might think of me, not less, but maybe they think I'm not yet fully integrated and fully involved" (Ahmed 2 October 2017). Therefore, he said: "Maybe they will think my idea is good, from the outside, but if they want to look at it from the community long-term, because I have still yet to get my full grasp of the laws, of the system, so I might say something not relevant" (Ahmed 2 October 2017).

Moreover, he argued that this disparity was not because he was a resident and not a citizen at the time of our interview. Rather, the issue was the short time he had lived in the United States:

> It's not because I'm not American yet or they are, but it's only how long you have been here, you know the community better, you know the country better, you know your city better. So, you know the laws better. So, for example, if I now go and protest against the [at the time of interview recently imposed] soda tax [in Chicago], okay I want to do that, but did I research the health implications on the American society and obesity? No, I did not. So, someone else might sit next to me: "How long have you been here?" And I would say: "twelve–thirteen months." They would say: "Okay, thank you for your opinion, but I might want to consider someone who has been here for the last thirty years of their life or [who was] born and raised and suffered health issues that affect all their lives and their families as well." (Ahmed 2 October 2017)

Sarah expressed uncertainty about her right to participate as a Green Card holder: "I don't know, which laws . . . allow me to participate. . . . I want to learn about this subject more from people, from organizations here. . . . I think some organizations here, talk about this subject. We are actually looking for it here" (30 November 2017).[7] She underscored this point, noting that as a resident she cannot vote. However, in the future, she said she would speak out if a candidate can "help the people, for example, to develop education, . . . health, many things. . . . We need the time to make this decision about which one we have to choose. . . . I want to learn. I want to learn first and then to, maybe, make a decision about that one (Sarah 30 November 2017).

Mohammed flatly answered "no" to the question whether it was his right to help decide what the laws are in the United States. He then elaborated:

> Do you know why? Because . . . any point in the Constitution, these are the American issues. It's difficult for me to understand the American life, and decide on any point, which is right for the American people. . . . This is the American right because you were born in America. You know what is needed in the American life. It's difficult, I don't have a lot of experience. If you asked me about Iraq, I will tell you: "Yes, 100 percent." Here, it's difficult. Just if you're reading about the tax system in America, you have to read like 100 books to understand it. (Mohammed 2 November 2017)

By way of example, Mohammed asked me to imagine I had moved to Iraq and had a car accident. There is no automobile insurance there, he said. To resolve the situation, one must work out with the other motorist who is at fault and who will pay for repairs. Sometimes in this process, the person at fault will argue over payment and families will become involved, he said. "You don't know about this process, right?" I said no. So, he said, this is difficult for a newcomer to understand. He also asked me to imagine I moved to Iraq, received three months of support services and, thereafter, was expected to find employment and make a new life. "It's really difficult" (Mohammed 2 November 2017). Yet, this is the expectation for resettled refugees. Mohammed volunteers to support newly resettled refugees in Upstate New York and often encounters clients who receive letters informing them of decisions made by various agencies that they do not understand. For example, they receive notice that their public assistance has been terminated because they missed an application deadline, or their credit has been negatively affected because of a missed gas bill payment. These routine matters are unfamiliar to newcomers and can be a challenge to understand.

Omar spoke about knowledge of the "tools" of democratic processes as necessary for democratic engagement, not as a barrier, but as a characteristic of such processes: "We are new and also beginners to these things. . . . I'm trying to educate myself in these democratic things, the tools. And so, we have a lot to learn" (14 December 2017). In his volunteer work, Omar educates community members about these processes as well: "We are also teaching our communities about these tools to use them. Right now, we have had a hard time to pull out our community to vote" (14 December 2017). For himself, Omar said: "Being able to also change the rules, I wish to. And I don't think there is an obstacle for that as far as I work for it and find the opportunities, I think, I will be able to do so" (14 December 2017).

Wissam offered that there ought to be more programs, available sooner, to educate refugees about the structures in American society, such as the purpose and uses of tax revenues:

For refugees, I think there should be more programs to teach them about these kinds of things that you guys know about: renting vs. buying, how to [file your] taxes, what do taxes mean, why do you pay them. Because most of these countries they come from they don't have any taxes. So, they don't know why. I mean, we do have some programs here, brief ones, about bank accounts, taxes, basically knowing your rights, what you can do, what you can say, . . . when you have the right to stay silent, things like that. (22 October 2017)

The wide array of programming Wissam described may or may not be available through nonprofit or resettlement agencies to those who have resettled, depending on several factors including the local resettlement context, whether one has legal status as a refugee, funding availability, and language learning and education support. Wissam argued: "It shouldn't be after getting citizenship [that one can] learn about all these things. It should be when you first come here. You learn about like: This is the Bill of Rights, these are twenty-seven amendments that we have, this is what people are discussing, these kinds of things. It should be available before they come, even before they come, yeah. Just to let them have an idea. And explain to them these kinds of things" (22 October 2017). Wissam was studying for his citizenship exam at the time of our interview, and I asked him whether he was learning about these issues now as he prepared. He said: "A lot of it, yeah. A lot of things I didn't know" (Wissam 22 October 2017).

For Hashim, specific subject area knowledge facilitated participation. At the time of our interview, he was completing a master's degree at a university in Chicago focused on healthcare management: "I'm studying policies and regulations, managing health institutions. This is something I'm going to be specialized in. It is something I can give an opinion about, you know?" (Hashim 1 October 2017). In his graduate work, he and his classmates spent significant time in seminars discussing the ethics and policy questions related to healthcare. As he put it: "This is something I can maybe give my opinion about. I can go into debates [on this topic] but not something related to different fields. So, yeah. I think I can participate in debates related to what I know about. What I'm doing" (Hashim 1 October 2017).

Marwa did not see an equal right to participate because "maybe Americans know more than me. I am still every day learning something" (25 November 2017). As she continued: "My kids now they are different. They know more than me. . . . I came already here, I'm an adult. I grew up there. I grew up in a different culture. I try my best to know. I try now. I try my best to know more. More, more, more. But I miss a lot" (Marwa 25 November 2017).

We returned to this subject later in our interview, and Marwa sketched her understanding of what it requires to make change in society: "It takes time," she said, "if I want to change something, I'm not going to give my opinion. . . . No, it needs research, it needs people who understand maybe . . .

more than me" (25 November 2017). Marwa's insights point toward the connection between time and knowledge. Sufficient time is required to learn about issues and to engage in democratic processes.

Finally, it is important to note there was a tension in the perception that many individuals lack time and/or knowledge for engagement in their communities and their activities. Individuals, including Mohammed, Marwa, and Ali, explained that they were very busy, which limited their time to engage. Nonetheless, each was involved in various forms of volunteering in addition to their paid jobs, as explored in the following chapter.

Engagement Requires undoing Authoritarian Acculturation

Marwa, Walid, Zaid, Omar, and Tariq suggested that living much of their lives under an authoritarian government had left them without experience to engage in democratic processes, and/or uninterested or afraid to do so. Marwa, for example, discussed how there was no freedom of speech in Iraq. She was highly critical of Saddam Hussein she said, but: "Even inside my home, I can't [criticize him]. Because my daughter . . . when she goes to school maybe . . . she will say: 'My mom and my dad they are talking about Saddam Hussein!' Believe me, the second day, we are going to be killed. That's how bad Saddam Hussein was" (Marwa 25 November 2017).

Conversely, Marwa said, "I like the freedom here. I like the free speech here" (25 November 2017). As a result, even though Marwa expressed several times in our interview that she did not want to participate in politics or political activities in the United States, she was clear that she does not remain silent if she has an opinion to share.

Although very active in his community, Walid still feared the repressive government in Iraq, which allowed no freedom to criticize it. "There is still fear," he said, "We came from a security government in Iraq if you say something about the government. . . . I lost my father, because my father, back in Iraq, he used to say things about the Ba'ath Party and they took him, they killed him, they took our home, confiscated it because of that" (Walid 27 September 2017).

In his view, such experiences meant "many Iraqis, they have this kind of fear. Don't talk about the government. So, don't talk about these things" (Walid 27 September 2017). Despite this fear, Walid engaged in activities such as protesting policies he did not support. He also invited many people he knows to attend marches organized against the 2017 travel ban, discussed in more detail in the following chapter. However, in his view, many were afraid to engage in such activities because: "They have trauma from police. Police there . . . are not supporting citizens. It's criminal, like they are criminals. They came to kill people . . . as part of the agenda of the government there. So, they have this kind of PTSD for now. I mean, many families if they see a police car, they freeze. So . . . they want to live peacefully without touching these things" (Walid 27 September 2017).

Zaid expressed the fear Walid identified in very similar terms. He explained that, in the Washington, DC, area where he now lives:

> Whenever I see a police car, I get this feeling that . . . they are going to arrest me. They are going to stop me, and they are going to find something wrong with my ID, with my car, with anything . . . because I came from this background when we really get scared when we see police anywhere. In Iraq, they just tend to harass people and try to get them into trouble and get as much as they can, like money or whatever. . . . So, it's completely on the contrary. People here feel safe when they see a police car. I get this kind of feeling. . . . By the way, I've never been stopped by a police car before. You know? But still. (Zaid 27 February 2018)

Considering this perception, Zaid described his views on participating in American democratic processes:

> I know it's not fair, it's actually selfish to say that [I am unable to participate in democratic processes] because I am gaining from this democracy . . . but on the other hand, I cannot participate in it. Maybe it's not just because I cannot, maybe I don't want to because . . . of my background, we came from this politically corrupt system. So, we have a very, very bad experience with being part of the system. I believe not just me, any people who came from that country, I believe that we would just rather stay away as much as possible from any kind of political system. We just want to live our life as far away as possible from any political things. (27 February 2018)

I asked Zaid if this included opting out of voting as well, and he said, "No, voting, I'm 100 percent with voting. . . . Voting is kind of practicing your democracy but, I don't think I can do anything other than that" (27 February 2018).

Omar, too, explained that even though he and other members of the Iraqi community had a right to engage in politics, he might hesitate: "Not because I'm scared of something," he said, "not because we still have the fear of expressing political views. It's related to back home. Even the community I'd say. Even it's our right. But sometimes we hesitated to express our perspective towards any case" (14 December 2017). He continued, "but we can do that in our community [of fellow Iraqis]. But with others, it is very hard because still, we have this influence from back home. . . . Because we don't know, what are the limits of our freedom" (Omar 14 December 2017).

When I asked Tariq whether he believed he was able to express his views and opinions about actions taken by the US government, he responded: "This is the part that I love. Because over there, you can [express views on the government]. But easily you can disappear, too. Here, you can do that;

you can express your views" (2 November 2017). Tariq was clear throughout our conversation that he opposed President Donald Trump's policies; however, he continued: "At least when I talk to people that support Trump, they're not going to kill me. At least they will listen and hear and then . . . it's up to you to decide if it's wrong or right" (2 November 2017).

Tariq juxtaposed this possibility with his life in Iraq. "Let me tell you something," he said, "I lived in Iraq twenty-seven years. I witnessed my whole life the dictatorship of Saddam Hussein. And we weren't allowed to talk. You were not allowed to express your opinions about government. So, it's very difficult for me to express my opinion now" (2 November 2017). Echoing Marwa, he said, "You can't even whisper because somebody will hear you, and then you're gone. Even with police. You can easily be taken by police over there. The police arrest you easily without any warrant, without anything. They just take you. Beat you up and leave you, that's easy" (Tariq 2 November 2017).

As a result of these experiences, Tariq was left with a lingering fear of government authorities and preferred not to interact with them or with the American legal system. As he explained: "I know . . . you have freedom of speech in the US. . . . You can express your feelings. But, it's still hard for me to say out loud because I still have fear that somebody will knock on the door, or probably break it down and take me out. It's difficult. It's not easy. That's why you guys, you Americans are lucky you didn't live through this situation" (Tariq 2 November 2017).

Taking a different angle on this same background of insecurity in Iraq, Wissam asserted that his experience under an authoritarian government gave him a special status to observe and comment on current events happening in American society. When I asked him if he believed it was his right to help decide what the laws are in the United States, he replied: "I believe so, yes, because to some extent, people live here in a bubble. This is unfortunate. But, for me, I got to live in a different society, different regime. . . . I had to go through all the processes. So, I know . . . how it starts because maybe I have a background about that. I know how it's going to go down the road because I've lived that, I can tell people what they can expect" (Wissam 22 October 2017).

Conclusion

This chapter has explored ways in which interviewees understood democratic membership in the United States as well as barriers many saw to exercising that status in substantive ways. Individuals' experiences point toward several important insights about how to bring democratic practices and processes closer to the ideal articulated at the opening of this chapter.

Indeed, these insights are not exclusive to resettled refugees, but likely apply to all members of American society. The need for time to put democratic membership to use and the need for information to engage productively in democratic processes are essential points.

Residents and citizens need sufficient time to engage in activities such as researching issues, voting, joining activist or advocacy organizations, or attending union meetings. A robust democratic society in the United States requires, as Mohammed suggested, an environment in which one need not choose between engaging in political activities and losing wages. Leaving aside whether it is an intentional government strategy, as Mohammed argued, citizens cannot engage in democratic practices if they must spend all their time working. This conundrum points to the realization that strong redistributive social and economic support mechanisms and structures are crucial to ensure that members of American society, resettled Iraqis, and others possess sufficient material security to engage in politics.

Moreover, as Wissam suggested, civil society organizations, political parties, and/or government agencies should prioritize and make educational programming as widely available as possible for residents and citizens to make clear how democratic processes and institutions that govern them function and to encourage widespread participation. Such processes and institutions are only democratic if individuals have meaningful influence within them, and wide and deep knowledge is necessary to exert such control effectively.

Beyond the institutional realm, for activists and those involved with social movements seeking to build a more democratic society, these insights speak to the importance of developing strategies and tactics that engage in the intertwined work of political education, fighting for reallocating resources away from war and toward public provision and social-democratic supports, and directly providing essential programs and services such as food and medical care when government does not.[8]

Finally, the lingering fear and unease individuals described about their experiences in Iraq under Saddam Hussein point to the need for government, media, and civil society to ensure that residents and citizens not only feel safe and protected by the law, but also are actually so treated in practice. It is not only a matter of attenuating the lingering effects of living under an authoritarian regime, but also about ensuring that those who live in the United States are guaranteed protection of their rights and safety. Democratic governance can only be approached in the United States if all residents have an equal right and substantive ability to participate and are guaranteed equitable treatment by governance institutions. This means ensuring that public agencies do not arbitrarily exercise their power against refugees, Muslims, and other groups and ensuring that members of those groups are confident that such will be the case. To realize this aim, it is essential to end the profiling, surveillance, and discriminatory policies that continue to target Arabs, Muslims, and refugees.

Critically as well, these experiences evince the need to listen to warnings such as Tariq's that actions by US government officials and agencies share qualities with the authoritarianism under which he lived in Iraq. As his interpretations shared in this and the previous chapter have highlighted, it is always possible for governments, local, state, and federal, to undermine the rights of particular groups. The Trump administration not only undercut and/or eliminated legal protections for immigrants and refugees, but also sought to strip protections from others, such as transgender Americans (Alonso-Zaldivar 2019). And, crucially, threats to legal protections are neither unique nor confined to the previous administration.

Consistent with Tariq's fears of expanding, arbitrary government power, while Trump's predecessor, Barack Obama, had a comparatively more progressive record on some issues, his administration nevertheless operated and vastly expanded a massive, clandestine domestic surveillance apparatus that aimed to collect all digital communications in the United States (Bamford 2016) and killed American citizens abroad without trial or conviction (Scahill 2015). Further, Obama's attorney general, Eric Holder, asserted in official communication with US Senator Rand Paul (Republican, Kentucky) that the United States military hypothetically had the right to kill American citizens within US borders (Holder 2013). Even though the latter thankfully did not happen, Holder's assertion sets a potential precedent for future administrations.

This is to say that threats to democratic culture do not come exclusively, or even primarily, from "outsiders,"[9] nor from only one side of the mainstream American political spectrum. Nor, for that matter, is there significant reason to assume that native-born citizens possess or strive to embrace and express a democratic ethos (Carens 2013). There is always potential for the degradation of a democratic ethos and practices among those who have been born and raised in a particular society. Given the critiques of existing institutions of American representative democracy, there is clearly a need to democratize democracy in the United States. Returning to Bloemraad and Ramakrishnan, although there can be barriers to democratic participation, "The immigrant experience can thus create obstacles to political and civic incorporation, but it can also rejuvenate or transform norms and practices in host societies" (2008, 5). Creating and maintaining a substantively democratic society is a perpetually unfinished process. It requires continual work on the part of members to inculcate, defend, and expand norms and institutions that foster participation. Many of the individuals with whom I spoke sought to take part in such processes, and their experiences provide insights into barriers to such engagements.

Chapter 4 builds upon these findings, examining the activities that interviewees have engaged in, such as discussion and debate with coworkers, friends, and fellow community members, and volunteering with civil society organizations. I also analyze my interviewees' activism, both their own and how native-born Americans' advocacy efforts affected them. As I explore, support, welcoming, and commitment to advocating publicly for the rights of vulnerable groups, including refugees, by native-born Americans are important to pushing government and the population at large to uphold its commitments to creating and perpetuating an open, tolerant, and multicultural society.

Notes

1. A series of US Supreme Court decisions beginning with the 1976 *Buckley v. Valeo* case and culminating in *Citizens United v. FEC* in 2010 have equated "political spending with political speech" (Levinson 2013, 885), upholding limits on direct contributions to politicians while allowing unlimited total expenditures in support of particular candidates or parties. This arrangement has created a system in which "people have as much speech . . . as they can buy" (Levinson 2013, 901). Legalized unlimited political spending has allowed those with money to "buy special access to politicians and [given them] an outsized voice in the political debate" (Levinson 2013, 901–2).
2. Although he did not explicitly name it, Tariq was likely referring to the system of household and internal migration registration called *hukou*, which provides disparate public benefits to Chinese citizens depending upon registration type and location and, as some have argued, has created a type of second-class citizenship within China (Tyner and Ren 2016).
3. Ali expressed a similar view that government, in this case the Iraqi rather than American, keeps individuals focused on daily concerns. He suggested that this was a tactic to prevent organizing against government policy and power: "They [the government] are making people run and care about electricity, care about their life, care about how they are going to feed their children because they don't want them to get involved with politics. They don't want them to get involved to do some kind of revolution against the government right now" (Ali 14 January 2018).
4. US military spending far exceeds that of any other country. According to the *Stockholm International Peace Research Institute (SIPRI)* military expenditure database (https://www.sipri.org/databases/milex), the United States spent $778 billion in 2020. This figure is approximately the same amount spent by the next twelve countries combined including China, India, Russia, the United Kingdom, Saudi Arabia, Germany, France, Japan, South Korea, Italy, Australia, and Canada.
5. A 2018 report by the Costs of War project at Brown University's Watson Institute for International and Public Affairs estimated that the so-called War on Terror cost $5.9 trillion between fiscal year 2001 and fiscal year 2019 (Crawford 2018b).

6. Mohammed's interpretation of a fundamental tension between the US government maintaining a vastly more expensive and powerful military than any other country in the world and its ability to provide basic services to its population echoes former US president Dwight D. Eisenhower's famous 1953 speech, "The Chance for Peace." In this speech, Eisenhower argued that a superpower arms race between the Soviet Union and the United States would most likely end in nuclear war or, failing that catastrophic outcome, would nonetheless result in perpetual fear, tension, and wasting of strength and wealth in both societies. As Eisenhower (2019) famously remarked: "Every gun that is made, every warship launched, every rocket fired signifies, in the final sense, a theft from those who hunger and are not fed, those who are cold and are not clothed." Eisenhower called for "solemn agreements" between nations to limit the size of militaries around the world and the resources devoted to such purposes. Given the United States's continued imperial pursuit of global military, economic, and cultural hegemony, pushing the American government to adhere to such commitments and limits, as Mohammed has suggested, is as relevant today as it was in 1953.
7. Later in our conversation, Sarah and I discussed the high barriers to home ownership in New York City. I asked her whether this topic, which she cared a great deal about, is something she would consider discussing with a local government representative. She said: "Actually, it's no problem for me. It's no problem because everyone can talk about this subject" (Sarah 30 November 2017). She then asked me: "For the new people here, it's no problem if we wanted to talk with them about that?" I said yes, it is legal, and she has the right to do so, to which she said: "Because we don't want to have a problem, especially me and my sister. We don't want to make a problem [by] talking with someone about subjects that are no good" (Sarah 30 November 2017).
8. The Black Panther Party, founded in 1966, provides a useful example of an organization that combined Black power, anti-imperialist and antiwar activism, political education, and social programs in its work. The Black Panthers ran community breakfast programs that at one time fed as many as ten thousand children every day in cities across the country (Bloom and Martin Jr. 2013). Programs like those the Black Panthers operated not only addressed a need, but also demonstrated that existing government programs were inadequate.
9. Consider, for example, a 2017 Pew Research Center poll that found that while large majorities of Americans surveyed believed that representative (86 percent) or direct democracy (67 percent) was somewhat or very good, a significant number believed that rule by experts (40 percent), a "strong leader" (22 percent), or the military (17 percent) was a good way to govern the country (Gramlich 2017). Certainly, rule by experts, a strong leader, or the military would not qualify as democratic.

4

Forms of Participation

Dialogue, Civil Society, and Resistance

People had come from all different nationalities just to say that we're welcome and then we started running around the court square and having all these signs with us. Then, there was another parade and there was a community session from the refugee office. . . . So, there was plenty of stuff happening just to make people feel welcome.

−Nora, 6 February 2018

Introduction

The previous chapter explored how interviewees regarded democratic membership in the United States and the particular barriers and requirements to its exercise. With that discussion in mind, this chapter considers the experiences that those with whom I spoke shared regarding their participation in various activities and the potential for resettled Iraqis to exercise democratic membership at multiple scales and sites—both formal and informal—in the United States. I use the term "participation" throughout this chapter to frame all of the experiences interviewees shared concerning engaging with fellow members of American society in democratic spaces.

This chapter first sets out the forms of participation interviewees described. I then narrow my focus to the three most salient modes and sites of engagement that recurred in interviews. The first is discussion and debate, broadly conceived, about the issues that affected interviewees' lives. Second, I explore the role of volunteering and nonprofit organizations in the locations where this study's interviewees lived, including Upstate New York, and the Shenandoah Valley Region of Virginia. Third, I reflect on the 2017 US travel ban targeting individuals from select predominately Muslim countries and the ways interviewees interpreted and participated in activism organized against it. Throughout this chapter, I draw on the argument offered in Chapter 2 that exchange among newcomers and native-born Americans is essential to widening participatory spaces and opportunities for all members of society.

Defining Participation and Locating Spaces for Engagement

Interviewees reflected on their experiences participating and engaging with democratic processes and practices. They shared many examples and definitions of what it meant to them to participate and what constituted the exercise of democratic political agency. Those with whom I spoke referenced a wide range of activities in which they had already engaged and/or that they wished to pursue. Those activities included completing surveys, protesting, voting, volunteering, attending Parent Teacher Association (PTA) and other school meetings, educating others, writing to and meeting with government representatives, and serving on nonprofit organization governing boards.

Many interviewees said that voting was an important way to participate in their communities. Some, including Kasim and Walid, who were citizens, had voted, and viewed doing so as important. Others, including Ahmed and Ali, could not yet vote, but said that they looked forward to doing so in the future. As discussed in Chapter 3, for individuals such as Marwa and Zaid, voting was the only way in which they wished to participate. Zaid, for example, said voting is important because it is "practicing your democracy" (27 February 2018). However, beyond that, he wanted to live his life "as far as possible from anything political" (Zaid 27 February 2018).

In addition to voting and engaging in a formal, institutionalized democratic process, three overlapping primary modes and sites of participation recurred in interviews. As Abdullah observed, for example, "I think the main thing that I can do is just to try to convince people not to vote for that person [who would harm others and to vote] for the other person" (14 January 2018). This observation touches on voting, but also on the first mode of participation I will explore: discussion, debate, and dialogue. Thereafter, I examine individuals volunteering with nonprofit and community initiatives engaged in the pursuit of various goals. Finally, I consider the 2017 travel ban and interviewees' interpretations of and, in some cases, participation in protests organized against that ban.

Participating in Discussion, Debate, and Conversation

Interviews examined whether and where interviewees engaged in discussion, dialogue, or debate about issues affecting their lives. Most individuals interacted with friends, family, or coworkers on such topics in various ways.

In many cases, discussion was informal, while in others they participated in activities sponsored by organizations in their communities.

Sarah, for example, said, "We talk about [government policies] a little. But not too much. [Primarily] at work, when on break" (30 November 2017). Mohammed and I discussed several contested issues in American politics at length, including healthcare provision and policy and the large student loan debt many Americans incur to attend college. He said that he speaks with friends of all backgrounds, fellow refugees and native-born Americans, about such issues and said that he "100 percent" had an equal right and ability to offer his views in such conversations.

In our exchange about sharing his views and experiences with others, Ahmed said that "sometimes I feel I have more than equal share" of space to do so "because sometimes people . . . want to listen to something different from . . . their perspective. Actually, I was given really more than enough share" (2 October 2017). For example, he explained that at a recent monthly office lunch, the subject of the 11 September 2001 terrorist attacks came up. When Ahmed began expressing his views, his coworkers focused their attention on him; "I was just telling them my experience," he said, "and instead of going around the table they just stopped, and they kept listening to me for the rest of the lunch. So, I think that was very considerate of them" (2 October 2017).

Despite interpreting his experiences as valued by colleagues, Ahmed voiced doubt about whether he had the right to try to persuade others to alter their views. Rather, he argued, it was the right of others to be exposed to new and different experiences and stories. As he put it: "If you never hear about things, you would only assume one certain way. So, it's your right to know the other stories, other people. So yes, I would say it's their right to hear me out. . . . Maybe they don't like my story, maybe they don't want stories about newcomers or they don't want to hear certain stories. But it's their right to hear it out and take whatever perspective they want to take" (Ahmed 2 October 2017)

Ahmed argued that this process requires listening as well as sharing your story, and there is no guarantee that it will be successful: "First of all, you need to listen to them. . . . Even if it's the most silly or stupid idea they have about the subject you are talking about, just listen to them. Try to talk sense into them. . . . And then, even if in the end you cannot change their views, you made them listen because you listened first. So, after that, you cannot do anything. You cannot force anyone to think in the same way you are thinking because who said you are right?" (2 October 2017)

As a newcomer, Ahmed suggested that it was important that he emphasize the positive aspects of life in the United States over its negative dimensions. Moreover, he argued, it was important to help Americans "understand that we don't all fit into one label. . . . The more they know about not only my story, my side of the story, but they know more about the partners in the community and how they are reacting to people. Maybe that would improve everything" (2 October 2017). "No society is perfect," he said, and learning from negative and positive experiences helps everyone, in his view.

"We are part of this community" in Chicago, Hashim observed; therefore, "for us, for everyone . . . we have to take care of others, to participate in setting up the rules and policies for that community" (1 October 2017). He explained how he viewed this role and his right to participate in doing so:

> I'm involved in everything. I'm involved with the daily challenges just like all the US communities face, so I think I can give my opinion exactly just like them. . . . Maybe three years is a short time for a new person to start giving their opinion and all of that, but I would say I have spent a lot of time reading policies, reviewing what . . . are my rights. . . . I mean we are part of this community, and we really want to keep this community growing and we really want this community to be better organized, safer for us. (Hashim 1 October 2017)

Returning to the example offered by Wissam, Omar, and Kasim in Chapter 3 about private gun ownership as an important issue in which they wished to engage, Wissam said, "I'm a newcomer," and as a result, Americans might react negatively to him offering a view on such a matter. They may say, "He just came here and he's trying to change my way of life" (22 October 2017). Indeed, gun ownership in the United States involves complex sets of "symbolic meanings that encompass personal identity, masculinity, power, freedom, racial attitudes, responsibility, morality, and views of governmental threat" (Boine et al. 2020, 7). Wissam continued: "So, in a way I also feel I don't have that right [to engage in discussions on topics such as gun control] to some extent because their ancestors were here before me, they fought for this country, I just came here and I'm trying to adapt" (22 October 2017).

Omar described how he had been involved with various discussions as a member and leader of a community organization, and I analyze that work in more detail in the following section. He offered two examples of the types of public dialogue the group had already organized or was planning for the future. In the first, the association members had held public discussions leading up to the 2016 election. Overall, Omar described those conversations as "very democratic" (14 December 2017). However, one member, originally from the Congo, left the group, concerned about what he perceived to be the character of its conversation. As Omar explained, "He didn't like the way we were debating, and he left the association. He thought that everyone in the association would definitely elect [Hillary] Clinton" (14 December 2017). Nonetheless, Omar refuted that perception, saying that every member of the group had a right to hold and express their views. Through later conversations, he and other participants learned of a specific policy that Clinton had supported concerning the Congo, prompting Congolese members to support Trump. "So, then I understood what happened," he noted, "and then the debate was very nice. . . . At the end, you get positive things" (Omar 14 December 2017).

In a second example, Omar described how one of his fellow organization coordinators, a white American, works part-time for the public transportation organization in the Shenandoah Valley Region. Omar's colleague told him that his fellow bus drivers "were talking about the immigrants, saying bad things. And he suggested to me that I should come and talk to them. I said, 'Well that's fine. I can'" (14 December 2017). Omar intended to do so, but at the time of our interview, he had not found the time to schedule that conversation. Such an event would be consistent with what he explained as the organization's ongoing project: "To go and listen to [members of the communities served], what are their issues. Trying to just listen, listen, listen. And then if there is an opportunity to try to explain or reveal anything that is maybe incorrect, by the media or other things. The ultimate goal is to have the city be welcoming for every immigrant" (Omar 14 December 2017).

Zaid spoke to the positive potential effects of dialogue as well. Even though he did not support Trump's election to the presidency, he viewed that outcome as a potential opportunity for American society. As he explained: "I'm okay with it. I think that having Trump as president is a very good thing to happen to the United States because there are issues. There are problems. People didn't really get the chance to talk about it, now they have the chance to talk about it. If you don't talk about it, it will never be on the table. It will never be discussed. It will never be solved" (Zaid 27 February 2018).[1] Democracy, Zaid went on to say, entails accepting other members of society and listening to a diversity of views, "I just want to show you my point of view. You want to show me your point of view. We are going to work on trying to meet in the middle, at least" (27 February 2018). As a result, "We don't have to agree on every single point, but at least we need to find a way to live and coexist with each other and live in harmony" (Zaid 27 February 2018). As Zaid argued, such processes might have a "rough period in the middle" (27 February 2018), but the outcome is likely to be a better collective future.

Speaking to Trump's election and policies as well, Ali described a local news interview with a young woman who came to New York as a refugee and lived near the location where we met. Ali related how she told the reporter that she disagreed with the travel ban and invited President Trump to her home to see what life is like for refugees: "It was a shock for me to hear from this . . . 19-year-old and she said that she would invite President Trump to come and visit us to see what refugees look like . . . and how they live" (14 January 2018). I asked Ali whether he would be willing to do the same and he laughed and said, "Sure. I'd love to. I would love to . . . convince him [to change his policies that harm refugees]" (14 January 2018).

Tariq, too, brought up the idea of inviting Trump to discuss the harm his policies had done to refugee communities. He argued that the policies Trump had enacted were "Creating . . . a tremendous amount of hate and killing us. . . . It's become a bigger and bigger issue" (Tariq 2 November 2017). Illustrating by way of analogy how to engage with Trump, Tariq said if he had a friend who was harming others, he would sit down with him to discuss why this was wrong, "Like my friend. I have a crazy friend. Doesn't mean he's bad. It's a crazy friend, that's it. I accepted it. He's my friend. But, when his decisions affect me, okay, stop. Come on. We got to sit and talk" (2 November 2017). And, in the case of Trump, Tariq observed, "your decisions hurt me and my family and many families. And, not one family, thousands of us" (2 November 2017).

For his part, Abdullah argued, "I think the greatest thing about the USA is the freedom of speech" (14 January 2018). He went on to say, "We don't actually have that in the Middle East. . . . People say we do. But, in reality, we don't actually" (Abdullah 14 January 2018). I understood this to be a reference to the post-2003 Iraqi constitutional guarantees to freedom of expression, press, and assembly (Associated Press 2005), but lack of substantive opportunities to put them into practice. As a US resident, Abdullah asserted that he was able to exercise his right to free speech anywhere in his community (New York City), "I could share my political views with anyone here . . . in conversation. . . . I don't feel threatened at all. Especially now, there is a lot of talk about the current president, and I could really say whatever I want" (14 January 2018). He argued that this right extended to himself as a resident, just as it did for citizens, "The only difference is on paper, and I cannot vote. But in terms of talking and sharing my ideas, no one has ever told me: 'You cannot say that because you aren't a citizen. You are not a citizen!' Never" (Abdullah 14 January 2018). Importantly, however, even though Abdullah has felt confident to express his views on US government policies, he said, "I feel that I don't have a say in [making those policies] because I don't have citizenship. So, I cannot vote. I cannot do anything" (14 January 2018). Moreover, despite being comfortable about speaking his mind, he explained: "I'm also careful with people who I talk with. Because sometimes you would talk with, I would say, ignorant people and you don't get anywhere from this conversation. So, I usually try to avoid talking [to those individuals]. I'm open to having a conversation with people who are willing to listen" (Abdullah 14 January 2018). A final caveat Abdullah brought up about his experience of exercising freedom of speech was the local context in which he lives: "Living here in New York is for sure, the place to do that [share his opinion]. I would imagine other places might be different" (14 January 2018).

Story Sharing

Several individuals framed sharing their stories as a discursive strategy that could potentially encourage others to shift their views of refugees. Nora, for example, had participated in public events to share her personal narrative to change negative perceptions. As she explained: "I mentioned my story in the university conferences. I went to [Virginia's capital] Richmond to the mental health conference. . . . I started going and talking, telling audiences it's not what you see on the news. . . . I was persecuted by both ISIS and the government, so that means I am [not] a terrorist" (Nora 6 February 2018).

Describing how he might make a positive change in his community, Ahmed said, "For me, it's making people just look at the glass half full, positive vibes, giving them real-life examples" and "sharing stories" (2 October 2017). This approach can influence those who hear these examples, he argued, "Because for me, I always think if you see a face and if you [hear] a story that would stick with you more" (Ahmed 2 October 2017). In elaborating how story sharing can lead to change, he went on to say:

> Let's take the travel ban, for example, and if you tell them I know this person with a name, he or she was affected by this travel ban and they were separated from their family, and for example, they both supported the US Army or the government, why are you doing that? If you keep telling that story, you can utilize social media, you can reach out to groups that support your cause. You can go to local authorities like the [Chicago City Council] alderman or someone within your state or city and write to them. . . . Maybe they can reach out actually to a wider audience that would help you. (Ahmed 2 October 2017)

For Ali, an aspect of his job is to speak with clients, largely immigrants and refugees from the Middle East and North Africa, and to gather their stories and help to disseminate them widely: "We can put them on media. Getting them interviewed. So, people will know the reality of refugees living in the United States. Their stories, they are normal people. They have families. They have a lot of responsibilities. The same, just like here. And it's doing a lot of good" (14 January 2018). The nonprofit organization for which Ali works also hosts a blog on which its staff post stories from clients about, among other things, their experiences as immigrants.

Although not part of his duties at the car dealership where he worked, Tariq suggested that sharing his personal story with his customers and coworkers is his "second job" and that he engages in that role daily. He does so:

Sometimes with nice people . . . they're nice, so I share it with them. . . . And then, the other group that, when I see them, you can tell from their reactions they know that you are a . . . foreigner. From your accent. And I tell them too. But when I tell them, I tell them the strong story. . . . This is why I'm here and why I came here, and this is what my expectation was and that [it was not met]. And then they are surprised, "Oh yeah, we didn't know that." (Tariq 2 November 2017)

He said that he considers it a success when his experiences provide new information for clients and prompt them to reconsider their views of refugees and the difficulties of the resettlement process.

Sarah, too, spoke about sharing her experiences with others and the importance of doing so: "It's important when I told some people [about my experiences] because some people don't care about this subject. I think it's good for me to tell these people about my experiences in my country and Syria and here in America. Maybe, some people will learn from me. Maybe, some people will discuss with me some of the questions you asked me. Maybe, when he asks me some questions, my answers will be useful to him. I think yes, I think also it's important to discuss these issues with the American people" (30 November 2017).

Limits of Discourse

Engaging in democratic deliberation is difficult. Even with intentional processes and mechanisms in place, fruitful deliberation in which everyone can participate presents a range of challenges (Guttman 2007). In addition to the possibilities and value of discussion and deliberation, several interviewees pointed out the limits to this form of democratic engagement. Ahmed, for example, discussed the need to avoid "alienating" those with whom you are interacting by ensuring conversations remain focused on issues and do not "get personal" (2 October 2017). As he put it: "If you alienate the person in front of you, that's it. You lost the discussion. . . . Even if they are not hostile, they will never come back and listen to you" (Ahmed 2 October 2017). Ahmed contended, "In the end, if they still cannot agree with me, that's fine. . . . The aim is not making them 100 percent agree with me, but the aim is to have a conversation, open their mind to my beliefs and my ideas and open my mind to their ideas and their beliefs. No one knows everything" (2 October 2017).

Wissam highlighted the challenge of securing "fruitful conversations" (22 October 2017). In his view, there is always a risk that certain participants will dominate a discussion, causing others to acquiesce to their position or perspective: "There are certain things here people discuss, . . . maybe a point of view, but it's not really valid. And they keep spending hours and hours on it so they can distract you from the main goal of the discussion.

And that will exhaust people and they just want to say, 'Okay let's just do that, this is never going to end'" (Wissam 22 October 2017). Determining what are legitimate or important topics for discussion is difficult, he said: "Because you don't want to shut everybody out and say: 'Shut up! I know what I'm doing, let's go with it.' But, it's between getting a fruitful conversation and wasteful conversation. It's very hard to balance between those. So, I don't know" (Wissam 22 October 2017).

Concluding this point, he laughingly said, "It's the government's job to figure out, not mine" (Wissam 22 October 2017). Wissam continued on the topic of discourse and dialogue, identifying the "paradox of tolerance" (Popper 1947, 226) as a particular challenge to the exercise of speech. He explained by way of an extended example an area in which it seemed to him that speech *should* be limited for the safety of others and in which expression violates the basic principles that American democracy claims to uphold and defend. As he explained:

> There are things that I can't really understand. For example, with the citizenship exam, they ask you were you a member of the Nazi regime.[2] At the same time, you see . . . what happened in Charlottesville [Virginia],[3] they're wearing all the swastikas and they are having conventions, things like that. . . . I know it's their right, but there must be a limit to that. . . . There shouldn't be a freedom to oppress people, to kill people, things like that. This is not freedom. This is like a lunatic. (Wissam 22 October 2017)

Wissam gave another example of a public event planned by well-known white supremacist and neo-Nazi Richard Spencer at the University of Florida in early 2017 (Levenson 2017). Students organized protests in response to the event, intending to prevent Spencer from giving a speech. "So," he noted, "There are a lot of contradictions. So, why do you ask people not to belong to these parties at the same time you allow people to have conventions, seminars and talk about [such ideas]? These kinds of things make you think, 'What's going on?'" (Wissam 22 October 2017).

Wissam opined that a large university like the University of Florida should not allow individuals or groups to have a platform to speak about white supremacy. In his view: "These things should be a matter of the past. I mean America fought a lot for that, they lost lots, hundreds and hundreds of soldiers, for that and now these people just come and speak about it. That doesn't make sense" (Wissam 22 October 2017).

Strategic Silence

Another concern this study explored in-depth was contexts that interviewees perceived as difficult, unproductive, or dangerous in which to share their views or opinions. In such cases, several individuals described how engaging in *strategic silence*–choosing not to engage in dialogue or debate– can be prudent and is itself an agentic choice and act. As Ahmed explained, since coming to the United States, he had "not yet" encountered a situation in which he kept his views to himself. However, in Iraq, he had routinely done so. Echoing Marwa's comment in Chapter 3 concerning the dangers of expressing opinions about the Saddam Hussein government, even in the apparent privacy of one's own home, Ahmed said, "You used to be silent because that's a way you can express yourself about certain subjects.... It is a tool you can use. Sometimes you better just say nothing" (2 October 2017). In his view, freedom of speech protections in the United States allowed individuals to "say whatever you want, as long as you are not offending people" (Ahmed 2 October 2017). However, choosing not to engage may be better "if you think maybe that someone will be impacted negatively," he said (Ahmed 2 October 2017). Another context in which keeping one's opinions to oneself may be prudent, according to Ahmed, is when "there is a safety issue, although I have never experienced this so far.... If you will be personally harmed, then it would be better to find a better occasion to speak about the issues you want to speak about" (2 October 2017). Tariq, too, explained that although he regularly shares his personal story with his clients, he also often withholds his views, "Oh yeah. A lot ... of the time, I just avoid that" (2 November 2017). But, he continued, that "doesn't mean that I'm going to say nothing whatsoever. No. I will say it later" (Tariq 2 November 2017).

For his part, Abdullah noted, "If I am seeing someone who is saying extremely racist things, I really don't see the point of talking to them" (14 January 2018). In such a case, "I just try to ignore it and then I hope that person will wake up" (Abdullah 14 January 2018). For example, Abdullah related a situation in which a stranger shouted at his friend on the New York City subway. The man yelled disparaging remarks about Islam and about individuals from the Middle East. Abdullah noted that his friend is also Iraqi, but is Christian, not Muslim. He attributed this incident more to the individual's mental state rather than to prejudice. He did not take the encounter personally because the person began harassing other passengers when Abdullah and his friend ignored him.

Another topical area that Abdullah said he avoids discussing on social media is politics. Although, as described above, he argued that it was his right, he often has chosen not to do so: "Because it really creates problems.... People back home, we have different sects and if you say something people will take the wrong way.... So, we end up losing friends if you share your political views about stuff back home, which is sad.... So, I try to avoid that so I don't, you know, lose people" (Abdullah 14 January 2018).

Nonetheless, Abdullah said that if he sees a post on social media about "something that is wrong" he will engage with it. For example, Abdullah said that if someone expresses a racist sentiment or if they are "attacking a certain sect or certain religion, I have to say something, and I usually do" (14 January 2018). As I explore in more detail below, Walid similarly explained that in his work with members of the refugee communities in Upstate New York, it can be better to avoid discussing certain sensitive topics in order, first, to build sustainable relationships.

Zaid expressed unease about discussing political subjects with anyone other than friends or family, "It's not that I don't feel safe. This is a big word. But I don't feel really comfortable discussing these ideas with people I don't know.... I would rather keep these discussions with the people that I know" (27 February 2018). For example, as we sat down for our interview, he received a phone call from a friend who had voted for Trump. He said, "I have no problem with that. I know this person. I know his background. I feel safe discussing these things with him" (Zaid 27 February 2018). "For example," he observed with a laugh, "When Trump suggested that he wants to give weapons to teachers to protect the kids, I just asked him: 'Okay, so are you happy with your president now?' But I don't really feel comfortable discussing these things with people I don't know" (Zaid 27 February 2018).[4] When I asked whether he would consider attending a public event or discussion on such a topic he responded, "Never."

During our interview, Nada chose to remain silent on the topic of US government policies. She said that she was comfortable sharing her views and opinions about life in the United States with Americans, Iraqis, and others in her life. However, when I asked her whether she would feel secure discussing her views concerning explicitly political issues, such as her perspective on President Trump, she laughed and responded that it was a "difficult question." Elaborating her answer, she suggested: "Anyone when he hurts another person, he deserves to be punished. And this, this is what our God said. Anyone. From any religion. From any country. This is the rule for our life. I will just say that. And you understand me, of course" (Nada 1 November 2017).

I attempted to clarify if she meant that if a president were doing something wrong, they should be punished for hurting others. She laughed and said, "I don't know. I don't know. Pass" (Nada 1 November 2017). Considering our full conversation, I understood her to mean that she disagreed with some of Trump's policies and that he ultimately would face punishment for those actions. However, she chose not to make that point explicitly.

Finally, Mohammed related a story about a time when, after remaining silent, he had decided to speak his mind. To improve his English language skills, Mohammed had enrolled in English as a second language (ESL) classes at a community college in Upstate New York. He described the course instructor as having "some issues with the refugees.... I was very careful to talk with him because I know he's a little bit racist" (Mohammed

2 November 2017). However, when his teacher spoke about the war in Iraq and its consequences, without–in Mohammed's view–sufficient knowledge or understanding, he confronted him. When his instructor said, "We helped the people in Iraq," Mohammed refuted that claim, saying: "No. Listen to me, I don't want to talk about politics . . . but really, Saddam Hussein was a bad guy, I know that. And he was a dictator, 100 percent. But, when he was deposed, we now have 100 dictators in Iraq, the same thing. . . . I don't know which democracy you are talking about, which freedom. We don't have freedom. . . . We have a mafia right now in our government in Iraq" (2 November 2017). Mohammed interpreted that his instructor held this discussion against him saying, "And this is the point I failed in the class. He didn't like me, and I changed my class finally and I passed it. . . . He didn't accept my opinion. But he started to ask me about my opinion, and I told him my opinion" (2 November 2017).

Community Engagement: Volunteering and Nonprofit Organizations

Moving from discussion and dialogue, civil society organizations constituted the second primary site and mode of engagement for interviewees. Some individuals, such as Mohammad and Wissam, volunteered with nonprofit organizations. Others, including Ahmed and Ali, worked for such organizations, and still others, including Walid and Omar, had founded their own. Interviewees engaged in a range of activities with those entities, such as providing services to other refugees and immigrants, building knowledge and awareness of US law and institutions, creating bonds among diverse members of their communities, and participating in discussions and dialogue. As described by Nora, Ali, and Omar, such organizations and activities served, in many cases, as spaces to inculcate and expand robust norms of belonging, diversity, and understanding among individuals of different backgrounds.

In Chicago, for example, Wissam has served as a board member for an organization working with immigrants from the Middle East and was, at one time, the chair of that group. Recalling the discussion in Chapter 3 about time constraints as a barrier to engagement, Wissam reported with a laugh, "I'm still on the Advisory Council, but I couldn't keep up because I have to do like ten hours a week. It was very demanding. So, I couldn't" (22 October 2017). The nonprofit provides services such as job placement, assistance applying for Green Cards, citizenship exam preparation, parenting programs, and Arabic classes.

Ahmed works full-time for another nonprofit that serves immigrant communities in Chicago. When I asked him whether he would like to become involved outside of work with other activities, he said, "I think yes. If I care for the cause, if the cause is close to heart . . . especially if in the end this would help spread the cause in a different part of the society" (Ahmed 2 October 2017). Elaborating on what sorts of issues these might be, he said that a coworker had asked him if he would be willing to speak at a high school located on Chicago's Southside to bring new and different perspectives to the school's students. Ahmed's coworker thought of him because of his Iraqi background. Ahmed referenced the term "Chiraq," a portmanteau of Chicago and Iraq, as a reason his colleague thought Southside students might respond to his experiences. This contested neologism purports to describe a level of violence experienced by Chicago residents equal to, or greater than, that of Iraq after 2003 (Williams-Harris, Ford, and Crepeau 2015). Ahmed had spoken with those Southside students when we met and described it as a positive experience and an example of an activity in which he would like to engage again.

Omar began our discussion on volunteering by explaining why he had become involved in many activities in the Shenandoah Valley Region. He said there was a "will inside . . . to show to this community . . . you have kind of an obligation . . . because every single person from the community represents me. And I also represent him. So, if you did bad, that will influence me. If I did good, that will influence him. So, yeah. That's the reason. Being a volunteer in different things, in different places. Volunteering everywhere" (Omar 14 December 2017).

When he first settled in Virginia, Omar and several other individuals created a volunteer group to welcome newly arrived refugees at the airport, organize transportation to their homes, prepare meals for them, and provide translation. This work was carried out via a formal agreement with the local resettlement agency. The group engaged in this work for several years, leading to a program to create the first Arabic translation of the Virginia Department of Motor Vehicles (DMV) driving exam booklet. This group also provided Arabic classes for children in cooperation with a municipal community center.

Omar went on to describe the process of founding several other initiatives in the area, "I started to form a group and after one or two years that group vanished or reformatted into another group. . . . The aim was to help the refugees and to make them productive members [of the community]" (14 December 2017). The organization undertook surveys of residents to advocate for them more effectively. Among the activities held, were public events for immigrants to discuss elections and the pros and cons of candidates and government policies. Omar stressed that in such discussions: "We had a lot of perspectives. . . . Some, they were [in favor of] electing Trump, for example. Some were against. And we took that in a freedom way and in a [democratic] way that each can express and is not prevented from [disagreeing]" (14 December 2017). As an organization comprised of members of various immigrant and refugee populations, they also meet with local government representatives to put forward plans and ideas for their communities.

Omar described a focus of his work as uniting communities, "That's strength. If I'm [a member of the] Iraqi community, maybe working alone will not give me power or my voice will not be heard by others" (14 December 2017). However, he argued, "if I have other communities working together and supporting each other" (Omar 14 December 2017), they can create a base of support. For example, if the Iraqi community is targeted by another group or government authorities, "standing as one" (Omar 14 December 2017) with other immigrant or refugee communities will provide a basis from which to organize.

Nora has volunteered with Omar and been active in the projects described above, among many other activities, including working part-time for a resettlement agency in her city in Virginia. The organizations she is active with offer classes to prepare immigrants for the US citizenship exam, advocacy concerning such issues as child migrants and family separation, classes designed specifically to support women, and driving lessons and assistance navigating public transportation in the area. As described in the previous section, part of her work includes public engagement, and Nora has spoken about her life at conferences in several parts of Virginia.

Nora also described efforts that several community groups in the Shenandoah Valley Region had taken to create a welcoming, multicultural environment for the city's residents. For example, her local school system has recognized Spanish, Arabic, Kurdish, and Russian languages and certain schools in the district cater specifically to Russian and Arabic speakers. Omar had helped establish the Arabic language school, an accomplishment Nora called a "big step forward." Her city is "getting more open. People are starting to realize that there are different communities in the area," she observed (Nora 6 February 2018). Aligning with the cooperation between local churches and community groups noted by Omar in Chapter 3, Nora suggested, "the churches are doing an amazing job here with the community with the growing difference and highlighting what those differences are" (6 February 2018).

Walid shared, "I feel I have a responsibility . . . to do something for the community" (27 September 2017). As a result, he is very active in Upstate New York, founding and serving as chair of an Iraqi and Arab immigrant-serving nonprofit organization in Western New York. That organization provides services such as ESL and case management to teach parenting skills, for example. Walid described the organization's mission as building leadership skills for those with whom it worked. At the time of our interview, he was also serving as president of a local coalition with the goal of "empowering refugees, not only Iraqis but all of the communities that came from different parts of the world" (Walid 27 September 2017). He described the group's work this way:

> We work on different levels. On, education, public safety, immigration issues, ... housing, employment, so we try to address ... major issues for refugees in general including Iraqis. ... Each community has unique problems. For example, when we come to people from the Middle East, ... there's a lot of background checks and suspicion about where they come from, how long they've been in the Middle East, who are their friends. So, it's not easy to get the Green Card or become a US citizen. ... So, each community they do have a problem. It just depends on where they come from and the culture, on education, on where they live. (Walid 27 September 2017)

Walid also contended that "the empowerment part is making a big difference for participants to understand" their rights (27 September 2017). In his view, the process of understanding and exercising rights is part of practicing democracy. For example, Walid described how members of his community group approached the mayor's office of his city to create a "language line" for non–English speakers to call in case of emergencies. They based their petition on federal law mandating interpreter access for non–English speaking residents. They enlisted the help of lawyers to demonstrate that lack of such a line violated the law. Group members met with the mayor and city council members to discuss this issue. They were successful and were able to push the municipal government to set up the line. The city police department also hired a community liaison and began providing language services.

Walid is also active in a yearly event celebrating his area's immigrant communities. At the time of our interview, he and others were planning the 2018 program, and he invited me to attend their organizing meeting. He described several others similarly involved, some of whom are native-born Americans, as "very passionate about international issues. ... They love people from different backgrounds, so they attend our meetings because of their interest to support the event" (Walid 27 September 2017). For Walid, planning this occasion is "part of changing American culture." As he explained, to do so, "We invite twelve teams from different ethnicities, from different backgrounds, from the refugee community and immigrants. We cook food. ... It's open to the public in a local park which is close to here. ... We invite elected officials, we invite the community, we announce through the media ... to show them our culture, to show them folklore dancing, traditions and also try to break this kind of stereotyping about unknown people. I know you are scared of these people, but it's good to talk with them to know who they are, which reduces their fear" (Walid 27 September 2017).

Walid pointed out that the city he lives in is a divided city with significant segregation between residents of different racial backgrounds. When he moved there in 2008, his goal was to "bring the entire community together and also to invite the American people who have some concerns to build friendship and relationships with people [from different backgrounds] so at least they have no fear" (Walid 27 September 2017). However, sustained activism is difficult, in Walid's estimation, "There are a lot of activists in different communities, but . . . there is no support. . . . I found many leaders and activists who help one year, two years, and feel frustrated [because there are] not enough support" (27 September 2017) programs for resettled refugees. The lack of financial resources, language training, and access to other services leads many to turn away from public engagement and say, "Let's focus on our families" (Walid 27 September 2017). Organizing community members is particularly challenging in refugee communities, in Walid's view, because of existing tensions among members. For example, Walid reported, those from countries experiencing civil wars may be uncomfortable working with individuals who were on opposing sides of those conflicts.

By way of example, he explained how he had met with a Kurdish Syrian family and had to steer the conversation away from religion, politics, and Kurdish independence from Iraq. "Let's put politics or religion aside," he suggested, "I know you agree or disagree. Because if we talk about religion or politics, we won't be friends. We have different opinions about that. . . . So, some people they became very isolated because of these things" (Walid 27 September 2017). Therefore, he proposed, "Let's focus on the family, kids, . . . school, education, how to be successful here, how to benefit from this opportunity, being in this country" (Walid 27 September 2017).

Marwa worked with Walid to help establish the immigrant-serving nonprofit organization in Upstate New York, an entity with which Mohammed also volunteers. The organization had been operating for approximately four years at the time of our interview in November 2017. Marwa was particularly involved with the nonprofit's women's empowerment programming: "We do many events for the women. [For example], how to raise your kids here. How to get your necessary [immigration documents]. How to be independent. How to have power in your family. How to support your family and how to be involved with the community" (25 November 2017).

The nonprofit's events, often facilitated in both English and Arabic, may draw between 100 and 150 participants. According to Marwa, "My community, they are growing now. They are a huge number. Also, not just Iraqi. Now we make it for all Arabic speakers. Like Syrians, anyone. Not just Iraqis now" (25 November 2017). Marwa's nonprofit organization extends invitations to local government officials to give talks on various subjects as well. As a volunteer, she has shared her contact information with local police in case community members have questions or concerns or need an interpreter. Her organization also holds events to celebrate holidays such as Ramadan, inviting residents to share communal meals, discuss issues they may be having, and offer assistance. They provide Arabic classes for children as well.

Ali stressed the importance of working together with diverse others in his community in New York City during our conversation. To that end, he had participated at the time of our interview for four years in a row in the Brooklyn International Day of Friendship events, recruiting volunteers for that festival. The annual gathering is a major facet of then–Brooklyn borough president Eric Adams's "Embrace Your Hyphen" campaign, which seeks to encourage residents to celebrate and learn more about the diversity of individuals living in the community (Leonhardt 2018). The 2018 International Day of Friendship, which Ali was helping to prepare at the time of our interview, included a "Unity Parade of Flags" on a main Brooklyn thoroughfare, cultural events featuring traditional dance and music from Panama and Tahiti, and a "Global Village" of "tents from countries around the world showcasing their cultures, cuisines and customs" (Leonhardt 2018).

In his full-time job for an Arab American–serving nonprofit, Ali works closely with the borough president's office as he conducts outreach to Arab American and refugee communities in the New York area. He also works to educate donors who, in his view, are often misinformed about the level of support refugees receive for resettlement. "The problem is," he said, "Most of them they think the refugees when they come here the government pays everything for them. But, in reality, they are already in debt. When they were in another country, not their mother country, seeking refuge or asylum, they spent their last penny over there and then when they come to the United States, they face this challenge to pay their airfare. . . . So, it's a lot. They are already in debt" (Ali 14 January 2018).[5]

Nada works for a different Arab American–serving nonprofit in New York City that provides training on various topics as well as undertakes advocacy trips to the New York State capital, Albany, and to Washington, DC. The organization places particular focus on issues Muslim women face in the United States and women's rights more broadly. Women "want to know their rights. It's very important because they want to protect themselves. This is good for us," Nada said (1 November 2017). She said that in Iraq, unlike in other countries in the Middle East, she had rights as a woman, and "My family gave me my rights and my husband is good. We don't have any problems in our . . . family or my country" (Nada 1 November 2017). However, she went on, "always, I think I need to know the rights here. Of course, not just as a woman, everybody should know their rights here. How they can protect them. How they can protect their kids. This is the most important. And . . . I'm learning that from my association" (Nada 1 November 2017). Nada was engaged in teaching others about their rights, while simultaneously seeking to build such knowledge herself.

No Ban, No Wall: Pro-refugee Protests Invoke Norms of Welcoming and Support

After speaking of Muslims and refugees as dangerous and irrational during his campaign, newly elected President Trump moved almost immediately to enact policies to prevent immigrants and refugees, particularly those from Muslim-majority countries, from entering the United States. On 27 January 2017, seven days after his inauguration, Trump signed Executive Order 13769, which sought to lower overall refugee resettlement to the United States in the long-term, to suspend all such admissions for 120 days, and to block new entry into the United States by individuals from seven countries: Iran, Iraq, Libya, Somalia, Sudan, Syria, and Yemen (Hersher 2017), all of which have Muslim-majority populations. This fact, and Trump's pledge to ban Muslims from entering the country while campaigning (Johnson 2015), prompted many opposed to the policy to frame the executive order as a Muslim ban (BBC 2017). As noted in Chapter 2, several thousand individuals were detained at airports upon arriving in the United States, some for multiple days, immediately upon the order's initial implementation (Cheng 2017). The US State Department denied thirty-seven thousand visa applications in 2018 as a result of the executive order (Torbati 2019).

The ban sparked immediate protests, with thousands occupying major airports such as John F. Kennedy (JFK) in New York City and gathering in large numbers in squares, parks, and other public spaces in many cities around the country. A common slogan of these protests was "No Ban, No Wall," linking opposition to the travel ban to another Trump anti-immigrant policy of expanding and further militarizing a partially constructed border wall located along the Mexico-US border (Rodgers and Bailey 2019). The American Civil Liberties Union launched a legal challenge to the ban, and a federal judge temporarily ordered a stay against the action (Hersher 2017). On 6 March 2017, Trump issued a superseding executive order, 13780, removing Iraq and Sudan from the list of targeted nations, after intense diplomatic pressure and negotiations with those governments (K. Liptak 2017). He added North Korea and Venezuela to replace those countries. At the time of interviews, the final status and legality of the ban were uncertain. However, in June 2018, the US Supreme Court upheld its constitutionality (Totenberg and Montanaro 2018). When Joe Biden assumed the presidency in 2021, he signed an executive order reversing the ban; however, the harm that this policy caused was fresh and salient at the time of the interviews.

The ban created increased precarity and uncertainty for those refugees already in the United States, as I turn now to explore. For some, including

Abdullah, Ali, Nora, and Ahmed, the pro-refugee responses to the executive orders, such as protests in airports and marches in city squares, were significant. They indicated a type of welcoming from native-born Americans toward refugees—particularly those from the Middle East—that these interviewees found new and meaningful. Those actions entailed a significant invocation and mobilization of norms by many Americans, such as welcoming newcomers, diversity, and openness to difference.

Only one individual with whom I spoke, Kasim, remarked that the travel ban was unimportant. At the time of our interview, Iraq had already been removed from the list of banned countries. Kasim dismissed the ban with a shrug, saying it "doesn't affect Iraqis and I have all my family here" (27 February 2018). He went on to say, "I mean, I understand [Trump's] point of view. But he's doing this for show" (Kasim 27 February 2018). Because, he argued, "Obama's administration did their best to vet everybody who comes in. Trump can't put any more security measures. But he's just saying that. I don't think it's applicable. The law is the law. You have to go by the book, and he cannot do anything to change the process. I mean, they did their best, Obama's administration, what can you add? It's just, he's trying to get more publicity and votes" (Kasim 27 February 2018).

All of the other interviewees who spoke about the ban viewed it as having consequences for themselves, their families, and others in their communities. For example, Tariq responded to Trump's action with incredulity. He called the initial decision to include Iraq on the banned country list "crazy," and observed, "We are the only country fighting ISIS. And you banned us? That doesn't make sense" (Tariq 2 November 2017). He then put it in personal terms, saying, "I served with the US Marines. He [Trump] didn't serve in his life. I served with your Marines, and I got the death threat, and I was forced to leave the country. And you ban me from coming? It doesn't make sense" (Tariq 2 November 2017).

Tariq paraphrased the US military's "Soldier's Creed" (Rawlings 2012) "leave no one behind" principle to support his argument against the Trump travel ban. As he put it: "We don't leave anybody behind, and this is our rule in the military. . . . This is what I learned from US Marines. We can't leave anybody behind. We got to get them, no matter what. And now you leave these people like me? Before, we put my life and my family's life in danger. I had death threats. They came to my house" (Tariq 2 November 2017). To reiterate his point, Tariq asked rhetorically if Trump faced death threats because he had worked as an interpreter with US Marines, would he support a policy that put him and his family at risk? The self-evident answer for Tariq was no.[6]

Whereas Tariq spoke about the danger the executive order potentially created for those still living in Iraq, others, including Abdullah, spoke about the precarity it created for their lives in the United States. Before the executive order was signed, Abdullah suggested: "I felt I'm protected. . . . I have rights. This country believes in human rights and I'm staying here. Finally, something good, you know? And then, he came up with that order and I felt that my rights got stripped away from me" (14 January 2018). Trump banned "seven countries and I was from one of those countries," Abdullah said, "I really felt that I was going to be kicked out. When I heard of it, I did not even leave my place. I stayed in my room. I was so depressed, stressed, I was like, I don't know what to do and I felt unsafe" (14 January 2018).

However, the efforts by many Americans to oppose the ban began to ameliorate some of Abdullah's fears. Soon after its initial enactment, "American friends started texting me," he noted, "they are trying to come up with a solution. It was like, 'We are there for you if you need anything'" (Abdullah 14 January 2018). After that, Abdullah began to see groups of people in New York City creating social media campaigns and organizing protests in Battery Park and at JFK Airport. *CBS New York* reported that ten thousand protesters participated in a rally and march opposing the ban held at Battery Park in lower Manhattan. US senators for New York, Chuck Schumer and Kirsten Gillibrand attended along with New Jersey senator Corey Booker and New York mayor Bill de Blasio (Falzon 2017). "They started protests," Abdullah said, "So, I felt these people, they made me like so much safer" (14 January 2018).

These protests, as Abdullah understood it, had "pushed people, certain judges . . . to make the right decisions for this country" (14 January 2018) and at least to temporarily block the ban from taking effect. He compared these rallies to earlier resistance movements, such as the large-scale marches organized against the 2003 Iraq War, noted in Chapter 1. As he said, "I don't know of any other protest that had this direct effect. I have heard there were some protests against the war in Iraq, but they didn't change anything. But that specific one [against the travel ban], it actually changed something" (Abdullah 14 January 2018). Before the protests in reaction to the travel ban, Abdullah was not involved in any political or activist activities. However, Trump's action pushed him to become engaged in such efforts. As he put it: "I contacted some people, and they were at JFK airport because there were a lot of people who were held at JFK. And they were asking for translators. So, I contacted some of my friends [to tell them] people need translators: 'Are you guys willing to go to JFK?' All of them said, 'Yeah, of course.' And then we were going to go. But then, by the time I wanted to put my name, there were a lot of people who were already signed up for this" (Abdullah 14 January 2018).

While he had been willing to provide translation, Abdullah said: "I didn't feel safe to go and protest, because anything could go wrong, I could get picked up. They could deport me" (14 January 2018). However, "there were a lot of Americans, really good Americans, who stood up for us and protected us. That was so beautiful to see" (Abdullah 14 January 2018).

Like Abdullah, Ali witnessed the protests against the ban unfold in New York City. He viewed the executive order unambiguously as a "Muslim ban," saying, "I cried when I saw the ban, my first response" (Ali 14 January 2018). He went on to say the "Trump administration, I don't know what he is going to do, the next step, to be honest with you. . . . It's hard when you think about that. Like, it's not only me. It's a lot of people in the community. And I'm listening and I'm hearing they are in fear" (Ali 14 January 2018). This fear for Ali was based on material impacts the ban had already had on those he knew. For example, he reported, "When the ban happened, the first one. I have a friend he's a citizen. Country of birth: Iraq. They didn't allow him to enter the United States. And then there were lawyers and . . . the ban was blocked" (Ali 14 January 2018).

However, in response to the ban, the first who went out to the airports and to squares to protest, Ali noted, "were Americans and they were born here. And they work in, some of them, in government, they work . . . a lot of places. The first response, they went" (14 January 2018). The fact that so many native-born Americans went out to protest was significant for Ali, who said, "I cried when I saw this scene in front of me" (14 January 2018). He described the effect of this response in the following way: "The Arab people now have this courage, come, like we [Americans] are protecting you. Just come, go out, let's be hand in hand. And I went to the airport at that time to give translation service, whatever. And, it was a huge thing for me" (Ali 14 January 2018).

The fact that government officials attended the protests was meaningful for Ali as well. "I love New York. I love the government of New York," Ali told me: "I love what they are doing because they are working not for only a specific community. Not only for a specific religion. They are working for all as Americans. . . . Let's have the federal government [do the same], just like the New York government" (14 January 2018). The government should "protect the American people," he argued, "not divide the American people" (Ali 14 January 2018).

Nora described how, after the executive order was signed, a protest in her city's downtown area drew a large crowd of several hundred residents. According to Nora, protestors gathered with signs, some expressing "welcome" in multiple languages. "I was there," Nora declared, "and it was very emotional" (6 February 2018). Several of her friends also attended and one, who is the leader of a local activist group, spoke to the crowd. As she explained, in addition to the initial protest, local organizations planned events for immigrants in the area: "People had come from all different nationalities just to say that we're welcome and then we started running around the court square and having all these signs with us. Then, there was another parade and there was a community session from the refugee office. . . . So, there was plenty of stuff happening just to make people feel welcome" (Nora 6 February 2018).

Nora also saw local residents come to the resettlement office where she works and inquire about volunteering because of the ban. The new volunteers asked how they could "support families so they don't feel they are alone because of the ban" (Nora 6 February 2018). These responses gave Nora a sense of belonging, she said, and she interpreted the protests and outreach as Americans saying, "Trump doesn't represent me, I welcome you in here. . . . We're here for you. We support you, we're completely with you" (6 February 2018). She compared this sentiment to refugees/Iraqis/Muslims asserting that extremists or terrorists do not represent them. Nora repeated that strangers had no obligation to go out of their way to show their support for refugees, and yet they had done so after Trump issued his executive order. In addition to receiving supportive reactions from other members of the community, after the ban was signed, Nora and Omar organized and held a "know your rights" workshop for immigrants residing in the area. This event covered topics such as what to do if you are approached by the police or ICE agents, when to contact a lawyer, and what support services are available.

Walid reported that, in Upstate New York, "when the ban happened . . . we saw a lot of people in this park [where we held our interview]. They came marching and supporting refugees" (27 September 2017). Many of the protesters were Americans, according to Walid: "It was a huge number of Americans talking about the ban, which made me feel really happy to see the democracy and the people who don't agree about the . . . injustice or [policies] that harm other people. . . . Really, I felt proud about this society that cares about unknown people or a refugee or an immigrant and they want to get justice" (27 September 2017).

Ahmed opposed the ban, although he said there could be an alternative way to "implement and improve" vetting potential refugees to prevent abuse of the system. When the president issued the order, his colleague called to check on him. "How do you feel?" his coworker had asked, to which Ahmed had replied, "I really feel wonderful. . . . And I said I feel wonderful for two reasons: One I have never seen support for the country I came from, or even the region, from American people like this. And second, I have never seen the power of the people like this in my life" (2 October 2017).

He went on to say that "you get accustomed, especially after all the events in the last twenty years that happened, you get a certain stereotyped image about the Middle East" (Ahmed 2 October 2017). "So," he continued, "when you see someone go and block three major airports in the nation . . . protesting [in support of those who have been negatively stereotyped] against the ultimate power in the country. . . . I have never seen such support" (Ahmed 2 October 2017). The potential for such protests to exercise the "will of the people," in Ahmed's words, was "one of the reasons why this country is great" (2 October 2017). Without the freedom of speech protections enshrined in the Constitution and law, Americans "would not be able to go to the airport to protest," he said (Ahmed 2 October 2017).

Finally, Zaid interpreted Trump's election in similar terms to Ahmed's view of the travel ban. He characterized Trump's policies as "radical," "extreme," and "racist." However, "To be honest," he said with a laugh, "it's not that I felt happy that he won. But I felt kind of relaxed. I felt kind of comfortable knowing that there are so many, the majority of people are against these ideas, and they are fighting on our behalf" (Zaid 27 February 2018). The fact that the majority of Americans rejected Trump's racist views and policies was important to Zaid because, "just as I told you earlier," he said, "I can't really say what's on my mind any time or anywhere I want. So, I'm so happy that I have this privilege that there are so many people who are like fighting this fight, this war for me" (27 February 2018).

Conclusion

This chapter has explored the various activities in which interviewees engaged to participate in their communities. Many of those with whom I spoke sought opportunities to discuss issues they found important with their friends, families, and colleagues. In some cases, this effort meant putting forward their personal stories and narratives to challenge negative perceptions held by a significant percentage of Americans concerning refugees, Iraqis, Muslims, and Arabs. As several interviewees pointed out, to have productive discussions and interactions that hold the potential to change views, reciprocal listening is important. As Ahmed and Omar similarly observed, to change beliefs and values, one must be willing to hear others' views and attempt to understand their perspectives, with the expectation that they will do the same. This mutuality can entail, as Tariq and Ali described, engaging with individuals with whom one fundamentally disagrees and who may actively be harming you.

Importantly, as Wissam argued, there may be limits to the degree to which one can participate in dialogue with individuals who harbor views that are counter to fundamental democratic norms. One cannot necessarily engage in dialogue with individuals, such as white supremacists and neo-Nazis, who espouse hate and support violence against particular groups within society. A fundamental precondition to engaging in dialogue with others is the assumption, implicit or explicit, that, because they are human, all participants are morally equal agentic individuals. Groups such as the neo-Nazis that Wissam referenced do not agree with the essential principle that all human beings are equal in this way, targeting in violent rhetoric and action various groups such as African Americans, Jews, and Muslims whom they deem inferior to themselves. Therefore, while interviewees indicated that discussion with individuals could be effective in changing views in some cases, in other instances, especially when confronting those who have a fundamental opposition to one's humanness, different strategies and tactics will be necessary to maintain and expand the rights of the groups they target.

This tension speaks to the need for multiple forms of democratic activities and participation: deliberative dialogue and engagement, civil society initiatives, and agonistic struggles with a strong emphasis on collective action. Unlike Ali and Tariq, I am not optimistic that individuals—such as Trump; his immigration advisor and author of the travel ban, Stephen Miller (Levitz 2019; Darby 2019); or the right-wing militia members who illegally detained fifty-six hundred migrants at gunpoint near the Mexico/US border between February and March 2019 (Hay 2019)—who advocate and use violence to exclude and expel those different from themselves can be convinced to welcome newcomers by discussion, interpersonal interaction, or increased understanding of the difficulties of displacement and resettlement.

Indeed, some of what may be required to push back against these reactionary forces is reflected in the activities and activism of civil society as described by interviewees. The volunteering and nonprofit work individuals such as Walid, Omar, and Nora described included providing essential services, supplementing the supports offered by government and resettlement agencies, facilitating discussions on important political issues, and working directly with individuals from diverse backgrounds to build connections and relationships among members of different communities. One of the themes woven throughout interviewees' experiences volunteering for events such as the Brooklyn International Day of Friendship and the Upstate New York immigrant festival was the desire on the part of both newcomers and native-born Americans to foster and reinforce the positive norms of diversity, inclusion, and multiculturalism, and to bring people together to have meaningful interactions and to learn about varied cultural expressions. These activities are the public version of the experiences with interpersonal exchange among participants and their friends, neighbors, and coworkers discussed in Chapter 2.

An even more direct strategy to confront a politics of exclusion, as Omar described, involves bringing individuals together to build power collectively. He contended that community and social movement organizing with residents of all backgrounds is likely better able to confront government repression than isolated individuals. The resistance to the travel ban as described in this chapter suggests the aptness of this insight. Educating immigrants about their rights, as Nada and Nora explained, is an avenue through which to prepare newcomers to assert their position as equal members of a democratic community. The large-scale protests and airport occupations are examples of individuals acting in concert to pressure government officials to reverse exclusionary policies and targeting of vulnerable populations. These actions represented a moment in which it was possible, as Ahmed framed it, for the "power of the people" to resist the "ultimate power in the country" (2 October 2017). As Nora, Ali and Walid explained, this effort involved significant numbers of native-born Americans joining with those directly targeted to demonstrate their opposition.

As Abdullah and others pointed out, rights such as the freedom of expression are written into the US Constitution. Newcomers and native-born Americans can mobilize existing rights, even limited ones, to push back at oppressive social and political structures toward further expansion of rights and protections. As multiple interviewees pointed out, the lack of even limited protections to protest and oppose the government in Iraq under both Saddam Hussein and the new American-imposed regime left significantly more circumscribed possibilities for action. The rights those living in the United States have are neither static nor ahistorical (Benhabib 2006). They have been contested through legal challenges (ACLU 2019), civil society, and agonistic conflict between progressive and reactionary forces. In some cases, formerly oppressed groups have succeeded in expanding such rights through those struggles. It is incumbent upon those Americans who wish to see a democratic, diverse, and multicultural society to use these rights and to demonstrate publicly that this is a society that should be open and welcoming to newcomers and that ensures the equal right to belonging and democratic membership for those who seek them. Finally, as Abdullah, Ali, and Nora's experiences with the protests against the travel ban demonstrated, "Individuals learn to participate by participating" (Pateman 2012, 10). Multiple examples of organizations and activities that began as part of the mass reaction against the travel ban have continued and expanded.[7] People learn democratic skills and attitudes by engaging in democratic processes. Those individuals can then go on to reproduce and expand a democratic ethos in the activities in which they later engage. Fully democratizing society, then, requires undoing undemocratic institutions and creating potentially new, more democratic norms and structures.

Notes

1. Zaid did not elaborate further on what specific issues he believed could be publicly addressed under a Trump presidency. From our full conversation, I interpreted that he was primarily referring to racism and other prejudice within American society.

2. Question 13 of the N-400 form asks: "Between March 23, 1933 and May 8, 1945, did you work for or associate in any way (either directly or indirectly) with: A. The Nazi government of Germany? B. Any government in any area occupied by, allied with, or established with the help of the Nazi government of Germany? C. Any German, Nazi, or S.S. military unit, paramilitary unit, self-defense unit, vigilante unit, citizen unit, police unit, government agency or office, extermination camp, concentration camp, prisoner of war camp, prison, labor camp, or transit camp?"
3. Here, Wissam was referencing the 11–12 August 2017 "Unite the Right" rallies held in Charlottesville, Virginia, organized by Ku Klux Klan, neo-Nazi, and other white supremacist groups. During the event, James Alex Fields Jr. intentionally drove a car into antiracist counterprotestors, killing Heather Heyer and injuring nineteen others (Caron 2017; Stolberg and Rosenthal 2017).
4. On 24 February 2018, Trump tweeted in support of training and arming teachers in schools as a way to deter school shootings (Landers 2018). These comments came in response to the massacre at Marjory Stoneman Douglas High in Parkland, Florida on 14 February 2018. A gunman entered the school and shot and killed seventeen people including fourteen children and three staff members. Seventeen other individuals were injured (Landers 2018). Such massacres are regular occurrences in the United States, and the Parkland shooting was the most recent before my interview with Zaid, occurring less than two weeks before.
5. As a condition of resettlement through the USRAP, individuals who do not pay for their airfare to the United States upfront are required to pay back the cost of their flight to the United States government (Westcott 2015).
6. Tariq questioned more broadly the disparity between Iraqis who worked for the United States and Americans who served in the occupation forces. Although some of his friends had been injured or died while working with the US military, he explained, "We're locals so we don't have any of the services that help us" (Tariq 2 November 2017). Because Tariq and Iraqis like him are not officially US military veterans, they are ineligible for any of the basic benefits veterans may receive, including GI Bill education benefits or Department of Veterans Affairs healthcare.
7. One such example is the Yemeni American Merchants Association (YAMA), an organization that began as an effort to resist the travel ban and has continued and branched out into other activities since its founding. When Trump signed the initial version of the ban, a group of Yemeni Americans quickly organized a temporary work stoppage/strike among Yemeni businesses in the city. More than one thousand Yemeni stores in New York temporarily closed on 2 February 2017 (Nigro 2019). Organizers and supporters of the strike also held a rally at Brooklyn's Borough Hall, drawing a large number of participants and support from elected officials such as then–Brooklyn borough president Eric Adams (Stack 2017). These actions brought together individuals who sought to continue the momentum from this organizing to create a shared space for ongoing activism. The NY merchants' protest of Trump's action led to the founding of the YAMA of New York. In its relatively short existence, the organization has assisted individuals whose family members were affected by the travel ban and offered support to families with members separated by it (Iqbal 2019). By

August 2019, YAMA had worked with ten families. Former congressman Max Rose (Democrat, New York) supported this work, and YAMA members have participated in activities such as a Congressional Briefing on Temporary Protected Status for Yemen and Somalia. In April 2019, YAMA launched a boycott of the *New York Post* by Yemeni-owned and operated bodegas in New York City. The action came as a response to a *Post* front page showing an out-of-context quotation by US Representative Ilhan Omar (Democrat, Minnesota)–herself a former refugee–alongside an image of the 11 September 2001 World Trade Center attack. By the end of June, five thousand businesses were boycotting sales of the *Post* in their establishments. In addition to participation leading to more participation, YAMA's work speaks to the importance of building relationships and organizing across communities, issues, and goals. For example, in 2019, several YAMA founders created Arab Women's Voice, a political consulting firm focused on issues/candidates of importance to Arab American and Muslim communities (Touré 2019). They have also worked to build other organizations such as Yalla Brooklyn, a civic organization that spun out of the strong, but unsuccessful, city council race of Khader El-Yateem, a Palestinian-born Lutheran Pastor who ran as a Democratic Socialist and came in second in the Democratic Primary in 2017.

Conclusion
The Local, National, and Cosmopolitan Work to Be Done

Throughout this book, resettled Iraqis' experiences of displacement and resettlement have demonstrated that constraints and challenges can exist simultaneously with opportunities for action. For example, deteriorating safety and social bonds can prompt one to leave one's home to seek more stable conditions elsewhere within one's home country or to seek refuge abroad. Persistent demands on one's time to work long hours to support a family can exist at the same time as desire and opportunities to participate in community-building work. Fear of government policies and agents and the material effects they can have on one's life can be and were partially mediated for a share of this study's interviewees by public demonstrations of support and resistance by others within society.

Therefore, a key takeaway from this research is the necessity for those in stronger, more secure positions within American society to find opportunities to work with and support those who suffer discrimination, violence, and are otherwise often placed in marginalized social, political, and economic positions. This work is urgent and imperative. Individuals with more privileged positions must engage in such work in ways deemed most helpful by those whom they would assist. This requires listening actively and empathetically to those targeted to understand what their goals and needs are.

Democratic Participation at a Local Scale

One of the threads that came through strongly across these interviews was the intersections and interplay of the local scale of engagement (interpersonal, in community organizations) and national-level political policies and discourses. Interviewees were rightly concerned about what the federal government did and said, and it is that level at which immigration policies about who can come into the United States are largely made. However, for the most part, they engaged in politics at the local level. I encountered several nonprofit leaders and community organizers drawing on norms of welcoming, multiculturalism, exchange, and dialogue to ground their advocacy and service work on behalf of refugees, immigrant communities, and the wider American society. Many of the activities and experiences described by interviewees had at their core the goal of interacting and working with others to change how belonging and democratic membership were constituted in US society. I found many examples of individuals invoking and (re)iterating norms concerning the issue of who has a right to come and stay in the United States, and where and what the boundaries of belonging and democratic membership ought to be.

I also found frequent quotidian opportunities for interviewees to engage with others, talk through various issues, interact with friends and share cultural practices and traditions, work with others to build welcoming spaces, organizations and communities, and occasionally, when acute moments of targeting against vulnerable groups appeared, to join with and draw support from other United States residents to press government officials to modify or reverse unjust policies. For those interested in working to build a more open, tolerant, and just society, such opportunities are one means by which to seek to do so. As elaborated throughout this book, building upon, and reinforcing norms of welcoming, diversity, and multiculturalism as values American society should strive to realize is vitally important given the recent acute period of violent and exclusionary anti-immigrant and anti-refugee policies and rhetoric emanating from the former Trump administration and the persistent resistance to newcomers—particularly Arabs and Muslims—among significant numbers of Americans.

My respondents largely considered democratic citizenship regularly in relation to their local communities, such as New York City or the Shenandoah Valley of Virginia, rather than at the state, national or international levels. Indeed, when interviewees Omar and Nora sought to build "welcoming cities," for example, they did so by working with local nonprofit resettlement organizations and with churches and other religious entities, as well as municipal governments. Simultaneously, when the macropolitical situation affected or intersected with their lives, they undertook local initiatives to address those factors and forces.

This insight might be combined with theories and practices of domicile citizenship, granting full membership to all residents "independent of ancestry or location of birth" (Bauder 2014, 79), to envision new, and reimagine existing, practices of citizenship at the level of the city or locality. Benhabib has similarly argued that "modalities of non-national citizenship" such as what she calls denizenship have developed alongside national citizenship, providing opportunities to exercise "proto-citizenship rights . . . at local and regional as well as supra- and transnational levels" (2006, 172). Indeed,

New York City, where four of the individuals interviewed for this book live, passed a law in early 2022 that will allow noncitizen, legal permanent residents to vote in municipal elections starting in 2023 (Ashford 2022). It is important to continue to explore how changes in citizenship rights and practices can occur at various scales; the city, the state, and inter-or-transnationally to provide opportunities for democratic decision-making to everyone, including those with temporary or no legal immigration status, stateless persons and others excluded under existing legal regimes.

In many ways, the initiatives in which Omar, Nora, and others reported participating are doing just that informally. They are working to enact politics and democratic citizenship–participating in dialogue, civil society, and activism–with and across organizations in their localities even as, in Nora's case, she did not yet have permanent status in the US at the time of our interview. Increasing opportunities and mechanisms for newcomers to engage in democratic processes at the scale(s) that have direct impacts on their lives may be a fruitful avenue to pursue for those interested in assisting this population.

Moreover, even when acting at a local scale in the United States, one must understand the global implications of decisions, particularly those taken by the American government. For example, one must understand the decades of American conflict waged against Iraq to understand refugee resettlement from that country in the United States. The United States and Iraq have intertwined transnational genealogies (Dewachi 2017). American imperial violence has forcefully (re)shaped Iraqi society and the resettlement of Iraqis in the United States will no doubt continue to alter the United States. Perhaps building deeper understandings of how US militarism, refugee resettlement, and democratic membership are intertwined can help analysts, scholars, and others to conceptualize more democratic and less violent approaches to American actions around the world, including within its current borders.

Envisioning New Forms of Cosmopolitan Democracy

Emphasizing the geopolitical nature of refugee resettlement also prompts (re)consideration of forms and processes of democratic participation that can be created beyond existing political communities. I take as a starting point for this reconceptualization what Fraser calls the "all-subjected principle." This principle is useful for determining "who" is allowed to participate in democratic deliberations about the substance of justice (2008, 411). Fraser has described it this way: "all those who are subject to a given governance structure have moral standing as subjects of justice in relation to it" (Fraser 2008, 411). This principle considers groups of people "fellow subjects of justice" not necessarily through state-centered citizenship, but through "subjection to a structure of governance, which sets the ground rules that govern their interaction" (Fraser 2008). The all-subjected principle moves beyond membership strictly defined as citizenship to a nation-state and recognizes that decisions have consequences that cannot be contained within national borders. As Fraser notes, this principle can be applied to those who are not already officially accredited members of a structure of governance. Therefore, and understood through this lens, those living in Iraq and facing an impending United States invasion *become* subjected to the American structures of governance, for example.

Iraqis have been bound by the decisions of the US government and have had to live under that country's jurisdiction, directly and indirectly for decades. Several interviewees pointed toward such a conception of democratic standing. As Abdullah and Walid noted, decisions made in the United States affect not only those within its borders, but also have impacts that reverberate around the world. Unlike other interviewees, Abdullah's entry to the US on a student visa does not provide him a direct path to lawful permanent residence or citizenship. As a result, "it's tricky," he said, to answer the question of whether he had a right to participate in decision making about laws and policies in the United States. As he explained: "Because at the end of the day, it's not my country and if it is not my country, I don't think I have the right to do that" (Abdullah 14 January 2018). However, he argued the United States' position as a global superpower gave him the right to participate in American politics: "So, I believe people from outside the USA, they should get involved in US politics. Because really, who you choose to be in power could affect other countries, other people."

Abdullah suggested that on certain issues, perhaps, he did not have a right to participate in decision-making processes. He noted US immigration policy, for example, as one such issue because even though he had views on the subject, in his understanding it is a domestic policy issue. "But," he said, "In terms of voting for a president, I think it's very important and I think because I could tell other people: 'Please don't vote for that candidate. Vote for the other candidate because [the first candidate] might cause wars and it would affect people from outside the USA.' . . . I don't know how I would affect, how would I change that. But I think the main thing that I can do is just to try to convince people not to vote for that person, and for the other person. And I think that is legit" (ibid.).

Similarly, describing his views on the 2016 presidential election, Walid said he disagreed with Trump and that he was a Bernie Sanders supporter during the Democratic Party primaries. As he observed:

> I'm a Democratic [Party supporter] and I was thinking about Hillary Clinton, but she decided to [support the invasion of] Iraq. She has a bad reputation. I was encouraging people about [Sanders] because he didn't vote for Iraq, he didn't vote for the war. . . . Yes, there are a lot of good candidates in this

country, they can do something good overseas. I mean, when you think about participating in democracy, you have to think about how much they do good here and also good outside of the United States. So, I didn't have any choice at that time [in 2016]. We disagree about President Trump . . . and we were thinking about the person who's caring about us and also caring about the people overseas because we know the United States plays a big role in many countries. (Walid 27 September 2017)

Abdullah and Walid's comments engage with the recurring central questions for democratic decision-making of who has standing to participate in deliberations, and how standing can be enlarged to incorporate those subjected to particular decisions (Benhabib 2011). These concerns highlight the important reality that decisions such as launching wars not only affect those beyond the borders of the belligerent state(s), but also in many ways subject those individuals to the governing structures of the warring states. This important empirical reality strengthens the argument that those former "outsiders" subjected to American military attack, including not only Iraqis but Afghans, Syrians, Yemenis, and others, have moral standing to participate in, consent to, and dissent from, decisions that affect their lives, including American decisions to invade, bomb and sanction their countries.

This insight, and the global scale and harm caused by conflicts waged by the United States described in this book, reinforce the argument that those who resettle in the United States ought to have full standing to participate in decision-making processes. It further points toward the need to reconceptualize democratic decision-making beyond the globally predominant form of territorially bounded sovereign states. Even though it remains an important political and social formation (Brubaker 2010), the nation-state is not, nor need it be, the sole site or scale of democratic attachments (Benhabib 2006). Rather, it is important to continue to envision other decision-making modes and mechanisms that can be exercised at all levels from the local to the inter-or-transnational. And, crucially, there is an urgent need to build substantively democratic organizations, movements, and institutions that can offer alternatives to the violent domination of imperial powers like the United States.

Implications for Policy and Activism

I close by reiterating the key insights for fostering and enriching a democratic ethos, practices, and institutions in the United States that my discussions with resettled Iraqis illuminated. I present the following recommendations aimed at government officials, non-governmental organization representatives, and activists and advocates working to expand the democratic spaces and opportunities for individuals to help to shape the rules, policies, and laws that govern their lives in the United States. Crucially, while this work has focused on those Iraqis displaced by the 2003 American invasion of their country, the recommendations here and requirements for participation identified in this research are not necessarily confined only to this group or, more generally, to resettled refugees. As the Biden administration's tenure proceeds, activists will need to assess the opportunities and risks of pushing for more open and less violent immigration policies with a less explicitly hostile administration, but also one that has already demonstrated it will use Trump-implemented policies to continue preventing asylum-seekers from entering the country. There is little indication that Biden will make a sharp break with the long-standing bipartisan commitment to punitive and violent immigration policies (Beltrán 2020).

Moreover, the Biden administration will certainly continue the global project of violent American military domination that has so often caused population displacement in the past. A change in presidential administration or party control of the US Congress is not sufficient to fundamentally alter the structures of US empire. The United States's ongoing wars around the world will no doubt continue to prompt resettlement of new populations. For example, the official end to the twenty-year occupation of Afghanistan in late 2021 is poised to spur significant numbers of Afghans to seek refuge in the United States. The suggestions outlined below are likely generalizable to such newcomer populations as well as to other residents of the United States who seek more substantive democracy. The experiences of the resettled refugees profiled in this book suggest that there is an urgent need to generate alternatives to American military violence; create and enlarge spaces for diversity, difference, and exchange; understand interconnected relationships between barriers and requirements for democratic participation; and engage in struggles for justice across multiple sites and modes of action with diverse strategies and tactics.

Generate Alternatives to American Military Violence

The United States is not a normal country; it is the preeminent imperial power that has sought to maintain its economic and military dominance throughout the world. As I hope this book has clearly demonstrated, that imperial project has caused immense suffering for the people of Iraq. We will likely never know exactly how many people have been injured and killed as a result of the war. What is known, as the experiences of those interviewed for this book demonstrate, is that the war tore apart Iraqi society, and caused hundreds of thousands of people to leave their homes and seek safety elsewhere. It is critical that Americans face the destruction their government has caused and begin the work of ameliorating that damage. That work entails creating mechanisms to hold the architects of the war against

Iraq accountable and developing reparations programs that can begin to redress the harm inflicted by the United States.

Moreover, the war against Iraq is only one of many conflicts the United States has waged in pursuit of expanding its influence and control. The twenty-year American war against Afghanistan, which officially ended in August 2021, is another example of the tremendous damage American imperial violence has done. One of the United States's final acts as it completed its withdrawal of troops was a drone bombing that killed ten civilians, including seven children (Liebermann and Kaufman 2022). Millions of Afghans, Libyans, Syrians, Palestinians, Yemenis, and many others have similarly strong claims to redress and reparation for the conflicts waged and supported by the United States against them.

As I noted in the introduction, this book is grounded in a pacifist ethic that refuses to legitimize war and military violence. Invading other countries, dismantling their governments, and imposing new economic and political structures are crimes against humanity that cannot be justified. Although often ignored and dismissed by policy makers and scholars of international relations (Jackson 2019), there are always alternatives to violence. It is incumbent upon Americans to reject the violent imperial project of their government in favor of seeking out more peaceful ways of interacting in the world.

Create and Enlarge Spaces for Diversity, Difference, and Exchange

The United States is a multicultural society. The anti-immigrant right wing may wish it were otherwise, but the historical and contemporary reactionary violence of white supremacy cannot undo this reality (Beltrán 2020). The experiences shared by participants in this study demonstrate the possibilities for those of diverse backgrounds to live together in their communities and to share and learn from one another. This requires more than simply repeating symbolic rhetoric that "we're all immigrants" or that the United States is uniquely successful at creating a "land of opportunity" (Crane 2021). Building a society in which diverse members can live together requires creating and supporting initiatives in advocacy groups, religious organizations, social movements, and elsewhere that enact ideals of multiculturalism, mutual exchange, and democracy.

The types of intentional efforts to this end that interviewees described, such as sharing of food and cultural practices; community interfaith meetings discussing differences and commonalities; festivals incorporating the traditions of a wide array of community members; and efforts to convince national, state, and local governments to adopt a welcoming, multicultural ethos, all point toward activities and programs that governments, NGOs, and activists might develop and adopt to create opportunities for deep engagement among those living in particular areas. Such undertakings may assist in developing and spreading the cosmopolitan viewpoint that every human being is entitled to equal rights, protections, and opportunities to express their own identities, practices, and cultures.

Understand the Interconnected Relationships between Barriers and Requirements for Democratic Participation

Democracy is time consuming. Participating in democratic processes can require devoting considerable time to any number of activities such as attending meetings, organizing events, or engaging in discussions. Moreover, it takes time to build the individual and collective knowledge that enables members of a political community to understand mechanisms and structures of democratic participation. As Pateman (2012) notes, when "ordinary citizens" have sufficient time and information, they are more than capable of participating in deliberations about complex public issues that affect them. By devoting time to developing deep knowledge, members of a community can also build the confidence to engage with questions of effective strategies and tactics to achieve their goals.

Not only are ensuring sufficient time and the need for deep knowledge to participate intertwined, but both are likely also necessary to begin to ameliorate lingering fear of authoritarian government and, importantly, to understand what mechanisms are available to confront state authority. Interviewees' perception that state authorities in the United States would arbitrarily use their power against them is well-founded. This fear is grounded in their experiences living in Iraq under repressive governments as well as in the knowledge that American police, spy agencies, and other repressive state institutions have targeted Arabs and Muslims for illegal surveillance, imprisonment, and violence. Democracy requires dismantling those repressive programs and capacities.

Moreover, as several of this study's participants noted, the lack of time to engage and build the knowledge necessary to participate in democratic processes is, at least in part, a function of the neoliberal political-economic arrangements in the United States. Many people in the United States are compelled to work long hours to support themselves and their families because there are few redistributive or public programs through which to meet needs such as healthcare or housing. The violent suppression of socialist, anarchist,[1] and other approaches within and beyond US borders (Lens 2008; Bevins 2020), has thus far succeeded in preventing alternative forms of social, political, and economic organization to flourish.

As multiple interviewees in this book pointed out, there is a need for programs that provide vital services to the population and resources to repair neglected infrastructure. Millions of Americans live in towns and cities with dangerous levels of lead contamination in their drinking water (Mulvihill 2021). Millions more are denied adequate food, housing, and medical care because of the pervasive ideological commitment to privatizing and marketizing life-sustaining essentials. In 2022, there is no lack of resources that could be marshaled to provide healthcare, education, and housing to everyone in the United States. The work of democratizing the United States requires moving beyond the myth of scarcity that perpetuates the fear that equitable (re)distribution of resources to those formerly excluded will require "taking something" from others (Pharr 1996). As Mohammed and Wissam pointed out about US military spending, the vast resources are there; but they are used for destructive purposes rather than constructive ones. What is lacking is not ample resources to meet the needs of every member of American society, citizens and noncitizens alike, but rather mechanisms that can translate policy preferences into programs (Gilens and Page 2014).

Substantive democracy must extend to all areas of life, including the economy. In a democratic society, members are able to make decisions about what to produce, how, and who gets the profits (Wolff 2012). An increased level of material security and comfort for all residents would enable everyone to have the time to engage in, and to pursue knowledge about, the decisions that affect their lives. Therefore, critically, actively building programs and institutions that improve material well-being and security, reduce inequalities, and (re)distribute resources must be key goals of social movements and any government that calls itself democratic.

Engage in Struggles for Justice across Multiple Sites and Modes of Action with Diverse Strategies and Tactics

Those who participated in this research described a wide array of activities in which they had engaged, including protesting, forming NGOs, community organizing, voting, contacting government representatives, translating, teaching children and adults with the goals of improving the material circumstances of their fellow residents, building relationships within and across communities, and defending and expanding their rights and the rights of others. Participants pursued all those goals through direct service provision, education, advocacy, and engagement with government officials and direct action organizing to bring together diverse members of communities to petition and challenge state authorities and build collective power. This research has demonstrated that all these forms of activism are vitally important to confront and push back against the sort of attacks on refugees, migrants, and other marginalized groups that were acute during the Trump administration and to envision and build more democratic and just alternative public policies and programs.

Participants described engaging in dialogue and deliberation, but also the limits to discussion. Any democratic society will likely include deliberation, even if deliberation is not taken as the core element of democracy (Parkinson and Mansbridge 2012). Deliberation may be necessary, but it is certainly not sufficient (Pateman 2012). Democracy, and the expansion of substantive opportunities to participate in American society, culture, and politics, also require struggle. There are members of American society who are committed to the violent exclusion of difference. Many of those people are in positions of power that allow them to carry out exclusionary policies. It is not about convincing such individuals that they are wrong through rational discussion and dialogue. Contestations and confrontations are needed that challenge existing structures of power that commit violence against refugees, immigrants, and many others.

Many formerly excluded individuals have engaged in ongoing struggles to answer the question of who gets to belong in American society. Those struggles have often required confronting cruel and violent systems of exclusion. Philip Hallie argues that people often fail to act to end cruel systems because they assume that only "vast ideologies and armies" can do so (1981, 28). The experiences shared in this book demonstrate that within limits imposed upon them (Inhorn and Volk 2021), resettled refugees as individuals, and collectively with other newcomers and native-born Americans, can engage in such contestations. Building a democratic society will involve complex interactions of deliberation (Parkinson and Mansbridge 2012), dialogue, confrontation, and conflict. Those engaged in struggles to create a better world must assess each context and situation to determine what will be most effective. Rather than a one-size-fits-all approach, taking action is better conceived of as a complex ecology of individual action, the aggregate effects of individuals acting, and collective work to transform the world (Nunes 2021). Much needs to be done to dismantle American military domination, democratize democracy in the United States, and create a society that is welcoming of newcomers. The task is to keep our horizons of possibilities open while assessing what we can feasibly do in each moment to pursue those goals.

Note

1. Such approaches, like pacifism, are also often dismissed or ignored by mainstream scholars (Rusche 2022). However, the anarchist tradition has much to offer those interested in building substantively democratic organizations, structures, and societies.

References

Abrahams, Fred. 2003. "Hearts and Minds: Post-War Civilian Casualties in Baghdad by U.S. Forces." New York: Human Rights Watch. Retrieved 18 September 2022 from https://www.hrw.org/report/2003/10/20/hearts-and-minds/post-war-civilian-casualties-baghdad-us-forces.

American Civil Liberties Union (ACLU). 2007. *Documents Received from the Department of the Army in Response to ACLU Freedom of Information Act Request.* Retrieved 18 September 2022 from https://www.aclu.org/sites/default/files/webroot/natsec/foia/log.html.

———. 2019. "Freedom of Expression." Retrieved 18 September 2022 from https://www.aclu.org/other/freedom-expression.

Agger, Ben. 1998. *Critical Social Theories: An Introduction.* Boulder, CO: Westview Press.

Ahtisaari, Martti. 1991. *Report to the Secretary-General on Humanitarian Needs in Kuwait and Iraq.* Retrieved 18 September 2022 from http://www.casi.org.uk/info/undocs/s22366.html.

Ainsley, Julia Edwards. 2017. "Exclusive: Trump Administration Considering Separating Women, Children at Mexico Border." *Reuters,* 3 March. Retrieved 18 September 2022 from https://www.reuters.com/article/us-usa-immigration-children-idUSKBN16A2ES.

Alba, Richard, and Nancy Foner. 2015. *Strangers No More: Immigration and the Challenges of Integration in North America and Western Europe.* Princeton, NJ: Princeton University Press.

Ali, Tariq. 2000. "Throttling Iraq." *New Left Review* 5 (Sept/Oct): 5–14.

All Things Considered. 2013. "Danger In Conflation: Separating Islam from Acts of Terror." *NPR,* 21 April. Retrieved 18 September 2022 from https://www.npr.org/.2013/04/21/178291522/danger-in-conflation-separating-islam-from-acts-of-terror.

Alonso-Zaldivar, Ricardo. 2019. "Administration Moves to Revoke Transgender Health Protection." *The Associated Press,* 24 May. Retrieved 18 September 2022 from https://www.apnews.com/44494a468abe4e009b0388798c16a197.

Amnesty International. 2004a. "Amnesty International Report 2004–Iraq." *Amnesty International.* Retrieved 18 September 2022 from https://www.refworld.org/docid/40b5a1f710.html.

———. 2004b. "Iraq: One Year on the Human Rights Situation Remains Dire." *Amnesty International,* 18 March. Retrieved 18 September 2022 from https://www.amnesty.org/en/documents/mde14/006/2004/en/.

———. 2017. "Iraq: Civilians Killed by Airstrikes in Their Homes after They Were Told Not to Flee Mosul." *Amnesty International*, 27 March. Retrieved 18 September 2022 from https://www.amnesty.org/en/latest/news/2017/03/iraq-civilians-killed-by-airstrikes-in-their-homes-after-they-were-told-not-to-flee-mosul/.

Anderson, Perry. 2014. *American Foreign Policy and Its Thinkers*. London: Verso.

Arnetz, Bengt B., Carissa L. Broadbridge, Hikmet Jamil, Mark A. Lumley, Nnamdi Pole, Evone Barkho, Monty Fakhouri, Yousif Rofa Talia, and Judith E. Arnetz. 2014. "Specific Trauma Subtypes Improve the Predictive Validity of the Harvard Trauma Questionnaire in Iraqi Refugees." *Journal of Immigrant and Minority Health* 16(6): 1055–66. https://doi.org/10.1007/s10903-014-9995-9.

Asad, Talal. 2011. "Muhammad Asad between Religion and Politics." In *Dr. Mohammad Asad–A Life for Dialogue*. Riyad: King Faisal Center for Research and Islamic Studies.

American Society of Civil Engineers (ASCE). 2021. "2021 Infrastructure Report Card." Retrieved 18 September 2022 from https://www.infrastructurereportcard.org/.

Ashford, Grace. 2022. "Noncitizens' Right to Vote Becomes Law in New York City." *The New York Times*, 9 January. Retrieved 18 September 2022 from https://www.nytimes.com/2022/01/09/nyregion/noncitizens-nyc-voting-rights.html.

Associated Press. 2005. "Full Text of Iraqi Constitution." *The Washington Post*, 12 October. Retrieved 18 September 2022 from http://www.washingtonpost.com/wp-dyn/content/article/2005/10/12/AR2005101201450.html.

Bakewell, Oliver. 2008. "Research beyond the Categories: The Importance of Policy Irrelevant Research into Forced Migration." *Journal of Refugee Studies* 21 (4): 432–53. https://doi.org/10.1093/jrs/fen042.

Bamford, James. 2016. "Every Move You Make." *Foreign Policy*, 7 September. Retrieved 18 September 2022 from https://foreignpolicy.com/2016/09/07/every-move-you-make-obama-nsa-security-surveillance-spying-intelligence-snowden/.

Barnard, Anne. 2004. "Inside Fallujah's War: Empathy, Destruction Mark a Week with US Troops." *The Boston Globe*, 28 November. Retrieved 18 September 2022 from http://archive.boston.com/news/world/articles/2004/11/28/inside_fallujahs_war/?page=4.

Bauder, Harald. 2014. "Domicile Citizenship, Human Mobility and Territoriality." *Progress in Human Geography* 38 (1): 91–106. https://doi.org/10.1177/0309132513502281.

BBC. 2021. "Covid: Biden to Continue Trump's Title 42 Migrant Expulsions." *BBC*, 23 August. Retrieved 18 September 2022 from https://www.bbc.com/news/world-us-canada-58077311.

———. 2011. "Iraq War in Figures." *BBC*, 14 December. Retrieved 18 September 2022 from https://www.bbc.com/news/world-middle-east-11107739.

———. 2018. "Trump Migrant Separation Policy: Children 'in Cages' in Texas." *BBC*, 28 June. Retrieved 18 September 2022 from https://www.bbc.com/news/world-us-canada-44518942.

———. 2017. "US Expands Travel Ban to Include N Korea." *BBC*, 25 September. Retrieved 18 September 2022 from https://www.bbc.com/news/world-us-canada-41382585.

Beaumont, Peter. 2006. "Sunnis Change Names to Avoid Shia Death Squads." *The Guardian*, 9 October. Retrieved 18 September 2022 from https://www.theguardian.com/world/2006/oct/10/iraq.peterbeaumont.

Beinart, Peter. 2018. "How Trumpian Nativism Leads to Anti-Semitism." *The Atlantic*, November 2. Retrieved 18 September 2022 from https://www.theatlantic.com/ideas/archive/2018/11/anti-semitism-inherent-trumps-nativism/574672/.

Beltrán, Cristina. 2020. *Cruelty as Citizenship: How Migrant Suffering Sustains White Democracy*. Minneapolis and London: University of Minnesota Press. https://doi.org/10.5749/j.ctv17z84bh.

Benhabib, Seyla. 2006. *Another Cosmopolitanism*. New York: Oxford University Press.

———. 2011. *Dignity in Adversity: Human Rights in Troubled Times*. Malden, MA: Polity Press.

Bevins, Vincent. 2020. *The Jakarta Method: Washington's Anticommunist Crusade and the Mass Murder Program That Shaped Our World*. New York: Hachette Book Group.

Beydoun, Khaled A. 2013. "Between Muslim and White: The Legal Construction of Arab American Identity." *The New York University Annual Survey of American Law* 69 (1): 29–76. https://doi.org/10.1017/S0008197300123359.

Bin Laden, Osama. 2002. "Full Text: Bin Laden's 'Letter to America.'" *The Guardian*, 24 November. Retrieved 18 September 2022 from https://www.theguardian.com/world/2002/nov/24/theobserver.

Black, Beverly M., Lisa M. Chiodo, Arlene N. Weisz, Nada Elias-Lambert, Poco D. Kernsmith, Jina S. Yoon, and Linda A. Lewandowski. 2013. "Iraqi American Refugee Youths' Exposure to Violence." *Violence Against Women* 19 (2): 202–21. https://doi.org/10.1177/1077801213476456.

Blain, Michael, and Angeline Kearns-Blain. 2018. *Progressive Violence: Theorizing the War on Terror*. London: Routledge.

Blake, Aaron. 2021. "Trump's Pressure Campaign to Overturn the 2020 Election: A Timeline." *The Washington Post*, 12 August. Retrieved 18 September 2022 from https://www.washingtonpost.com/politics/2021/08/06/trumps-brazen-attempt-overturn-2020-election-timeline/.

Blanford, Andrea. 2017. "Judge Orders Documents in Case against Alleged Chapel Hill Shooter Craig Hicks Released to Defense." *ABC11*, 14 March. Retrieved 18 September 2022 from https://abc11.com/news/judge-give-documents-in-chapel-hill-shooting-to-defense/1800425/.

Bloemraad, Irene, and S. Karthick Ramakrishnan, eds. 2008. *Civic Hopes and Political Realities: Immigrants, Community Organizations, and Political Engagement*. New York: Russell Sage Foundation.

Bloom, Joshua, and Waldo E. Martin Jr. 2013. *Black against Empire: The History and Politics of the Black Panther Party*. Berkeley: University of California Press.

Bohmer, Carol, and Amy Shuman. 2008. *Rejecting Refugees: Political Asylum in the 21st Century*. New York: Routledge.

Boine, Claire, Michael Siegel, Craig Ross, Eric W. Fleegler, and Ted Alcorn. 2020. "What Is Gun Culture? Cultural Variations and Trends across the United States." *Humanities and Social Sciences Communications* 7 (1): 1–12. https://doi.org/10.1057/s41599-020-0520-6.

Boot, Max. 2019. "Why Winning and Losing Are Irrelevant in Syria and Afghanistan." *The Seattle Times*, 30 January. Retrieved 18 September 2022 from https://www.seattletimes.com/opinion/why-winning-and-losing-are-irrelevant-in-syria-and-afghanistan/.

Bouckaert, Peter, and Fred Abrahams. 2003. "Violent Response: The U.S. Army in Al-Falluja." New York: Human Rights Watch.

Brands, Hal. 2022. "Russia Is Right: The U.S. Is Waging a Proxy War in Ukraine." *The Washington Post*, 10 May. Retrieved 18 September 2022 from https://www.washingtonpost.com/business/russia-is-right-the-us-is-waging-aproxy-war-in-ukraine/2022/05/10/2c8058a4-d051-11ec-886b-df76183d233f_story.html.

Brody, Reed. 2004. "The Road to Abu Ghraib." New York: Human Rights Watch. https://www.hrw.org/reports/2004/usa0604/usa0604.pdf.

Brown, Dee. 1970. *Bury My Heart at Wounded Knee: An Indian History of the American West.* New York: Henry Holt and Company, LLC.

Brubaker, Rogers. 2010. "Migration, Membership, and the Modern Nation-State: Internal and External Dimensions of the Politics of Belonging." *Journal of Interdisciplinary History* 41 (1): 61–78. https://doi.org/10.1162/jinh.2010.41.1.61.

Bruno, Andorra. 2019. "Iraqi and Afghan Special Immigrant Visa Programs." Washington, DC: Congressional Research Services.

Burnham, Gilbert, Riyadh Lafta, Shannon Doocy, and Les Roberts. 2006. "Mortality after the 2003 Invasion of Iraq: A Cross-Sectional Cluster Sample Survey." *The Lancet* 368: 1421–28. https://doi.org/DOI:10.1016/S0140-6736(06)69491-9.

Burns, Robert, Aamer Madhani, and Qassim Abdul-Zahra. 2021. "Biden Says US Combat Mission in Iraq to Conclude by Year End." *AP News*, 27 July. Retrieved 18 September 2022 from https://apnews.com/article/joe-biden-government-and-politics-middle-east-iraq-islamic-state-group-9397d9996703d7416f8571650 72a0a05.

Busby, Chris, Malak Hamdan, and Entesar Ariabi. 2010. "Cancer, Infant Mortality and Birth Sex-Ratio in Fallujah, Iraq 2005-2009." *International Journal of Environmental Research and Public Health* 7 (7): 2828–37. https://doi.org/10.3390/ijerph7072828.

Bush, George W. 2001. "Remarks by the President Upon Arrival." *The White House*, 16 September. Retrieved 18 September 2022 from https://georgewbush-whitehouse.archives.gov/news/releases/2001/09/20010916-2.html.

Cainkar, Louise. 2008. "Thinking Outside the Box." In *Race and Arab Americans Before and After 9/11: From Invisible Citizens to Visible Subjects*, edited by Amaney Jamal and Nadine Naber, 46–80. Syracuse: Syracuse University Press.

CAIR. 2017. "The Empowerment of Hate." Washington, DC: Council on American-Islamic Relations.

Cameron, Bobby Thomas. 2014. "Reflections on Refugee Studies and the Study of Refugees: Implications for Policy Analysts." *Journal of Management & Public Policy* 6 (1): 4–13.

Campbell, Madeline Otis. 2016. *Interpreters of Occupation: Gender and the Politics of Belonging in an Iraqi Refugee Network.* Syracuse: Syracuse University Press.

Capps, Randy, and Ariel G. Ruiz Soto. 2018. "A Profile of Houston's Diverse Immigrant Population in a Rapidly Changing Policy Landscape." Washington, DC: Migration Policy Institute. https://www.migrationpolicy.org/research/profile-houston-immigrant-population-changing-policy-landscape.

Carens, Joseph H. 2013. *The Ethics of Immigration.* New York: Oxford University Press.

Caron, Christina. 2017. "Heather Heyer, Charlottesville Victim, Is Recalled as 'a Strong Woman.'" *The New York Times*, 13 August. Retrieved 18 September 2022 from https://www.nytimes.com/2017/08/13/us/heather-heyer-charlottesville-victim.html.

CBS News. 2015. "Arabic Speaker Detained from Flight after Nervous Passenger Complains." *CBS News*, 20 November. Retrieved 18 September 2022 from https://www.cbsnews.com/news/arabic-speaker-detained-from-flight-because-passenger-complained/.

Chappell, Bill. 2019a. "Americans Who Were Detained After Speaking Spanish in Montana Sue U.S. Border Agency." *NPR*, 15 February. Retrieved 18 September 2022 from https://www.npr.org/2019/02/15/695184555/americans-who-were-detained-after-speaking-spanish-in-montana-sue-u-s-border-pat.

———. 2019b. "Trump Pardons Michael Behenna, Former Soldier Convicted of Killing Iraqi Prisoner." *NPR*, 7 May. Retrieved 18 September 2022 from https://www.npr.org/2019/05/07/720967513/trump-pardons-former-soldier-convicted-of-killing-iraqi-prisoner.

Cheng, Amrit. 2017. "The Muslim Ban: What Just Happened?" *ACLU*, 6 December. Retrieved 18 September 2022 from https://www.aclu.org/blog/immigrants-rights/muslim-ban-what-just-happened.

Chilcott, John. 2016. "The Report of the Iraq Inquiry: Executive Summary." London: House of Commons. http://webarchive.nationalarchives.gov.uk/20171123124621/http://www.iraqinquiry.org.uk/media/247921/the-report-of-the-iraq-inquiry_executive-summary.pdf.

Chrisafis, Angelique, David Fickling, Jon Henley, John Hooper, Giles Tremlett, Sophie Arie, and Chris McGreal. 2003. "Millions Worldwide Rally for Peace." *The Guardian*, 16 February. Retrieved 18 September 2022 from https://www.theguardian.com/world/2003/feb/17/politics.uk.

Chulov, Martin. 2010. "Iraq Littered with High Levels of Nuclear and Dioxin Contamination, Study Finds." *The Guardian*, 22 January. Retrieved 18 September 2022 from https://www.theguardian.com/world/2010/jan/22/iraq-nuclear-contaminated-sites.

Cleveland, William L., and Martin Bunton. 2009. *A History of the Modern Middle East*. Boulder, CO: Westview Press.

CNN. 2003a. "Arab Leaders Declare Opposition to War in Iraq." *CNN*, 2 March. Retrieved 18 September 2022 from http://www.cnn.com/2003/WORLD/meast/03/01/sprj.irq.arab.ministers/.

———. 2003b. "Cities Jammed in Worldwide Protest of War in Iraq." *CNN*, 16 February. Retrieved 18 September 2022 from http://www.cnn.com/2003/US/02/15/sprj.irq.protests.main/.

———. 2003c. "Text of EU Statement on Iraq." *CNN*, 18 February. Retrieved 18 September 2022 from http://edition.cnn.com/2003/WORLD/meast/02/18/sprj.irq.europe.text/.

———. 2007. "Marine to Serve 8 Years in Killing of Iraqi." *CNN*, 17 February. Retrieved 18 September 2022 from http://www.cnn.com/2007/US/02/17/marines.hamdaniya/.

Cobain, Ian. 2016. "Senior British Officers Knew of 'wetting' of Iraqi Civilians, Inquiry Told." *The Guardian*, 4 July. Retrieved 18 September 2022 from https://www.theguardian.com/uk-news/2016/jul/04/senior-british-officers-knew-of-wetting-of-iraqi-civilians-inquiry-told.

Cockburn, Patrick. 2016. *The Age of Jihad: Islamic State and the Great War for the Middle East*. London and Brooklyn: Verso.

Coll, Steve, and William Branigin. 1991. "U.S. Scrambled to Shape View of 'Highway of Death.'" *The Washington Post*, 11 March. Retrieved 18 September 2022 from https://www.washingtonpost.com/archive/politics/1991/03/11/us-scrambled-to-shape-view-of-highway-of-death/05899d9a-f304-441d-8078-59812cdacc5c/.

Crane, Ken R. 2021. *Iraqi Refugees in the United States: The Enduring Effects of the War on Terror*. New York: New York University Press.

Crawford, Neta C. 2018a. "Human Cost of the Post-9/11 Wars: Lethality and the Need for Transparency." Providence: The Watson Institute for International and Public Affairs at Brown University. https://watson.brown.edu/costsofwar/files/cow/imce/papers/2018/Human Costs percent2C Nov 8 2018 CoW.pdf.

———. 2018b. "United States Budgetary Costs of the Post-9/11 Wars Through FY2019: $5.9 Trillion Spent and Obligated." Providence: The Watson Institute for International and Public Affairs at Brown University. https://watson.brown.edu/files/watson/imce/news/ResearchMatters/Crawford_Costs of War Estimates Through FY2019.pdf.

Crawford, Neta C., and Catherine Lutz. 2021. "Human Cost of Post-9/11 Wars: Direct War Deaths in Major War Zones, Afghanistan & Pakistan (Oct. 2001–Aug. 2021); Iraq (March 2003–Aug. 2021); Syria (Sept. 2014–May 2021); Yemen (Oct. 2002–Aug. 2021) and Other Post-9/11 War Zones." *Costs of War*. https://watson.brown.edu/costsofwar/files/cow/imce/papers/2021/Costs of War_Direct War Deaths_9.1.21.pdf.

Darby, Luke. 2019. "There's Nothing Controversial about Calling Stephen Miller What He Is." *GQ Magazine*, 9 April. Retrieved 18 September 2022 from https://www.gq.com/story/stephen-miller-is-a-white-nationalist.

Darweesh, Hameed. 2017. "I Risked My Life for the U.S. Army in Iraq. But When I Came Here, I Was Nearly Sent Back." *The Washington Post*, 10 February. Retrieved 18 September 2022 from https://www.washingtonpost.com/posteverything/wp/2017/02/10/i-worked-for-the-u-s-army-in-iraq-but-when-i-landed-in-america-i-was-detained/?utm_term=.c131fadf1a67.

Davis, Charles. 2021. "A New Low: In Biden's First Year, the US Is on Track to Resettle Even Fewer Refugees than under Trump." *Business Insider*, 12 August. Retrieved 18 September 2022 from https://www.businessinsider.com/number-of-refugees-resettled-in-us-lowest-since-1975-2021-8.

Democracy Now. 2022. "'We're Fundamentally at War': Rep. Moulton Says U.S. in Proxy War with Russia," 29 May. Retrieved 18 September 2022 from https://www.democracynow.org/2022/5/9/headlines/were_fundamentally_at_war_rep_moutlon_says_us_in_proxy_war_with_russia.

Deutsche Welle. 2021. "The End of the US Combat Mission in Iraq: A Meaningful Change?" *Deutsche Welle*, 18 December. Retrieved 18 September 2022 from https://www.dw.com/en/iraq-after-us-ends-combat-mission/a-60174121.

Dewachi, Omar. 2017. *Ungovernable Life: Mandatory Medicine and Statecraft in Iraq*. Stanford: Stanford University Press.

Dickerson, Caitlin. 2018. "Migrant Children Moved Under Cover of Darkness to a Texas Tent City." *The New York Times*, 30 September. Retrieved 18 September 2022 from https://www.nytimes.com/2018/09/30/us/migrant-children-tent-city-texas.html.

Docherty, Bonnie, and Marc E. Garlasco. 2003. "Off Target: The Conduct of the War and Civilian Casualties in Iraq." New York: Human Rights Watch. https://www.hrw.org/reports/2003/usa1203/6.htm.
Du Bois, W. E. B.. 1903. *The Souls of Black Folk.* Chicago: A.C. McClurg & Co.
Dyson, Tim. 2006. "Child Mortality in Iraq since 1990." *Economic and Political Weekly* 41 (42): 4487–96.
Eisenhower, Dwight D. 2019. "April 16, 1953: Chance for Peace." Miller Center of Public Affairs. https://millercenter.org/the-presidency/presidential-speeches/april-16-1953-chance-peace.
Elsouhag, D., B. Arnetz, H. Jamil, M. A. Lumley, C. L. Broadbridge, and J. Arnetz. 2015. "Factors Associated with Healthcare Utilization Among Arab Immigrants and Iraqi Refugees." *Journal of Immigrant and Minority Health* 17 (5): 1305–12. https://doi.org/10.1007/s10903-014-0119-3.
Espiritu, Yến Lê. 2014. *Body Counts: The Vietnam War and Militarized Refuge(es).* Oakland: University of California Press.
Falzon, Andrew. 2017. "Thousands Gather at Battery Park, March for Second Day of Protests." *CBS New York,* 29 January. Retrieved 18 September 2022 from https://newyork.cbslocal.com/2017/01/29/battery-park-protest/.
FBI. 2015. "Incidents, Offenses, Victims, and Known Offenders by Bias Motivation, 2014." Washington, DC: FBI. https://ucr.fbi.gov/hate-crime/2014/tables/table-1.
———. 2016. "Incidents, Offenses, Victims, and Known Offenders by Bias Motivation, 2015." Washington, DC: FBI. https://ucr.fbi.gov/hate-crime/2015/tables-and-data-declarations/1tabledatadecpdf.
———. 2017. "Incidents, Offenses, Victims, and Known Offenders by Bias Motivation, 2016." Washington, D.C.: FBI. https://ucr.fbi.gov/hate-crime/2016/tables/table-1.
———. 2018. "Incidents, Offenses, Victims, and Known Offenders by Bias Motivation, 2017." Washington, DC: FBI. https://ucr.fbi.gov/hate-crime/2017/topic-pages/tables/table-1.xls.
Ferrigno, Lorenzo. 2015. "Donald Trump: Boston Beating Is 'Terrible.'" *CNN,* 21 August. Retrieved 18 September 2022 from https://www.cnn.com/2015/08/20/politics/donald-trump-immigration-boston-beating/.
Fiddian-Qasmiyeh, Elena, Gil Loescher, Katy Long, and Nando Sigona, eds. 2014. *The Oxford Handbook of Refugee and Forced Migration Studies.* Oxford: Oxford University Press.
Frankovic, Kathy. 2015. "Americans 'remember' Opposing the Iraq War." *YouGov.Com,* 21 May. Retrieved 18 September 2022 from https://today.yougov.com/topics/politics/articles-reports/2015/05/21/americans-remember-opposing-2003-war-iraq.
———. 2019. "What Is Terrorism? For Americans, Who Matters More than What." *YouGov.Com,* 26 March. Retrieved 18 September from articles-reports/2019/03/26/terrorism-in-america-constitutional-rights.
Fraser, Nancy. 2008. "Abnormal Justice." *Critical Inquiry* 34 (3): 393–422. https://doi.org/10.1086/589478.
Frontline. 2014. "Secrets of His Life and Leadership: An Interview with Saïd K. Aburish." *Frontline.* https://www.pbs.org/wgbh/pages/frontline/shows/saddam/interviews/aburish.html.

Fu, Minnie. 2018. "F-1 Student Visa, Optional Practical Training Risks Continue." *The National Law Review*, 19 November. Retrieved 18 September 2022 from https://www.natlawreview.com/article/f-1-student-visa-optional-practical-training-risks-continue.

Gallup. 2021. "In Depth: Topics A to Z Iraq." *Gallup*. https://news.gallup.com/poll/1633/iraq.aspx.

———. 2011. "Views of Violence: What Drives Public Acceptance and Rejection of Attacks on Civilians 10 Years after 9/11." *Gallup*. https://news.gallup.com/poll/157067/views-violence.aspx.

Galvin, Gaby. 2021. "About 7 in 10 Voters Favor a Public Health Insurance Option. Medicare for All Remains Polarizing." *Morning Consult*, 24 March. Retrieved 18 September 2022 from https://morningconsult.com/2021/03/24/medicare-for-all-public-option-polling/.

Gangamma, Rashmi. 2018. "A Phenomenological Study of Family Experiences of Resettled Iraqi Refugees." *Journal of Marital and Family Therapy* 44 (2): 323–35. https://doi.org/10.1111/jmft.12251.

George, Nick. 2015. "I Was Arrested for Learning a Foreign Language. Today, I Have Some Closure." *ACLU*, 23 January. Retrieved 18 September 2022 from https://www.aclu.org/blog/speakeasy/i-was-arrested-learning-foreign-language-today-i-have-some-closure.

George, Susannah. 2016. "Iraqi City of Ramadi, Once Home to 500,000, Lies in Ruins." *The Seattle Times*, 17 January. Retrieved 18 September 2022 from https://www.seattletimes.com/nation-world/iraqi-city-of-ramadi-once-home-to-500000-lies-in-ruins/.

Gilens, Martin, and Benjamin I. Page. 2014. "Testing Theories of American Politics: Elites, Interest Groups, and Average Citizens." *Perspectives on Politics* 12 (3): 564–81. https://doi.org/10.1017/S1537592714001595.

Gjelten, Tom. 2015. *A Nation of Nations: A Great American Immigration Story*. New York: Simon & Schuster.

Glantz, Aaron. 2017. "Did Defense Secretary Nominee James Mattis Commit War Crimes in Iraq?" *Reveal*, 11 January. Retrieved 18 September 2022 from https://www.revealnews.org/article/did-defense-secretary-nominee-james-mattis-commit-war-crimes-in-iraq/.

Goldman, Adam, and Matt Apuzzo. 2012. "NYPD: Muslim Spying Led to No Leads, Terror Cases." *The Associated Press*, 21 August. Retrieved 18 September 2022 from https://www.ap.org/ap-in-the-news/2012/nypd-muslim-spying-led-to-no-leads-terror-cases.

Gomez, Alan. 2017. "Lawyers Try to Free Immigrants Still Trapped at U.S. Airports." *USA Today*, 30 January. Retrieved 18 September 2022 from https://www.usatoday.com/story/news/2017/01/30/immigrants-detained-at-us-airport-president-trump-executive-order/97253348/.

Gordon, Joy. 2010. *Invisible War: The United States and the Iraq Sanctions*. Cambridge: Harvard University Press.

Gramlich, John. 2017. "How Countries around the World View Democracy, Military Rule and Other Political Systems." *Pew Research Center*, 30 October. Retrieved 18 September 2022 from http://www.pewresearch.org/fact-tank/2017/10/30/global-views-political-systems/.

Greve, Joan E. 2022. "Biden's Record Defense Budget Draws Progressive Ire over Spending Priorities." *The Guardian*, 3 April. Retrieved 18 September 2022 from https://www.theguardian.com/us-news/2022/apr/03/biden-record-defense-budget-progressive-spending-priorities.

Grieco, Elizabeth. 2003. "Iraqi Immigrants in the United States." *Migration Policy Institute*, 1 April. Retrieved 18 September 2022 from https://www.migrationpolicy.org/article/iraqi-immigrants-united-states-0.

Guilliard, Joachim, Lühr Henken, Knut Mellenthin, Tim K. Takaro, Robert M. Gould, Ali Fathollah-Nejad, and Jens Wagner. 2015. "Body Count–Casualty Figures after 10 Years on the 'War on Terror.'" Washington, DC, Berlin, Ottawa: International Physicians for the Prevention of Nuclear War.

Guttman, Nurit. 2007. "Bringing the Mountain to the Public: Dilemmas and Contradictions in the Procedures of Public Deliberation Initiatives That Aim to Get 'Ordinary Citizens' to Deliberate Policy Issues." *Communication Theory* 17 (4): 411–38. https://doi.org/10.1111/j.1468-2885.2007.00305.x.

Haddad, Emma. 2008. *The Refugee in International Society: Between Sovereigns*. Cambridge: Cambridge University Press.

Hagopian, Amy, Abraham D Flaxman, Tim K Takaro, Sahar A Esa Al Shatari, Julie Rajaratnam, Stan Becker, Alison Levin-Rector, et al. 2013. "Mortality in Iraq Associated with the 2003–2011 War and Occupation: Findings from a National Cluster Sample Survey by the University Collaborative Iraq Mortality Study." *PLOS Medicine* 10 (10): 1–15.

Haldane, Joanne, and Angela Nickerson. 2010. "The Impact of Interpersonal and Noninterpersonal Trauma on Psychological Symptoms in Refugees: The Moderating Role of Gender and Trauma Type." *Journal of Traumatic Stress* 29: 457–65. https://doi.org/10.1002/jts.

Hallie, Philip. 1981. "From Cruelty to Goodness." *The Hastings Center Report* 11 (3): 23–28.

Harding, Scott, and Kathryn Libal. 2012. "Iraqi Refugees and the Humanitarian Costs of the Iraq War: What Role for Social Work?" *International Journal of Social Welfare* 21 (1): 94–104. https://doi.org/10.1111/j.1468-2397.2011.00780.x.

Harper, Andrew. 2008. "Iraq's Refugees: Ignored and Unwanted." *International Review of the Red Cross* 90 (869): 169–90.

Harris, Shane, and Matthew M. Aid. 2013. "Exclusive: CIA Files Prove America Helped Saddam as He Gassed Iran." *Foreign Policy*, 26 August. Retrieved 18 September 2022 from http://foreignpolicy.com/2013/08/26/exclusive-cia-files-prove-america-helped-saddam-as-he-gassed-iran/.

Hartig, Hannah. 2021. "Democrats Overwhelmingly Favor Free College Tuition, While Republicans Are Divided by Age, Education." *Pew Research Center*, 11 August. Retrieved 18 September 2022 from https://www.pewresearch.org/fact-tank/2021/08/11/democrats-overwhelmingly-favor-free-college-tuition-while-republicans-are-divided-by-age-education/.

Hassan, Carma, and Catherine E. Shoichet. 2016. "Arabic-Speaking Student Kicked off Southwest Flight." *CNN*, 18 April. Retrieved 18 September 2022 from https://www.cnn.com/2016/04/17/us/southwest-muslim-passenger-removed/index.html.

Hauck, Fern R., Elsbeth Lo, Anne Maxwell, and P. Preston Reynolds. 2014. "Factors Influencing the Acculturation of Burmese, Bhutanese, and Iraqi Refugees into American Society: Cross-Cultural Comparisons." *Journal of Immigrant & Refugee Studies* 12 (3): 331–52. https://doi.org/10.1080/15562948.2013.848007.

Hay, Andrew. 2019. "FBI Arrests Leader of Armed Group Stopping Migrants in New Mexico." *Reuters*, 20 April. Retrieved 18 September 2022 from https://www.reuters.com/article/us-usa-immigration-militia/fbi-arrests-leader-of-armed-group-stopping-migrants-in-new-mexico-idUSKCN1RW0O5.

Hersher, Rebecca. 2017. "Federal Judge Stays Trump Travel Order, But Many Visas Already Revoked." *NPR*, 3 February. Retrieved 18 September 2022 from https://www.npr.org/sections/thetwo-way/2017/02/03/513306413/state-department-says-fewer-than-60-000-visas-revoked-under-travel-order.

Hillyard, Vaughn. 2015. "Donald Trump's Plan for a Muslim Database Draws Comparison to Nazi Germany." *NBC News*, 20 November. Retrieved 18 September 2022 from https://www.nbcnews.com/politics/2016-election/trump-says-he-would-certainly-implement-muslim-database-n466716?nc=4444.

Hitchens, Christopher. 2007. "Defending Islamofascism." *Slate*, 22 October. Retrieved 18 September 2022 from https://slate.com/news-and-politics/2007/10/defending-the-term-islamofascism.html.

Holder, Eric. 2013. "Letter to: The Honorable Rand Paul, United States Senate." Washington, DC: Office of the Attorney General.

Horst, Cindy. 2006. *Transnational Nomads: How Somalis Cope with Refugee Life in the Dadaab Camps of Kenya*. New York: Berghahn Books.

House of Representatives Committee on Oversight and Government Reform. 2007. "Memorandum: Additional Information about Blackwater USA." Washington, DC: Congress of the United States House of Representatives Committee on Oversight and Government Reform.

Howard, Michael, and Rory McCarthy. 2003. "More Die as Troops Open Fire on Mosul Crowd." *The Guardian*, 16 April. Retrieved 18 September 2022 from https://www.theguardian.com/world/2003/apr/17/iraq.rorymccarthy.

Huber, Lindsay Perez. 2016. "Make America Great Again: Donald Trump, Racist Nativism and the Virulent Adherence to White Supremacy amid US Demographic Change." *Charleston Law Review* 10: 215–48.

Human Rights Watch. 2005. "Leadership Failure: Firsthand Accounts of Torture of Iraqi Detainees by the U.S. Army's 82nd Airborne Division." New York: Human Rights Watch. https://www.hrw.org/report/2005/09/22/leadership-failure/firsthand-accounts-torture-iraqi-detainees-us-armys-82nd.

———. 2017. "US Embraces Cluster Munitions." *Human Rights Watch*, 1 December. Retrieved 18 September 2022 from https://www.hrw.org/news/2017/12/01/us-embraces-cluster-munitions.

International Committee of the Red Cross (ICRC). 2004. "Report of the International Committee of the Red Cross (ICRC) on the Treatment by the Coalition Forces of Prisoners of War and Other Protected Persons by the Geneva Conventions in Iraq During Arrest, Internment and Interrogation." Geneva, Switzerland: International Committee of the Red Cross.

Immerman, Richard H. 2010. *Empire for Liberty: A History of American Imperialism from Benjamin Franklin to Paul Wolfowitz*. Princeton: Princeton University Press.

Immerwahr, Daniel. 2019. *How to Hide an Empire: A History of the Greater United States.* New York: Farrar, Straus and Giroux.
Inhorn, Marcia C. 2018. *America's Arab Refugees: Vulnerability and Health on the Margins.* Stanford: Stanford University Press.
Inhorn, Marcia C., and Lucia Volk, eds. 2021. *Un-Settling Middle Eastern Refugees: Regimes of Exclusion and Inclusion in the Middle East, Europe, and North America.* New York: Berghahn Books.
Iqbal, Zainab. 2019. "The Muslim Ban Separated Many Families. Ten Days Ago, One Was Reunited." *Bklyner,* 16 August. Retrieved 18 September 2022 from https://bklyner.com/yemen-muslim-ban-reunited-max-rose/.
International Refugee Assistance Project (IRAP). 2022. "One Year After Biden Signed Order to Restore Refugee Program, Progress Has Fallen Short." *International Refugee Assistance Project,* 4 February. Retrieved 18 September 2022 from https://refugeerights.org/news-resources/one-year-after-biden-signed-order-to-restore-refugee-program-progress-has-fallen-short.
Irwin, Neil, and Emily Badger. 2019. "Trump Says the U.S. Is 'Full.' Much of the Nation Has the Opposite Problem." *The New York Times,* 9 April. Retrieved 18 September 2022 from https://www.nytimes.com/2019/04/09/upshot/trump-america-full-or-emptying.html.
Jackson, Richard. 2019. "Pacifism and the Ethical Imagination in IR." *International Politics* 56 (2): 212–27. https://doi.org/10.1057/s41311-017-0137-6.
Jamail, Dahr. 2012. "Seven Years after Sieges, Fallujah Struggles." *Al Jazeera,* 4 January. Retrieved 18 September 2022 from https://www.aljazeera.com/indepth/features/2012/01/201212102823143370.html.
Jamil, Hikmet, Abir Aldhalimi, Bengt B. Arnetz, Bernadette Kumar, M Saugo, and Z Slonska. 2012. "Post-Displacement Employment and Health in Professional Iraqi Refugees vs. Professional Iraqi Immigrants." *Journal of Immigrant & Refugee Studies* 10 (4): 395–406. https://doi.org/10.1080/15562948.2012.717826.
Jen, K.-L. Catherine, Kequan Zhou, Bengt Arnetz, and Hikmet Jamil. 2015. "Pre- and Post-Displacement Stressors and Body Weight Development in Iraqi Refugees in Michigan." *Journal of Immigrant and Minority Health* 17 (5): 1468–75. https://doi.org/10.1007/s10903-014-0127-3.
Jensen, Tom. 2015. "Trump Lead Grows Nationally; 41% of His Voters Want to Bomb Country From Aladdin; Clinton Maintains Big Lead." Raleigh, NC: Public Policy Polling.
Johnson, Jenna. 2015. "Trump Calls for 'Total and Complete Shutdown of Muslims Entering the United States.'" *The Washington Post,* 7 December. Retrieved 18 September 2022 from https://www.washingtonpost.com/news/post-politics/wp/2015/12/07/donald-trump-calls-for-total-and-complete-shutdown-of-muslims-entering-the-united-states/?utm_term=.37a7812c2fc7.
Judt, Tony. 2006. "Bush's Useful Idiots." *London Review of Books* 28 (18). https://www.lrb.co.uk/v28/n18/tony-judt/bushs-useful-idiots.
Kaczynski, Andrew. 2016. "Michael Flynn in August: Islamism a 'Vicious Cancer' in Body of All Muslims That 'Has to Be Excised.'" *CNN,* 22 November. Retrieved 18 September 2022 from https://www.cnn.com/2016/11/22/politics/kfile-michael-flynn-august-speech/index.html.

Kagen, Robert. 2021. "A Superpower, Like It or Not: Why Americans Must Accept Their Global Role." *Foreign Affairs*, 16 February. Retrieved 18 September 2022 from https://www.foreignaffairs.com/articles/united-states/2021-02-16/superpower-it-or-not.

Kearns, Erin M., Allison E. Betus, and Anthony F. Lemieux. 2018. "Why Do Some Terrorist Attacks Receive More Media Attention Than Others?" *Justice Quarterly*, forthcoming, 1–53.

Kellner, Douglas. 2004. "Media Propaganda and Spectacle in the War on Iraq: A Critique of U.S. Broadcasting Networks." *Cultural Studies–Critical Methodologies* 4 (3): 329–38. https://doi.org/10.1177/1532708603262723.

———. 1992. *The Persian Gulf TV War*. London: Routledge.

Kennard, Matt. 2012. *Irregular Army: How the War on Terror Brought Neo-Nazis, Gang Members and Criminals into the US Military*. London: Verso.

Kennedy, Edward. 2006. "Limiting Diversity Visas Closes America's Doors." *The Hill*. http://thehill.com/blogs/congress-blog/politics/30478-limiting-diversity-visas-closes-americas-doors.

Keyel, Jared, 2020. "'The Country Is Completely Destroyed:' Toward a National Project of Recognition, Reparation, and Reconciliation for the American War against Iraq." *Peace Studies Journal* 12 (2): 167–86.

Kinzer, Stephen. 2007. *Overthrow: America's Century of Regime Change from Hawaii to Iraq*. New York: Times Books.

Kira, Ibrahim, Linda Lewandowski, Jina Yoon, Cheryl Somers, and Lisa Chiodo. 2012. "The Linear and Nonlinear Associations between Multiple Types of Trauma and IQ Discrepancy Indexes in African American and Iraqi Refugee Adolescents." *Journal of Child & Adolescent Trauma* 5 (1): 47–62. https://doi.org/10.1080/19361521.2012.633239.

Kitaba-Gaviglio, Bonsitu A, and Monica Andrade. 2017. "ICE Continues to Detain Hundreds of Iraqis Despite Lack of Evidence of Flight Risk or Danger." *ACLU*, 20 December. Retrieved 18 September 2022 from https://www.aclu.org/blog/immigrants-rights/ice-and-border-patrol-abuses/ice-continues-detain-hundreds-iraqis-despite.

Kramer, Ronald C., and Raymond J. Michalowski. 2005. "War, Aggression and State Crime." *British Journal of Criminology* 45 (4): 446–69. https://doi.org/10.1093/bjc/azi032.

Kramer, Ronald, Raymond Michalowski, and Dawn Rothe. 2005. "'The Supreme International Crime': How the U.S. War in Iraq Threatens the Rule of Law." *Social Justice* 32 (2): 52–81.

Kumar, Deepa. 2012. *Islamophobia and the Politics of Empire*. Chicago: Haymarket Books.

Landers, Elizabeth. 2018. "Trump Tweets Support for Arming Teachers, Says 'up to States.'" *CNN*, 24 February. Retrieved 18 September 2022 from https://www.cnn.com/2018/02/24/politics/trump-tweet-arming-teachers/index.html.

Leigh, David, and Maggie O'Kane. 2010. "Iraq War Logs: US Turned over Captives to Iraqi Torture Squads." *The Guardian*, 24 October. Retrieved 18 September 2022 from https://www.theguardian.com/world/2010/oct/24/iraq-war-logs-us-iraqi-torture.

LeMaster, Joseph W., Carissa L. Broadbridge, Mark A. Lumley, Judith E. Arnetz, Cynthia Arfken, Michael D. Fetters, Hikmet Jamil, Nnamdi Pole, and Bengt B. Arnetz. 2017. "Acculturation and Post-Migration Psychological Symptoms Among Iraqi Refugees: A Path Analysis." *American Journal of Orthopsychiatry* 88 (1): 38–47. https://doi.org/10.1037/ort0000240.

Lens, Sidney. 2008. *The Labor Wars: From the Molly Maguires to the Sitdowns*. Chicago: Haymarket Books.

Leonhardt, Andrea. 2018. "Celebrate the Diversity of Brooklyn at the 5th Annual International Day of Friendship." *BK Reader*, 1 August. Retrieved 18 September 2022 from https://www.bkreader.com/2018/08/01/celebrate-diversity-brooklyn-5th-annual-international-day-friendship/.

Levenson, Eric. 2017. "Protesters Heckle Richard Spencer at Univ. of Florida Talk." *CNN*, 19 October. Retrieved 18 September 2022 from https://www.cnn.com/2017/10/19/us/university-florida-richard-spencer-speech/index.html.

Levinson, Jessica A. 2013. "The Original Sin of Campaign Finance Law: Why Buckley v. Valeo Is Wrong." *University of Richmond Law Review* 47 (3): 881–938. https://doi.org/10.3868/s050-004-015-0003-8.

Levitz, Eric. 2019. "If You Are Defending Stephen Miller, You Are an Ally of Anti-Semitism." *New York Magazine*, 9 April. Retrieved 18 September 2022 from http://nymag.com/intelligencer/2019/04/ilhan-omar-is-right-stephen-miller-is-a-white-nationalist.html.

Liebermann, Oren, and Ellie Kaufman. 2022. "US Military Releases Videos of August Drone Strike That Killed 10 Afghan Civilians." *CNN*, 19 January. Retrieved 18 September 2022 from https://www.cnn.com/2022/01/19/politics/military-releases-videos-august-drone-strike-killed-civilians/index.html.

Liptak, Adam. 2017. "Supreme Court Allows Trump Travel Ban to Take Effect." *The New York Times*, 4 December. Retrieved 18 September 2022 from https://www.nytimes.com/2017/12/04/us/politics/trump-travel-ban-supreme-court.html.

Liptak, Kevin. 2017. "Why Iraq Was Removed from the Revised Travel Ban." *CNN*, 6 March. Retrieved 18 September 2022 from https://www.cnn.com/2017/03/06/politics/iraq-travel-ban/index.html.

Lister, Matthew. 2013. "Who Are Refugees?" *Law and Philosophy* 32 (5): 645–71. https://doi.org/10.1007/s10982-012-9169-7.

Long, Colleen, and Ricardo Alonso-Zaldivar. 2019. "Watchdog: Thousands More Children May Have Been Separated." *U.S. News and World Report*, 17 January. Retrieved 18 September 2022 from https://www.usnews.com/news/politics/articles/2019-01-17/watchdog-many-more-migrant-families-may-have-been-separated.

MacAskill, Ewen, and Julian Borger. 2004. "Iraq War Was Illegal and Breached UN Charter, Says Annan." *The Guardian*, 15 September. Retrieved 18 September 2022 http://www.theguardian.com/world/2004/sep/16/iraq.iraq.

MacAskill, Ewen, and Michael Howard. 2007. "US Soldier Sentenced to 100 Years for Iraq Rape and Murder." *The Guardian*, 23 February. Retrieved 18 September 2022 https://www.theguardian.com/world/2007/feb/23/usa.iraq.

Macguire, Eoghan, Ali Gostanian, and Erik Ortiz. 2017. "Trump Travel Restrictions Leave Refugees Stranded: Reports." *NBC News*, 23 February. Retrieved

18 September 2022 from https://www.nbcnews.com/news/world/trump-travel-restrictions-leave-refugees-stranded-reports-n713591.
MacLean, Nancy. 2017. *Democracy in Chains: The Deep History of the Radical Right's Stealth Plan for America.* New York: Viking.
Madley, Benjamin. 2016. *An American Genocide: The United States and the California Indian Catastrophe, 1846-1873.* New Haven: Yale University Press.
Mahajan, Rahul. 2001. "'We Think the Price Is Worth It.'" *FAIR.Org*, 1 November. Retrieved 18 September 2022 from http://fair.org/extra/we-think-the-price-is-worth-it/.
Mahmood, Mona, Maggie O'Kane, Chavala Madlena, and Teresa Smith. 2013. "Revealed: Pentagon's Link to Iraqi Torture Centres." *The Guardian*, 6 March. Retrieved 18 September from https://www.theguardian.com/world/2013/mar/06/pentagon-iraqi-torture-centres-link.
Mango, Oraib. 2012. "Arab American Women Negotiating Identities." *International Multilingual Research Journal* 6 (2): 83–103. https://doi.org/10.1080/19313152.2012.665823.
Marr, Phebe, and Ibrahim Al-Marashi. 2017. *The Modern History of Iraq*, 4th ed. Boulder, CO: Westview Press.
McCarthy, Justin. 2018. "U.S. Support for Central American Refugees Exceeds Norm." *Gallup*, 20 December. Retrieved 18 September 2022 from https://news.gallup.com/poll/245624/support-central-american-refugees-exceeds-norm.aspx.
McCarthy, Rory. 2004a. "'US Soldiers Started to Shoot Us, One by One.'" *The Guardian*, 21 May. Retrieved 18 September 2022 from https://www.theguardian.com/world/2004/may/21/iraq.rorymccarthy.
———. 2004b. "Wedding Party Massacre." *The Guardian*, 19 May. Retrieved 18 September 2022 from https://www.theguardian.com/world/2004/may/20/iraq.rorymccarthy.
McCarthy, Rory, and Peter Beaumont. 2004. "Civilian Cost of Battle for Falluja Emerges." *The Guardian*, 13 November. Retrieved 18 September 2022 from https://www.theguardian.com/world/2004/nov/14/iraq.iraq3.
Meng, Grace. 2021. "On Day One, US President Biden Reverses Odious Travel Ban." *Human Rights Watch*, 20 January. Retrieved 18 September 2022 from https://www.hrw.org/news/2021/01/20/day-one-us-president-biden-reverses-odious-travel-ban#.
Mulvihill, Keith. 2021. "Causes and Effects of Lead in Water." *The Natural Resources Defense Council.* https://www.nrdc.org/stories/causes-and-effects-lead-water.
Muslim Advocates. 2018. "Running on Hate: 2018 Pre-Election Report."
"National Survey Finds Just 1 in 3 Americans Would Pass Citizenship Test." 2018. *Woodrow Wilson National Fellowship Foundation.* https://woodrow.org/news/national-survey-finds-just-1-in-3-americans-would-pass-citizenship-test/.
Neiwert, David. 2017. "Trump's Fixation on Demonizing Islam Hides True Homegrown US Terror Threat." *Reveal*, 17 June. Retrieved 18 September 2022 from https://www.revealnews.org/article/home-is-where-the-hate-is/.
Neiwert, David, Darren Ankrom, Esther Kaplan, and Scott Pham. 2017. "Homegrown Terror." *Reveal*, 22 June. Retrieved 18 September 2022 from https://apps.revealnews.org/homegrown-terror/.
Nelson, Matthew, Julia Meredith Hess, Brian Isakson, and Jessica Goodkind. 2016. "'Seeing the Life': Redefining Self-Worth and Family Roles Among Iraqi Refu-

gee Families Resettled in the United States." *Journal of International Migration and Integration* 17 (3): 707–22. https://doi.org/10.1007/s12134-015-0441-1.

Neuman, Scott. 2017. "U.S. Appeals Court Tosses Ex-Blackwater Guard's Conviction In 2007 Baghdad Massacre." *NPR*, 4 August. Retrieved 18 September 2022 from https://www.npr.org/sections/thetwo-way/2017/08/04/541616598/u-s-appeals-court-tosses-conviction-of-ex-blackwater-guard-in-2007-baghdad-massa.

Newkirk II, Vann R. 2018. "Trump's White-Nationalist Pipeline." *The Atlantic*, 23 August. Retrieved 18 September 2022 from https://www.theatlantic.com/politics/archive/2018/08/trump-white-nationalism/568393/.

The New York City Commission on Human Rights, Somjen Frazer, and Erin Howe. 2018. "Xenophobia, Islamophobia, and Anti-Semitism in NYC Leading up to and Following the 2016 Presidential Election: A Report on Discrimination, Bias, and Acts of Hate, Experienced by Muslim, Arab, South Asian, Jewish, and Sikh New Yorkers." New York: NYC Commission on Human Rights.

Nguyen, Mimi Thi. 2012. *The Gift of Freedom: War, Debt, and Other Refugee Passages.* Durham: Duke University Press.

Nickel, Patricia Mooney, ed. 2012. *North American Critical Theory After Postmodernism: Contemporary Dialogues.* London: Palgrave Macmillan.

Nigro, Michael. 2018. "How Yemeni Immigrant Activists in NYC Are Changing a Whole Community's Mindset." *Law@theMargins*, 5 November. Retrieved 18 September 2022 from https://lawatthemargins.com/how-yemeni-immigrant-activists-in-nyc-are-changing-a-whole-communitys-mindset/.

Nunes, Rodrigo. 2021. *Neither Vertical nor Horizontal: A Theory of Political Organisation.* London: Verso.

Ó Tuathail, Gearóid. 2003. "'Just Out Looking for a Fight': American Affect and the Invasion of Iraq." *Antipode* 35 (5): 856–70. https://doi.org/10.1111/j.1467-8330.2003.00361.x.

Obama, Barack. 2010. "Remarks by the President on Comprehensive Immigration Reform." *The White House*, 29 January. Retrieved 18 September 2022 from https://obamawhitehouse.archives.gov/realitycheck/the-press-office/remarks-president-comprehensive-immigration-reform.

Owen, Tess. 2018. "ICE Says It Won't Arrest People Seeking Shelter from Hurricane Florence." *Vice News*, 4 September. Retrieved 18 September 2022 from https://news.vice.com/en_us/article/qvapdb/ice-says-it-wont-arrest-people-seeking-shelter-from-hurricane-florence.

Pappe, Ilan. 2006. *The Ethnic Cleansing of Palestine.* Oxford: One World.

Parkinson, John, and Jane Mansbridge, eds. 2012. *Deliberative Systems: Deliberative Democracy at the Large Scale.* Cambridge: Cambridge University Press.

Pateman, Carole. 1970. *Participation and Democratic Theory.* Cambridge: Cambridge University Press.

———. 2012. "Participatory Democracy Revisited." *Perspectives on Politics* 10 (1): 7–19. https://doi.org/10.1017/S1537592711004877.

Pew. 2017a. "Americans Express Increasingly Warm Feelings Toward Religious Groups." *Pew Research Center*, 15 February. Retrieved 18 September 2022 from https://www.pewforum.org/2017/02/15/americans-express-increasingly-warm-feelings-toward-religious-groups/.

———. 2017b. "U.S. Muslims Concerned about Their Place in Society, but Continue to Believe in the American Dream." *Pew Research Center*, 26 July. Retrieved 18

September 2022 from https://www.pewforum.org/2017/07/26/findings-from-pew-research-centers-2017-survey-of-us-muslims/.

Pharr, Suzanne. 1996. *In the Time of the Right: Reflections on Liberation.* Berkeley: Chardon Press.

Pilkington, Ed. 2018. "NYPD Settles Lawsuit after Illegally Spying on Muslims." *The Guardian*, 5 April. Retrieved 18 September 2022 from https://www.theguardian.com/world/2018/apr/05/nypd-muslim-surveillance-settlement.

Pillar, Paul R. 2003a. "Principal Challenges in Post-Saddam Iraq." *National Intelligence Council.*

———. 2003b. "Regional Consequences of Regime Change in Iraq." *National Intelligence Council.*

Popper, Karl R. 1947. *The Open Society and Its Enemies. Vol. I: The Spell of Plato.* London: George Routledge & Sons.

Poushter, Jacob. 2015. "In Nations with Significant Muslim Populations, Much Disdain for ISIS." *Pew Research Center*, 17 November. Retrieved 18 September 2022 from http://www.pewresearch.org/fact-tank/2015/11/17/in-nations-with-significant-muslim-populations-much-disdain-for-isis/.

Public Information Section. 2003. "Chronology: 1991 Gulf War Crisis." *United Nations High Commissioner for Refugees.* Retrieved 18 September 2022 from https://www.unhcr.org/subsites/iraqcrisis/3e798c2d4/chronology-1991-gulf-war-crisis.html.

Rawlings, Nate. 2012. "The Warrior Ethos: Why We Leave No One Behind." *Time*, 17 May. Retrieved 18 September 2022 from http://nation.time.com/2012/05/17/the-warrior-ethos-why-we-leave-no-one-behind/.

Rayburn, Joel D., Frank K. Sobchak, Jeanne F. Godfroy, Matthew D. Morton, James S. Powell, and Matthew M. Zais. 2019. "The U.S. Army in the Iraq War: Volume 1 Invasion, Insurgency, Civil War 2003-2006." Carlisle: Strategic Studies Institute and U.S. Army War College Press.

Refugee Processing Center. 2019. "Admissions & Arrivals." *Refugee Processing Center.* Retrieved 18 September 2022 from http://www.wrapsnet.org/Reports/AdmissionsArrivals.

Roberts, Joel. 2005. "6 Months For GI In Iraqi Drowning." *CBS News*, 12 June. Retrieved 18 September 2022 from https://www.cbsnews.com/news/6-months-for-gi-in-iraqi-drowning/.

Rodgers, Lucy, and Dominic Bailey. 2019. "Trump Wall–All You Need to Know about US Border in Seven Charts." *BBC*, 21 January. Retrieved 18 September 2022 from https://www.bbc.com/news/world-us-canada-46824649.

Roth, Kenneth. 2004. "War in Iraq: Not a Humanitarian Intervention." *Human Rights Watch*, 25 January. Retrieved 18 September 2022 from https://www.hrw.org/news/2004/01/25/war-iraq-not-humanitarian-intervention.

Rozansky, Michael. 2014. "Americans Know Surprisingly Little about Their Government, Survey Finds." *Annenberg Public Policy Center of the University of Pennsylvania.* Retrieved 18 September 2022 from https://cdn.annenbergpublicpolicycenter.org/wp-content/uploads/2018/03/Civics-survey-press-release-09-17-2014-for-PR-Newswire.pdf.

Rusche, Jonas. 2022. "Imagining Peace Outside of Liberal Statebuilding: Anarchist Theory as Pathway to Emancipatory Peacefacilitation." *Alternatives* 47 (1): 18–44. https://doi.org/10.1177/03043754221074618.

Saadi, Altaf, Barbara E. Bond, and Sanja Percac-Lima. 2015. "Bosnian, Iraqi, and Somali Refugee Women Speak: A Comparative Qualitative Study of Refugee Health Beliefs on Preventive Health and Breast Cancer Screening." *Women's Health Issues* 25 (5): 501–8. https://doi.org/10.1016/j.whi.2015.06.005.
Said, Edward W. 2003. *Orientalism*. London: Penguin Books.
Sanford, Jonathan E. 2003. *Iraq's Economy: Past, Present, Future*. Washington, DC: Congressional Research Service The Library of Congress.
Sassoon, Joseph. 2009. *The Iraqi Refugees: The New Crisis in the Middle East*. London: I.B. Tauris.
Scahill, Jeremy. 2015. "The Drone Papers." *The Intercept*, 15 October. Retrieved 18 September 2022 from https://theintercept.com/drone-papers/the-assassination-complex/.
———. 2018. "Legacy of Blood–The 55-Year U.S. War Against Iraqis." *The Intercept*, 21 March. Retrieved 18 September 2022 from https://theintercept.com/2018/03/21/us-war-iraq-legacy-of-blood/.
Schmidt, Michael S. 2011. "Junkyard Gives Up Secret Accounts of Massacre in Iraq." *The New York Times*, 14 December. Retrieved 18 September 2022 from https://www.nytimes.com/2011/12/15/world/middleeast/united-states-marines-haditha-interviews-found-in-iraq-junkyard.html.
———. 2012. "Anger in Iraq after Plea Bargain over 2005 Massacre." *The New York Times*, 24 January. Retrieved 18 September 2022 from https://www.nytimes.com/2012/01/25/world/middleeast/anger-in-iraq-after-plea-bargain-over-haditha-killings.html.
Schmitt, Eric. 2021. "U.S. Carries Out Airstrikes in Iraq and Syria." *The New York Times*, 21 August. Retrieved 18 September 2022 from https://www.nytimes.com/2021/06/27/us/politics/us-airstrikes-iraq-syria.html.
Schofield, Matthew. 2011. "WikiLeaks: Iraqi Children in U.S. Raid Shot in Head, U.N. Says." *McClatchy Newspaper*, 31 August. Retrieved 18 September 2022 from http://www.mcclatchydc.com/news/special-reports/article24696685.html.
Searcey, Dionne, and Emmanuel Akinwotu. 2018. "Nigerian Army Uses Trump's Words to Justify Fatal Shooting of Rock-Throwing Protesters." *The New York Times*, 2 November. Retrieved 18 September 2022 from https://www.nytimes.com/2018/11/02/world/africa/nigeria-trump-rocks.html.
Seville, Lisa Riordan, and Hannah Rappleye. 2018. "Trump Admin Ran 'Pilot Program' for Separating Migrant Families in 2017." *NBC News*, 29 June. Retrieved 18 September 2022 from https://www.nbcnews.com/storyline/immigration-border-crisis/trump-admin-ran-pilot-program-separating-migrant-families-2017-n887616.
Shacknove, Andrew E. 1985. "Who Is a Refugee?" *Ethics* 95 (2): 274–84.
Shaheen, Jack G. 2003. "Reel Bad Arabs: How Hollywood Vilifies a People." *The Annals of the American Academy of Political and Social Science* 588: 171–93. https://doi.org/10.1177/0002716203255400.
———. 1984. *The TV Arab*. Bowling Green: Bowling Green State University Popular Press.
Sharp, Jeremy M. 2022. "U.S. Foreign Aid to Israel." Washington, DC: Congressional Research Service.
Sherry, Virginia N. 1991. *Needless Deaths in the Gulf War: Civilian Casualties during the Air Campaign and Violations of the Laws of War*. New York: Human Rights Watch.

Shiblak, Abbas. 2005. *Iraqi Jews: A History of Mass Exodus.* London: Saqi.
Shoeb, Marwa, Harvey M. Weinstein, and Jodi Halpern. 2007. "Living in Religious Time and Space: Iraqi Refugees in Dearborn, Michigan." *Journal of Refugee Studies* 20 (3): 441–60. https://doi.org/10.1093/jrs/fem003.
Sides, John, and Dalia Mogahed. 2018. "Muslims in America: Public Perceptions in the Trump Era." Washington, DC: The Democracy Fund Voter Study Group.
Siegal, Mark. 1999. "Former UN Official Says Sanctions against Iraq Amount to 'Genocide.'" *Cornell Chronicle.* Retrieved 18 September 2022 from https://news.cornell.edu/stories/1999/09/former-un-official-says-sanctions-against-iraq-amount-genocide.
Sim, David. 2017. "The Devastation of Mosul After ISIS, in Photos." *Newsweek,* 30 September. Retrieved 18 September 2022 from https://www.newsweek.com/photo-report-victory-over-isis-mosul-comes-terrible-cost-634190.
Singh, Amrit. 2013. *Globalizing Torture: CIA Secret Detention and Extraordinary Rendition.* New York: Open Society Justice Initiative. https://doi.org/10.1017/CBO9781107415324.004.
Slater, Alice. 2018. "The US Has Military Bases in 80 Countries. All of Them Must Close." *The Nation,* 24 January. Retrieved 18 September 2022 from https://www.thenation.com/article/the-us-has-military-bases-in-172-countries-all-of-them-must-close/.
Smith, Alexander, Caroline Radnofsky, Linda Givetash, and Vladimir Banic. 2019. "New Zealand Mosque Shooting: Attacker's Apparent Manifesto Probed." *NBC News,* 15 March. Retrieved 18 September 2022 from https://www.nbcnews.com/news/world/new-zealand-mosque-terrorist-may-have-targeted-country-because-it-n983601.
SPLC. n.d. "ACT for America." *Southern Poverty Law Center.* Retrieved 18 September 2022 from https://www.splcenter.org/fighting-hate/extremist-files/group/act-america.
Stack, Liam. 2017. "Yemenis Close Bodegas and Rally to Protest Trump's Ban." *The New York Times,* 2 February. Retrieved 18 September 2022 from https://www.nytimes.com/2017/02/02/nyregion/new-yorks-yemeni-owned-bodegas-close-to-protest-trumps-immigration-ban.html.
Stolberg, Sheryl Gay. 2017. "Senate Passes $700 Billion Pentagon Bill, More Money Than Trump Sought." *The New York Times,* 28 September. Retrieved 18 September 2022 from https://www.nytimes.com/2017/09/18/us/politics/senate-pentagon-spending-bill.html.
Stolberg, Sheryl Gay, and Brian M. Rosenthal. 2017. "Man Charged After White Nationalist Rally in Charlottesville Ends in Deadly Violence." *The New York Times,* 12 August. Retrieved 18 September 2022 from https://www.nytimes.com/2017/08/12/us/charlottesville-protest-white-nationalist.html.
Stuster, J. Dana. 2013. "Mapped: The 7 Governments the U.S. Has Overthrown." *Foreign Policy,* 20 August. Retrieved 18 September 2022 from https://foreignpolicy.com/2013/08/20/mapped-the-7-governments-the-u-s-has-overthrown/.
Szczepanik, Marta. 2016. "The 'Good' and 'Bad' Refugees? Imagined Refugeehood(s) in the Media Coverage of the Migration Crisis." *Journal of Identity and Migration Studies* 10 (2): 23–34.

Taguba, Antonio M. 2004. *Article 15-6 Investigation of the 800th Military Police Brigade.* United States Army.
Taylor, Eboni M, Emad A Yanni, Clelia Pezzi, Michael Guterbock, Erin Rothney, Elizabeth Harton, Jessica Montour, Collin Elias, and Heather Burke. 2014. "Physical and Mental Health Status of Iraqi Refugees Resettled in the United States." *Journal of Immigrant and Minority Health* 16 (6): 1130–37. https://doi.org/10.1007/s10903-013-9893-6.
Telhami, Shibley. 2015. "American Attitudes Toward the Middle East and Israel." *Center for Middle East Policy at Brookings.*
Torbati, Yeganeh. 2019. "U.S. Denied Tens of Thousands More Visas in 2018 Due to Travel Ban: Data." *Reuters,* 26 February. Retrieved 18 September 2022 from https://www.reuters.com/article/us-usa-immigration-ban/u-s-denied-tens-of-thousands-more-visas-in-2018-due-to-travel-ban-data-idUSKCN1QF2KF.
Totenberg, Nina, and Domenico Montanaro. 2018. "In Big Win For White House, Supreme Court Upholds President Trump's Travel Ban." *NPR,* 26 June. Retrieved 18 September 2022 from https://www.npr.org/2018/06/26/606481548/supreme-court-upholds-trump-travel-ban.
Touré, Madina. 2019. "Facing Marginalization in the Trump Era, Arab Women Form Political Firm." *Politico,* 24 April 2019. Retrieved 18 September 2022 from https://www.politico.com/states/new-york/albany/story/2019/04/24/facing-marginalization-in-the-trump-era-arab-women-form-political-firm-988610.
Tucker, Jonathan. 2014. "American Firms' Supplying Iraq's Chemical Weapons Production." *The New York Times,* 14 October. Retrieved 18 September 2022 from https://www.nytimes.com/interactive/2014/10/14/world/middleeast/american-firms-supplying-iraqs-chemical-weapons-production.html.
Turse, Nick. 2021. "Will the Biden Administration Shine Light on Shadowy Special Ops Programs?" *The Intercept,* 20 March. Retrieved 18 September 2022 from https://theintercept.com/2021/03/20/joe-biden-special-operations-forces/.
Tyner, Adam, and Yuan Ren. 2016. "The Hukou System, Rural Institutions, and Migrant Integration in China." *Journal of East Asian Studies* 16 (3): 331–48. https://doi.org/10.1017/jea.2016.18.
US Department of Defense. n.d. "Our Story." U.S. Department of Defense. Retrieved 27 February 2019 from https://www.defense.gov/Our-Story/.
Ullman, Harlan K., and James P. Wade. 1996. *Shock and Awe: Achieving Rapid Dominance.* Washington DC: National Defense University.
United Nations. 2021. "ISIL Crimes against Yazidis Constitute Genocide, UN Investigation Team Finds." *UN News,* 10 May. Retrieved 18 September 2022 from https://news.un.org/en/story/2021/05/1091662.
"US and British Aircraft Attack Iraq." 2001. *The Guardian,* 2 March. Retrieved 18 September 2022 from https://www.theguardian.com/world/2001/feb/16/iraq.
US Department of Homeland Security. 2004. "Yearbook of Immigration Statistics." Washington, DC: United States Department of Homeland Security.
———. 2014. "Yearbook of Immigration Statistics." Washington, DC: United States Department of Homeland Security.
———. 2017. "Yearbook of Immigration Statistics." Washington, DC: United States Department of Homeland Security.

US Department of State. 2019. "Refugee Arrivals: From March 20, 2003 through September 30, 2017, Nationality of Iraq." Washington, DC: United States Department of State: Bureau of Population, Refugees, and Migration.

Valenciana, Christine, and Rosario Ordoñez-Jasis. 2012. "Unconstitutional Deportation of the 1930s: Learning from the Voices of the Past." *The Social Studies* 103 (2): 81–89. https://doi.org/10.1080/00377996.2011.571569.

Vandewalker, Ian, and Keith Gunnar Bentele. 2015. "Vulnerability in Numbers: Racial Composition of the Electorate, Voter Suppression, and the Voting Rights Act." *Harvard Latino Law Review* 18: 99–150.

Vine, David. 2015. *Base Nation: How U.S. Military Bases Abroad Harm America and the World.* New York: Metropolitan Books.

Walker, Christina. 2019. "10 Years. 180 School Shootings. 356 Victims." *CNN*, 24 July. Retrieved 18 September 2022 from https://www.cnn.com/interactive/2019/07/us/ten-years-of-school-shootings-trnd/.

Welcoming America. 2019. "What's the Difference between a Welcoming City and Sanctuary City?" *Welcoming America.* 2019. https://www.welcomingamerica.org/difference-between-welcoming-city-sanctuary-city.

Westcott, Lucy. 2015. "A Brief History of Refugees Paying Back the U.S. Government for Their Travel." *Newsweek*, 12 December. Retrieved 18 September 2022 from https://www.newsweek.com/brief-history-refugees-paying-back-us-government-their-travel-403241.

White, Josh. 2005. "Documents Tell of Brutal Improvisation by GIs." *The Washington Post*, 3 August. Retrieved 18 September 2022 from http://www.washingtonpost.com/wp-dyn/content/article/2005/08/02/AR2005080201941.html.

———. 2006. "Military Cleared in Raid on Iraq House." *The Washington Post*, 3 June. Retrieved 18 September 2022 from http://www.washingtonpost.com/wp-dyn/content/article/2006/06/02/AR2006060201796.html.

Whitlock, Craig. 2009. "Army Sergeant Pleads Guilty to Murder in Iraqi Prisoner Deaths." *The Washington Post*, 31 March. Retrieved 18 September 2022 from http://www.washingtonpost.com/wp-dyn/content/article/2009/03/30/AR2009033001352.html?noredirect=on.

Willard, Cynthia L, Mara Rabin, and Martha Lawless. 2014. "The Prevalence of Torture and Associated Symptoms in United States Iraqi Refugees." *Journal of Immigrant and Minority Health* 16 (6): 1069–76. https://doi.org/10.1007/s10903-013-9817-5.

Williams-Harris, Deanese, Liam Ford, and Megan Crepeau. 2015. "2 Dead, 6 Wounded, Including Rapper King Louie, in Chicago Shootings." *Chicago Tribune*, 23 December. Retrieved 18 September 2022 from https://www.chicagotribune.com/news/local/breaking/ct-chicago-shooting-violence-20151223-story.html.

Wise, David. 2009. "The CIA—Licensed to Kill for Decades." *The Los Angeles Times.* Retrieved 18 September 2022 from https://www.latimes.com/archives/la-xpm-2009-jul-22-oe-wise22-story.html.

Wolff, Richard. 2012. *Democracy at Work: A Cure for Capitalism.* Chicago: Haymarket Books.

Wright, A. Michelle, Abir Aldhalimi, Mark A. Lumley, Hikmet Jamil, Nnamdi Pole, Judith E. Arnetz, and Bengt B. Arnetz. 2016. "Determinants of Resource Needs

and Utilization among Refugees over Time." *Social Psychiatry and Psychiatric Epidemiology* 51 (4): 539–49. https://doi.org/10.1007/s00127-015-1121-3.
Wright, A. Michelle, Abir Dhalimi, Mark A. Lumley, Hikmet Jamil, Nnamdi Pole, Judith E. Arnetz, and Bengt B. Arnetz. 2016. "Unemployment in Iraqi Refugees: The Interaction of Pre and Post-Displacement Trauma." *Scandinavian Journal of Psychology* 57 (6): 564–70. https://doi.org/10.1111/sjop.12320.
Yako, Rihab Mousa, and Bipasha Biswas. 2014. "'We Came to This Country for the Future of Our Children. We Have No Future': Acculturative Stress among Iraqi Refugees in the United States." *International Journal of Intercultural Relations* 38 (1): 133–41. https://doi.org/10.1016/j.ijintrel.2013.08.003.
Yi, Jean, and Amelia Thomson-DeVeaux. 2022. "Where Americans Stand On Abortion, In 5 Charts." *Five Thirty Eight*, 6 May. Retrieved 18 September 2022 from https://fivethirtyeight.com/features/where-americans-stand-on-abortion-in-5-charts/.
YouGov. 2015. "YouGov: November 20–23, 2015." *YouGov.Com*. Retrieved 18 September 2022 from https://d25d2506sfb94s.cloudfront.net/cumulus_uploads/document/236fb46xyh/tabs_OP_National_Registry_20151123.pdf.
———. 2018. "HuffPost: Iraq War." *YouGov.Com*. Retrieved 18 September 2022 from http://big.assets.huffingtonpost.com/tabsHPIraqwar20180315.pdf.
Zielbauer, Paul Von. 2007a. "Army Says Improper Orders by Colonel Led to 4 Deaths." *The New York Times*, 21 January. Retrieved 18 September 2022 from https://www.nytimes.com/2007/01/21/world/middleeast/21abuse.html?_r=1.
———. 2007b. "Civilian Claims on U.S. Suggest the Toll of War." *The New York Times*, 12 April. Retrieved 18 September 2022 from https://www.nytimes.com/2007/04/12/world/middleeast/12abuse.html.
Zogby Analytics. 2017. "American Attitudes: Immigration, Civil Rights, Surveillance, Profiling, and Hate Crimes." *Arab American Institute*, 1 July. Retrieved 18 September 2022 from https://www.aaiusa.org/library/american-attitudes-immigration-civil-rights-surveillance-profiling-and-hate-crimes-2017.
Zogby International. 2010. "American Views on Arab and Muslim Americans." *Arab American Institute*, September. Retrieved 18 September 2022 from https://d3n8a8pro7vhmx.cloudfront.net/nnaac/pages/569/attachments/original/1411496549/AmericanViewsOnArabMuslimAmericans_2010ogby.pdf?1411496549.
Zwijnenburg, Wim, and Doug Weir. 2016. "Targets of Opportunity: Analysis of the Use of Depleted Uranium by A-10s in the 2003 Iraq War." Manchester: PAX and The International Coalition to Ban Uranium Weapons.

Index

2003 American-led invasion of Iraq, 1, 10, 11, 14, 16, 20, 24, 26, 29, 30, 31, 32, 33, 34, 35, 37, 38, 40, 45, 46n2, 46n3, 47n6, 48n9, 70, 83, 143, 156
   Abu Ghraib prison, 32
   Camp Bucca prison, 32
   death squads, 32. *See also* 2003 American-led invasion of Iraq: special police commando Wolf Brigade
   depleted uranium, 30
   cluster munitions, 30, 47n6
   murder of Abeer Qassim Hamza al-Janabi, 32
   sectarian violence, 32, 35
   siege of Fallujah, 30
   special police commando Wolf Brigade, 32. *See also* 2003 American-led invasion of Iraq: death squads
   torture, 9, 24, 32, 33

Adams, Eric, 140, 149n7
Afghanistan, 10, 46n4
   American withdrawal, 22n6, 43, 156
   US war against, 25, 113, 157
Albright, Madeleine, 28
all-subjected principle, 153–54
al-Qa'ida, 30, 32, 38, 46n3
American Civil Liberties Union (ACLU), 106, 141
anarchism, 158, 160n1

Ba'athist regime, 13, 26, 28, 34–35. *See also* Ba'ath Party
Ba'ath Party, 26, 117 *See also* Ba'athist regime
Belonging, 2, 17, 19, 20, 21, 23, 46, 49, 50, 54, 55, 56, 57, 58, 59, 60, 61, 74, 82, 83, 84, 87, 92, 93, 105, 135, 145, 148, 152
Biden, Joe, 7–10, 22n6, 25, 33, 42, 94, 141, 156
Black Panther Party, 123n8
Blair, Tony, 46n3
Booker, Corey, 143
British Joint Intelligence Committee, 46n3
Brooklyn International Day of Friendship, 140, 147
Bush, George H. W., 8
Bush, George W., 8, 9, 25, 28, 33, 43, 45, 46n3, 62

Council on American-Islamic Relations (CAIR), 73
Clinton, Bill, 8, 28
Clinton, Hillary, 127–28, 154
Chiraq, 136
Central Intelligence Agency (CIA), 9, 25, 26
chemical weapons, 26
child separation policy, 80, 93–94n5
citizenship exam, 116, 132, 135, 137
civil society, 96, 120, 122, 135, 147, 148, 153

cosmopolitanism, 21, 81, 153, 158

de Blasio, Bill, 143
democratic membership, 17, 19, 20, 23, 49, 93, 95, 96, 99, 100, 103, 105, 107, 119, 120, 124, 148, 152, 153
democracy, 3, 17, 18, 19, 21, 95–99, 100, 101, 104, 105, 107, 111, 112, 118, 121, 123n9, 125, 128, 132, 135, 138, 145, 153, 155, 156, 157, 158–59, 160
demographics of Iraq, 11–12
denizenship, 152
domicile citizenship, 152
drone wars, 25, 33, 46n4, 157
Du Bois, W. E. B., 50, 60–61

Egypt, 9, 13, 15, 41, 42
Eisenhower, Dwight D., 123n6
El-Yateem, Khader, 150n7
Embrace Your Hyphen Campaign, 140
English as a second language (ESL), 14, 16, 134, 137
Executive Order 13769, 141. *See also* Muslim ban; travel ban

Federal Bureau of Investigation (FBI), 9, 73, 93n1
Flying while Muslim, 73
Flynn, Michael, 70

Gillibrand, Kirsten, 143
Green Card, 15, 74, 77, 114, 135, 138
Gulf War, 1, 11, 106
    Highway of Death, 27

Halliday, Denis, 28
Heyer, Heather, 149n3
Holder, Eric, 121
Hussein, Saddam, 14, 23, 24, 26–28, 29, 33, 34, 37, 38, 39, 40, 41, 46n3, 77, 106, 117, 119, 120, 133, 135, 148

Iran-Iraq War, 26, 27
Islamic State in Iraq and Syria (ISIS), 1, 24, 30, 32, 33, 35, 37, 39, 47n5, 71, 72, 79, 100, 130, 142

Israel, 35
    military occupation of the West Bank and Gaza, 25
    Zionist militias, 6

Jordan, 15, 16, 17, 28, 41, 42, 43, 50, 58

lawful permanent residence, 154
Lebanon, 16, 42, 77
Libya, 10, 113, 141
    NATO war against, 25

Muslim ban, 141, 144. *See also* Executive Order 13769; travel ban

National Intelligence Council, 46n3
National Security Entry-Exit Registration System (NSEERS), 9
nativism, 6, 62
New York City Police Department (NYPD), 9, 73
No Ban, No Wall, 141
nonprofit organizations, 10, 13, 14, 15, 21, 43, 44, 51, 53, 54, 91, 93, 110, 116, 124, 125, 130, 135, 137, 139, 140, 147, 152
North Atlantic Treaty Organization (NATO), 25

Obama, Barack, 7, 8, 9, 25, 33, 43, 70, 75, 98, 121, 142
Omar, Ilhan, 150n7
Optional Practical Training (OPT), 15, 18, 75
Organisation of Islamic Cooperation (OIC), 71
Orientalism, 6, 12, 61

pacifism, 3, 157, 160n1
Pakistan, 10, 25, 46n4
Palestinian refugees, 6, 22n7
participation, 2, 17, 18, 19, 21, 49, 50, 96, 97, 107, 108, 109, 111, 116, 120, 121, 124, 125, 147, 150n7, 151, 153, 156, 158

refugee resettlement, 1, 6, 7, 12, 13, 16, 17, 22n3, 23, 36, 41, 42, 44, 48n9, 50–51, 52, 53, 54, 55, 67, 76, 82, 92, 93, 107, 131, 140, 141, 147, 151, 153, 156
resettlement agency, 51, 52–53, 67, 110, 136, 137
resettlement flight debt, 140, 149n5
Rose, Max, 150n7

sanctions, 28, 39, 85
Sanders, Bernie, 154
Schumer, Chuck, 143
Somalia, 10, 25, 46n4, 68, 93n2, 141, 150n7
Special Immigrant Visa (SIV), 1, 11, 14, 15, 18, 29, 42, 43, 51, 56, 74, 75, 110
Sudan, 68, 141
surveillance of Arabs and Muslims, 9, 73, 107, 121, 158
Syria, 10, 11, 13, 14, 15, 25, 33, 36, 41, 42, 43, 44, 50, 85, 131, 141

terrorism, 34, 37, 46n3, 62, 64–65, 72, 76, 78, 79, 81, 102, 106, 126, 130, 145
travel ban, 6, 7, 9, 21, 74, 77, 117, 128, 130, 141–48, 149n7. *See also* Executive Order 13769; Muslim ban
Trump administration, 6, 41, 77, 78, 93–94n5, 106, 121, 144, 152, 159
Trump, Donald, 6, 7, 8, 9, 22n6, 25, 48n11, 50, 62, 65, 68, 69, 70, 72, 73, 74, 75, 76, 77, 78, 79, 80, 81, 92, 93–94n5, 98, 105, 106, 119, 121, 128, 129, 134, 136, 141, 142, 143, 145, 146, 147, 149n4, 149n7, 154–55, 156

United Nations High Commissioner for Refugees (UNHCR), 22n7, 46n3, 50–51
United Nations Relief and Works Agency for Palestine Refugees in the Near East (UNRWA), 6
United States Agency for International Development (USAID), 15, 42, 54
United States Border Patrol, 106
United States Constitution, 68, 76, 99, 115, 146, 148
United States Customs and Border Protection, 93n4
United States Immigration and Customs Enforcement (ICE), 8, 77, 106, 145
United States military budget, 10, 112
United States Refugee Act of 1980, 50
United States Refugee Admissions Program (USRAP), 1, 6, 13, 14, 16, 18, 42, 43, 50, 51, 149n5
United States Supreme Court, 6, 97, 109, 122n1, 141
Unite the Right rallies, 149n3

War on Terror, 70, 122n5. *See also* war on terrorism
war on terrorism, 62. *See also* War on Terror
Welcoming America, 91
welcoming city, 91, 152

xenophobia, 3, 7, 21, 50, 62, 74

Yemen, 10, 16, 25, 46n4, 141, 150n7
Yemeni American Merchants Association (YAMA), 149–50n7

www.ingramcontent.com/pod-product-compliance
Lightning Source LLC
Chambersburg PA
CBHW051547020426
42333CB00016B/2137